This is a render-free zone

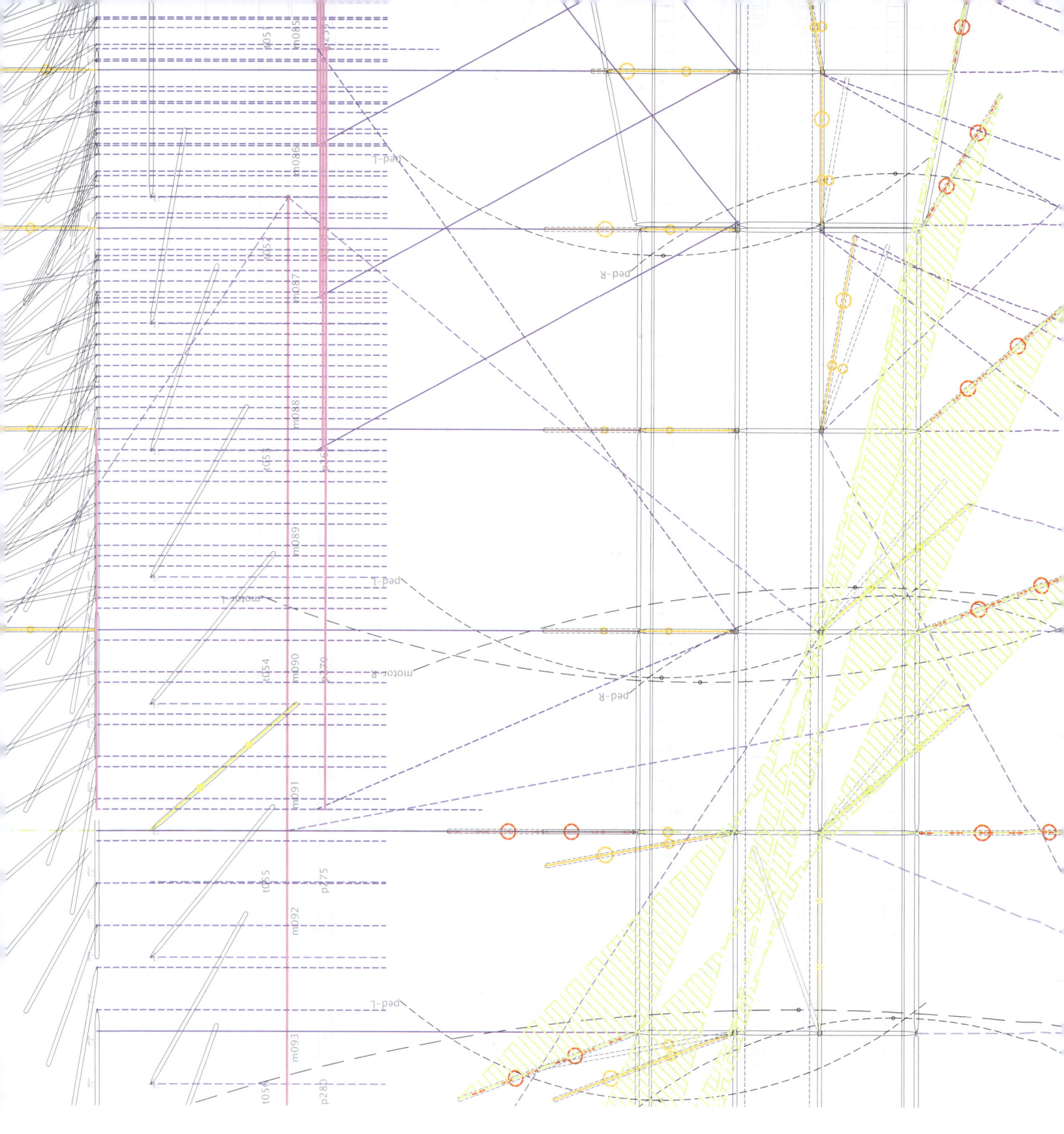

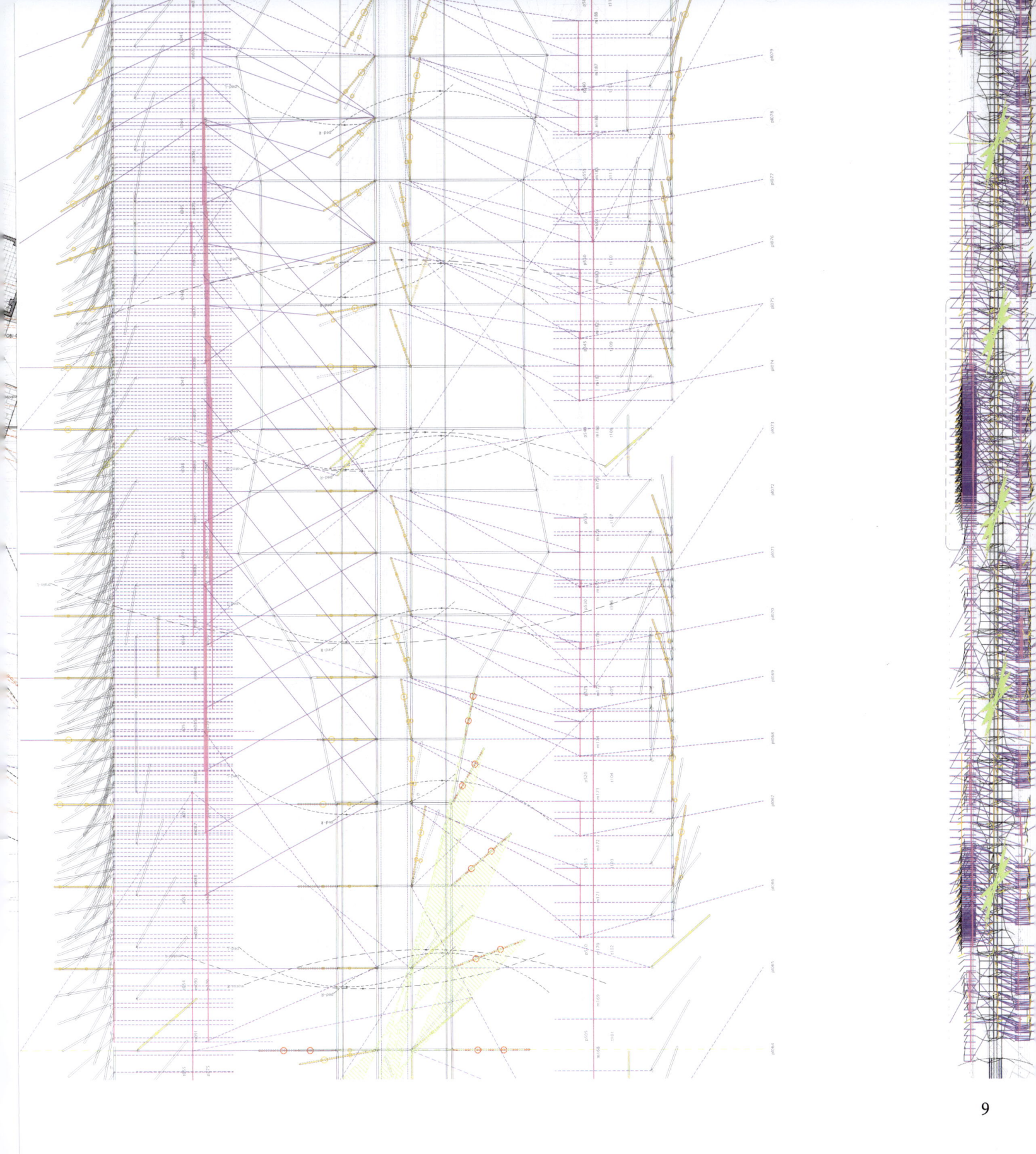

9

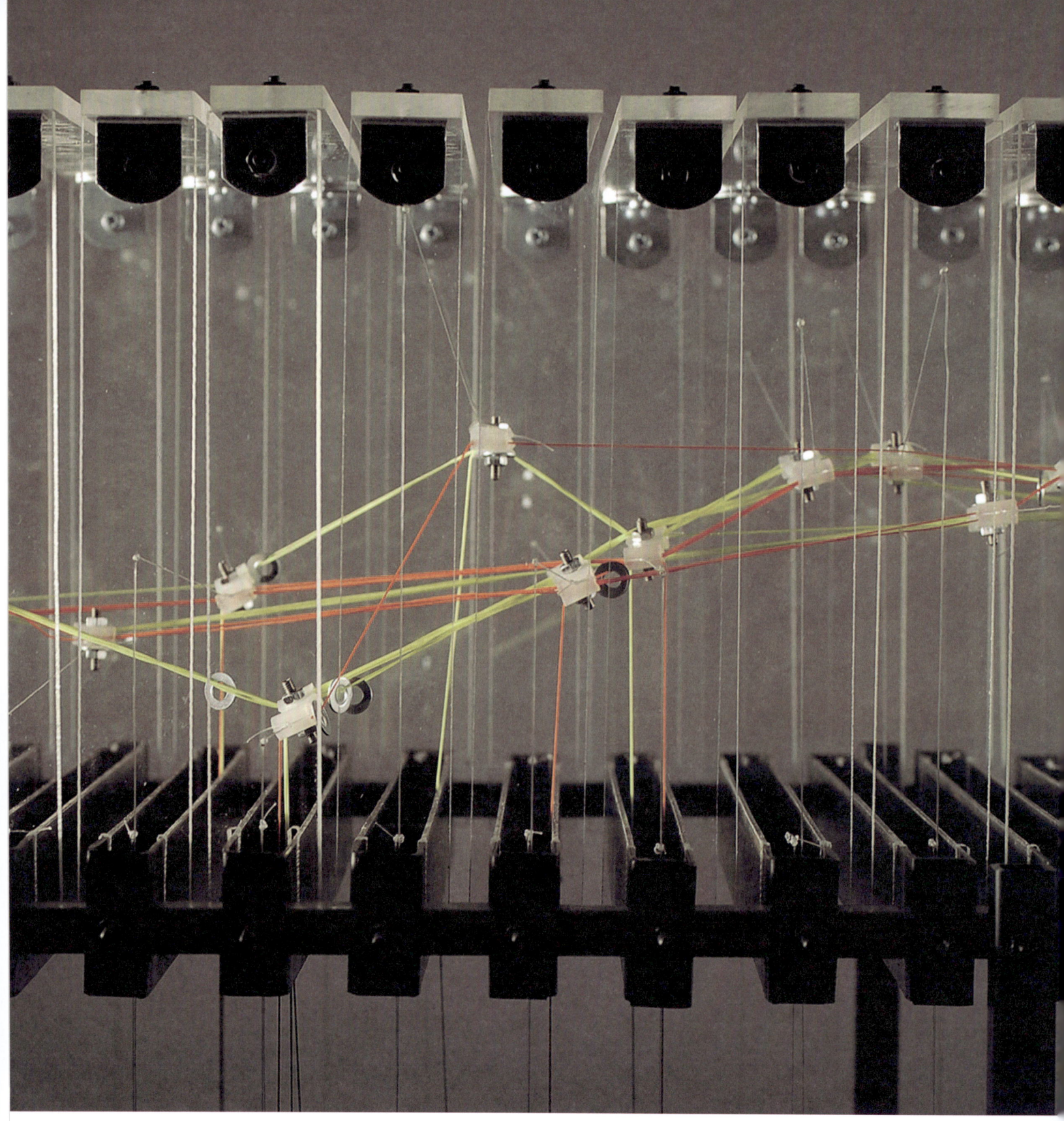

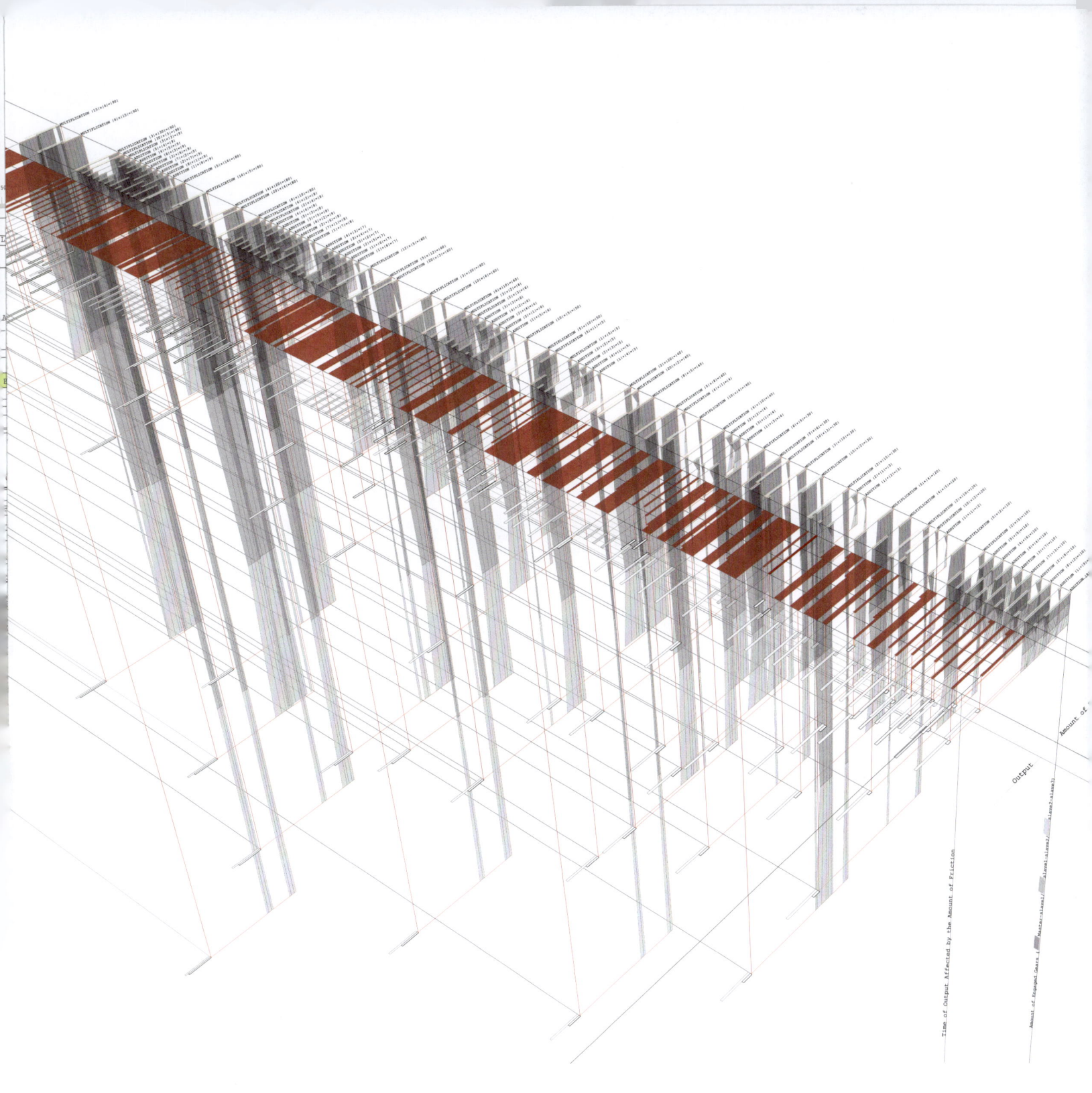

Time of Output Affected by the Amount of Friction

Output

Amount of Engaged Gears (Master-Slave1, Slave1-Slave2, Slave2-Slave3)

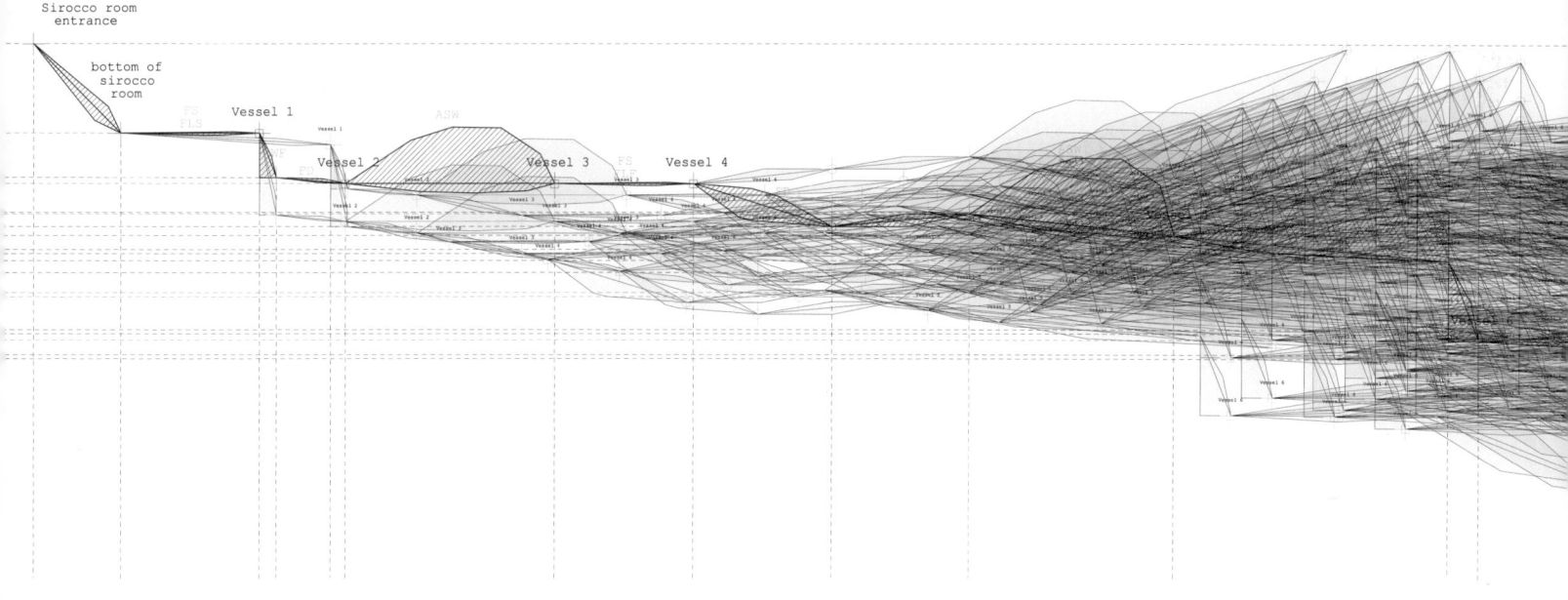

Sirocco room
entrance

bottom of
sirocco
room

Vessel 1

Vessel 2

Vessel 3

Vessel 4

17

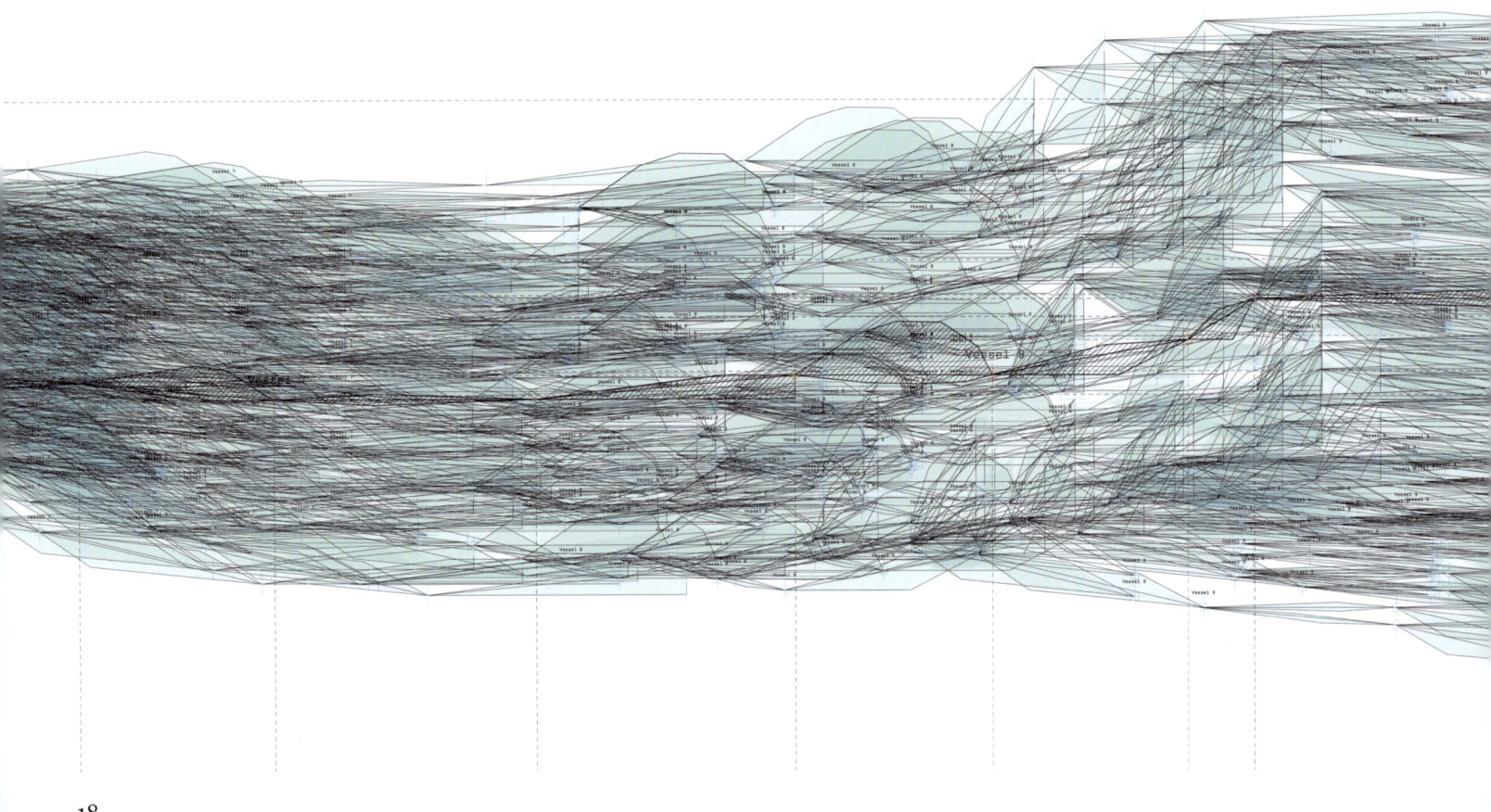

Introduction — Francesca Hughes

The drawings in this volume were produced by the students of AA Diploma Unit 15 between 2004 and 2010. This was a period of great transition, not only for the AA, but also, more broadly, from the tail end of one era to the beginning of another. Production paradigms shifted radically during these years: the parametric peaked and then nose-dived, and the narrative returned, accompanied by an alarming resurgence of figuration. For better or for worse, our work somehow always stood outside these currents.

In the first phase of teaching with Rita Lambert, our research began by proposing adaptations to extreme cultural, political and economic environments: the tax havens of Gibraltar and Ceuta, the demilitarised zones of the Panama Canal. Wary of the metaphoric, and especially of biological metaphors, our striving for specificity was a critique of the prototypical in the digitalised designs flourishing around us. The processing power of the computer, rather than being harnessed for the specificity of the locale, was instead engendering generic architectural production that would be equally at home and equally alien anywhere. Somehow, the computer was undoing context, though why was not clear.

Two years on, Noam Andrews – a superbly bright student we had taught in the first year of the unit – stepped into Rita's shoes, and we picked up where we had left off, the post-colonial questions of Panama still ringing in our ears. We turned to Hanoi, where imperial China, colonial France and a brief but efficient Soviet occupation have left a physical context overwhelmed by the artifice of a triple-fold nostalgia. Eating croissants as we stood in a tropical downpour by the gates of an imperial palace looking onto a Soviet monument, we repeatedly asked ourselves: where exactly are we? Over the course of the last century the palace had undergone a series of transformations, becoming first an embassy, then a school and finally a museum. In each instance type – that most effective of colonising tools, being itself, by definition, a-contextual – had served as a vehicle for rewriting context, for the political reconfiguration of a repeatedly occupied Hanoi. The promiscuity of Hanoi's architectural type taught us an important lesson: go all out, cut the cord between context and geography. Hanoi undid physical location as context, much as the digital production methods were about to. After Hanoi we would have to think more radically, and bring the students along with us.

p21
Derin Ozken
*Hanoi Hypercontext
Analysis Model*

So we turned to the two supercontexts that are behind all of architecture's 'contexts': the idea of Antiquity and, the oldest context of all, the Future. Antiquity was viewed through the prism of the Grand Tours of the eighteenth and nineteenth centuries, and mediated via a list of supertype vehicles: the ruin, the copy, the collection, the fragment, the dead city, the triumph and the Alpine passage. The Future was mediated by that thing that always promises access to the very next future: technology.

When we presented our work on the artifice of Antiquity as a kind of supercontext, many of our colleagues at the AA simply did not get it, understanding our engagement to be thematic rather than a systemic analysis of the space of indeterminacy that is antique scholarship. But the classicist Mary Beard really got it. She got what the students were doing with the artifice of classical scholarship: with the delineating of its mechanism, the description of its material operations, the spatialisation of time. Curiously, the following year, when our site was 'The Future' and we took technology, with the aid of David Edgerton, to stand as its not unproblematic proxy, our colleagues felt much more at home with the work. Perhaps there had just been an institutional delay of adjustment. Perhaps, as Noam suggests in his essay here, the historical had become an alien land in architectural pedagogy, whereas technology was deemed a familiar enough site, even if it was old technology (we were focusing on the late-nineteenth-century proliferation of technologies of representation, transportation and communication).

Equally at home with the cultural content of technology and the technological content of culture is Matthew Wells, engineer, teacher and writer, who would teach alongside us from each January and bring to bear his extraordinary ability to disregard all disciplinary boundaries, all sense of academic propriety, and impart knowledge on seemingly any topic in both the most sophisticated and eclectic terms. Scratch the surface of the paper architecture here and you will find his material interrogation of as yet material-free conceits that is fed back into each and every line. Matthew's annual effect was to induce this acutely architectural trauma and pleasure that marked the turning point of each student's own educational passage. Over the years his gentle, sometimes quizzical but always precisely aimed comments helped steer our ongoing enquiry. At the same time, the brief but incisive scholarly interventions of Mary Beard and David Edgerton have had lasting effect on our work and thinking. Sometimes cross-disciplinary exchange does manage to evade the fetishisation of the unfamiliar or the exotic and actually raise the game for all concerned. We are grateful to them all for seriously raising ours.

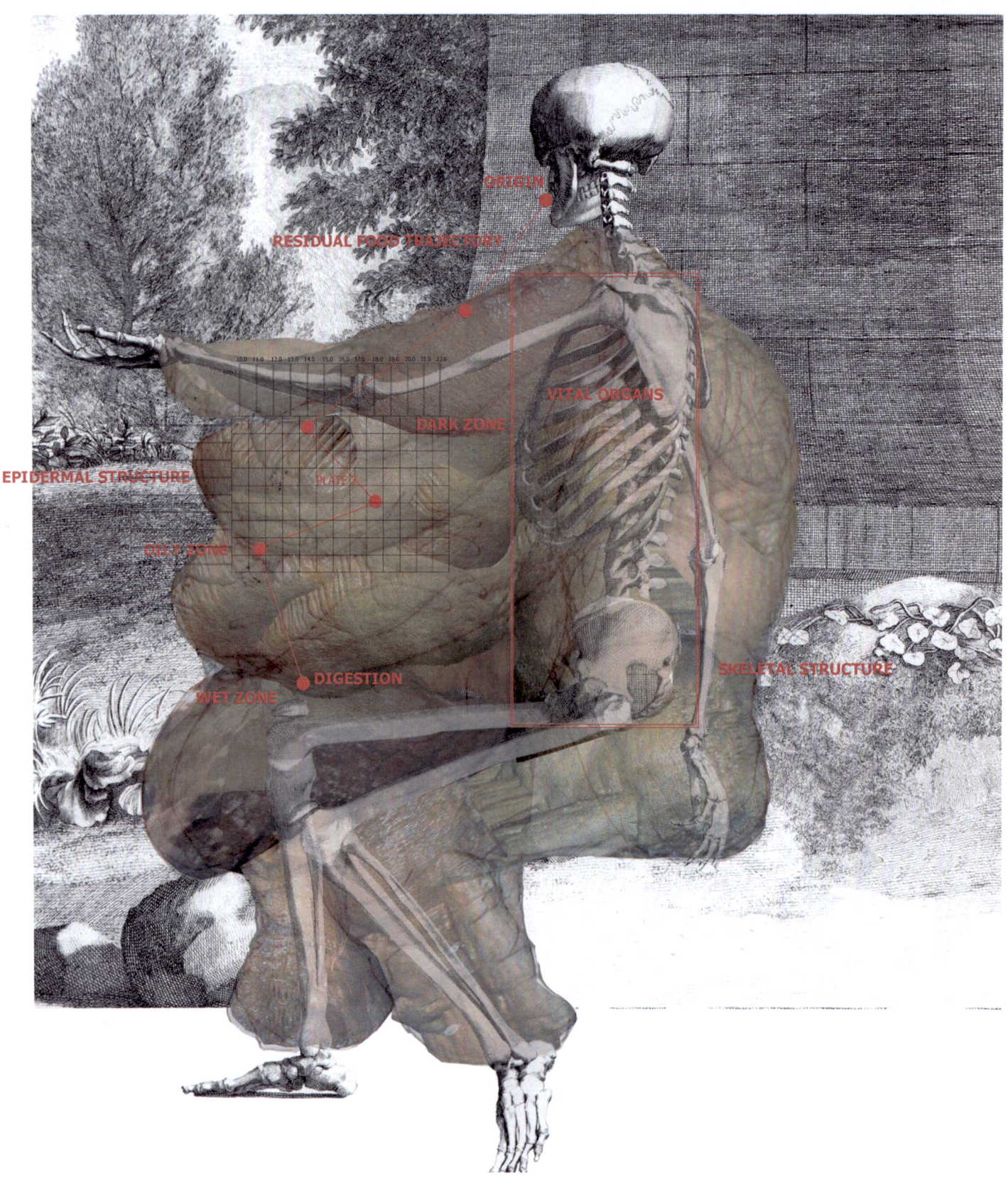

ORIGIN

RESIDUAL FOOD TRAJECTORY

VITAL ORGANS

DARK ZONE

EPIDERMAL STRUCTURE

PLATE 2

OILY ZONE

SKELETAL STRUCTURE

DIGESTION

WET ZONE

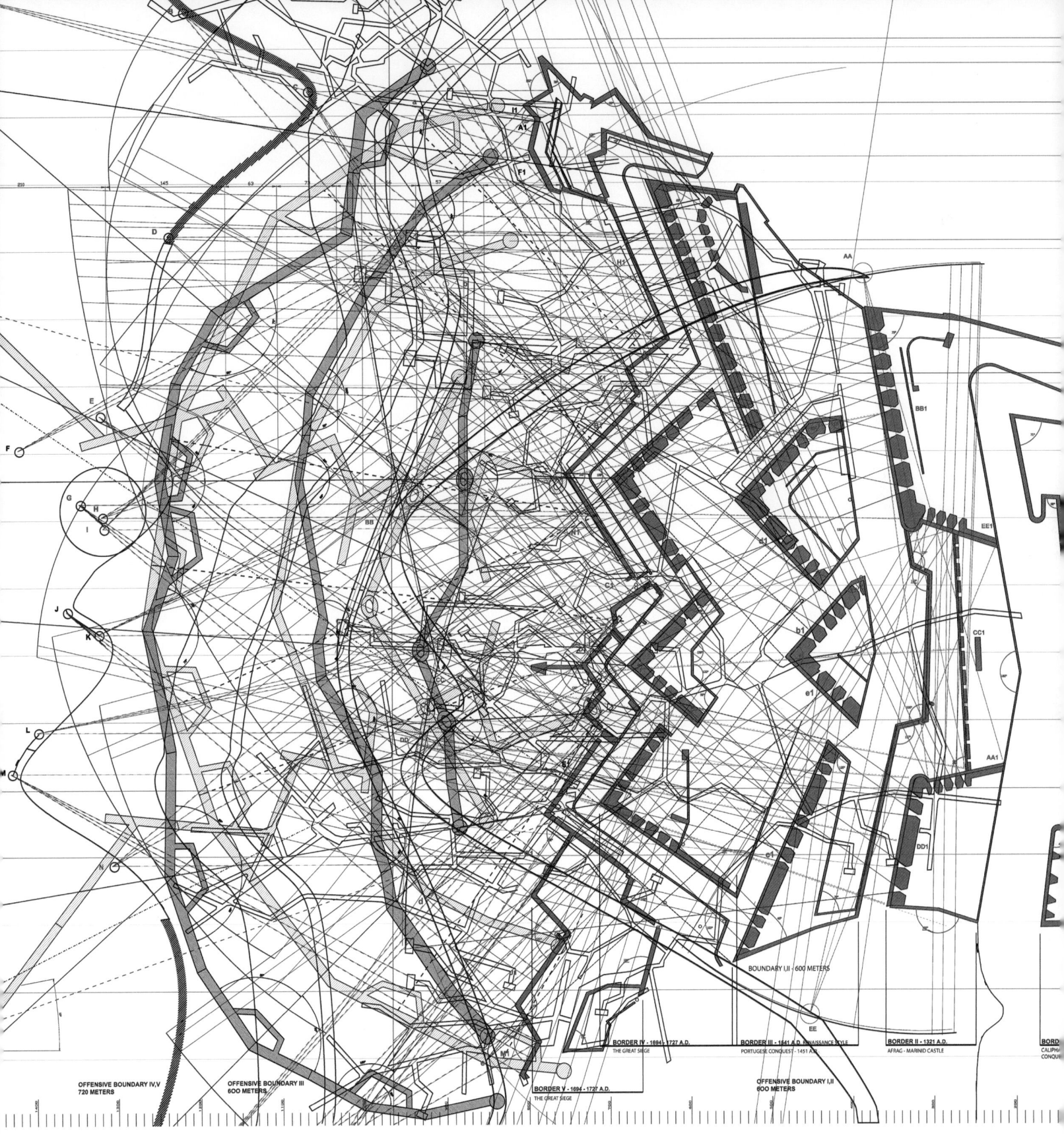

OFFENSIVE BOUNDARY IV,V
720 METERS

OFFENSIVE BOUNDARY III
600 METERS

BORDER V · 1694 - 1727 A.D.
THE GREAT SIEGE

OFFENSIVE BOUNDARY I,II
600 METERS

BOUNDARY I,II - 600 METERS

BORDER IV · 1694 - 1727 A.D.
THE GREAT SIEGE

BORDER III · 1541 A.D. RENAISSANCE STYLE
PORTUGESE CONQUEST · 1451 A.D.

BORDER II · 1321 A.D.
AFRAG · MARINID CASTLE

BORD
CALIPHA
CONQU

EE

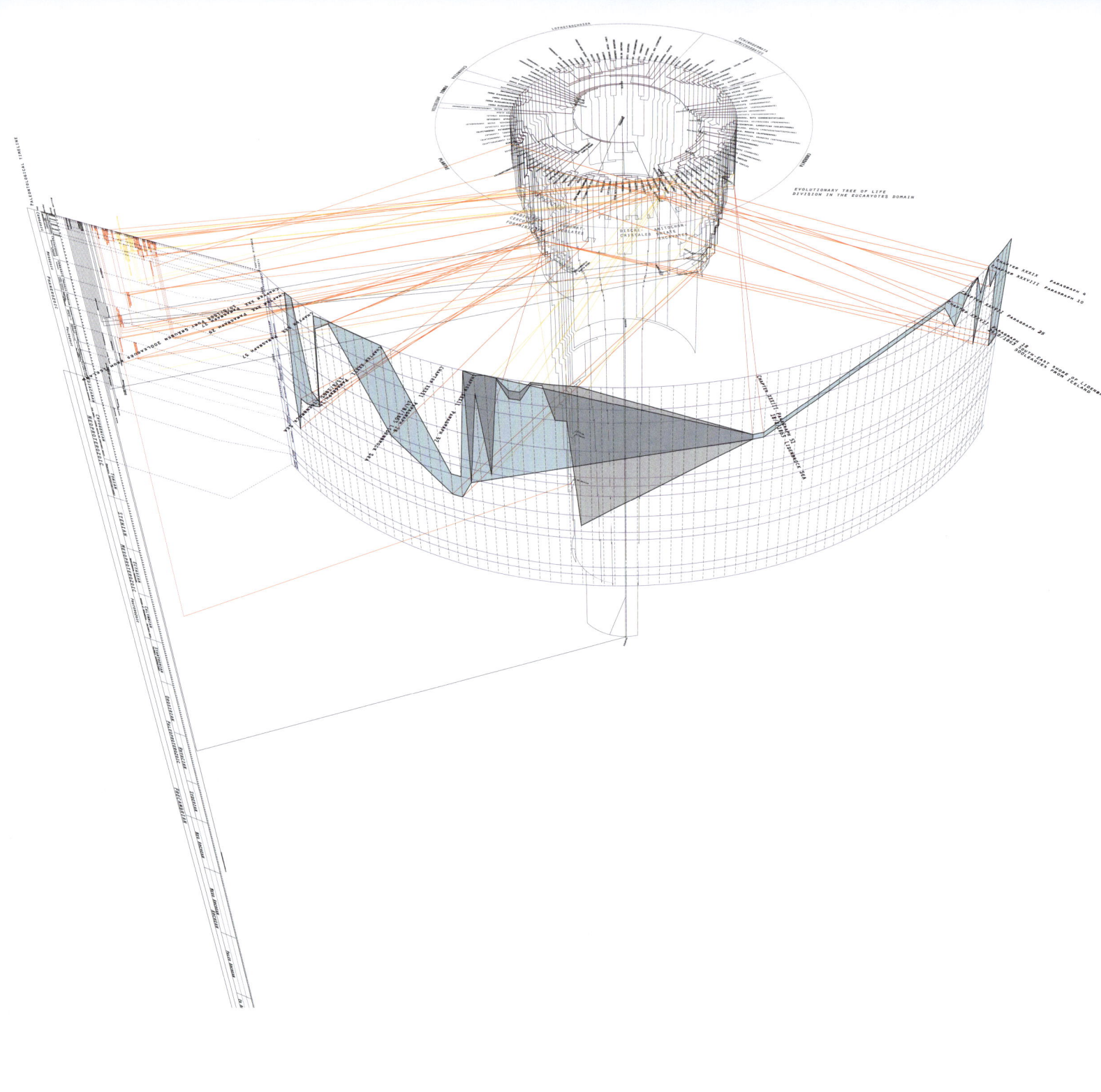

EVOLUTIONARY TREE OF LIFE
DIVISION IN THE EUCARYOTES DOMAIN

Context is...

— Francesca Hughes

*Rome is dead, gone. But every time
I step out of my door, I am in Rome.*
– Mary Beard, AA Dip 15 seminar,
19 January 2009

Consider 'context', that most fickle of categories in architecture's bag. To name but a few of its guises, it has been cast as: counterpoint (always flattering and thus subservient); alibi (as in 'the context made me do it this way'); *raison d'être* (source of the problem that the architectural cavalry arrives to fix); canvas and backdrop; *tabula rasa* (another kind of canvas that is never what it promises); accessory (to the architectural assassination); loom and matrix (for the textural *bricoleurs*); mirror (rarely); ecology (providing resource and constraint as well as metaphoric complexity); surface only (for camouflage and other strictly surface games, not to mention the more complex, performative business of mimicry that necessarily gets under the surface); or retreat position (when architecture remembers its ultimately conservative roots – *genius loci*, Critical Regionalism and other forms of vernacular *manqué*). Despite its Luddite reputation, 'context' is nothing if not a promiscuous survivor. At first seemingly undone by the hermeticism of digitalised production, it has now been reconfigured yet again within its productive operations. Doubly so: firstly, in the form of the reductive parameter set in the engineered neutrality of the 'optimised' and the strange new breed of determinism it paradoxically espouses; then, more craftily, evading this regime, in the peculiar conflation of geographical context with the machinic context of production itself – the software, the interface with the CNC, or the setting on the rapid prototyping machine. Especially in more simulative design strategies, any distinction between production and context is frequently, and perhaps conveniently, lost.

Within the realm of architectural representation – the prison and the fun park of architectural pedagogy – the nod to context is found in the figurative, in those tortured trees that haunt rendered perspectives. Or, more recently, as some measurable local parameter that is fed into a form-generating algorithm whose final iteration is garnished with the same tortured trees. Both are strange

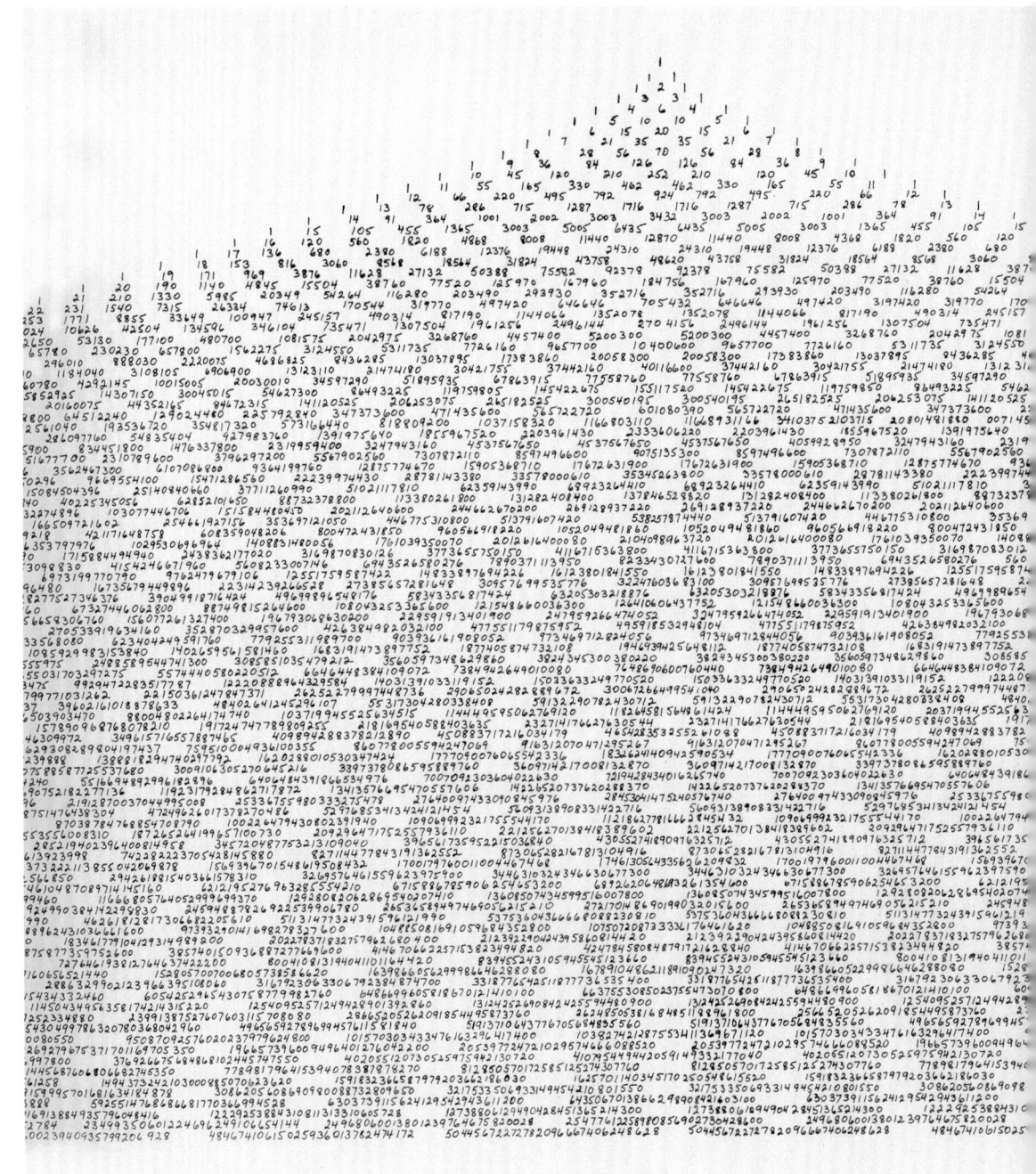

forms of censorship of the very process they are meant to stand for – the rereading and rewriting of context within a given proposal. Both neuter the potency of context as a generator, as a critical engine of specificity and above all resistance. But how might context be newly radicalised as a generator? How might the question of context become not an accommodating proxy but itself critically acute?

We were asking these questions in the academy, not on the site. Our engagement with context and its potential action was to be mediated by a whole other extraordinary context itself: architectural representation. To work on the question of context – conscious that we were necessarily doing so within and through the context of architectural representation, and its own problematic relations to the pictorial – was to work in a hall of mirrors. We needed to devise and develop a representational medium that would cut through the auto-reflexive nature of this paradox without dumbing down the artifice at stake. So we drew and we drew: but there were no trees, no cars, no people, no sky, no light, no shadow nor any caressing line extruding from a latent landmark figure. We got tired of guileless set questions from some quarters: 'But if you are working on context why can't I see it in the drawing?' 'Why doesn't it *look* like that place?' Hounded by the geographic we eventually cut context loose from place. Indexicality came to our

rescue, bringing the relief of its abstraction but also the onerous burden of rigour and graft demanded by its currency of iterative notation. Mark upon mark, context had to be registered, read and rewritten as a factory of hypercontextual inventions. This medium needed to be not just message but maker too. There were crucial instructive precedents: the work of Vija Celmins, as well as the earlier and lesser known work of Agnes Denes, such as *Pascal's Triangle, Drawing No 3* (1973–75) <u>p 26</u>, for example, where a tiny hand on red graph paper draws, in figures and not figure, the spiralling shifts of probability distribution across the 16ft-span of the drawing. The labour evidenced is silent, apparently effortless. Denes notes nonchalantly: 'If the structure were continued to a height of 22.9ft, the base would be one mile long. If the base were extended from here to the sun (93 million miles), the tip of the structure would still be only 133 miles high.' Drawings like this put us architects firmly in our place.

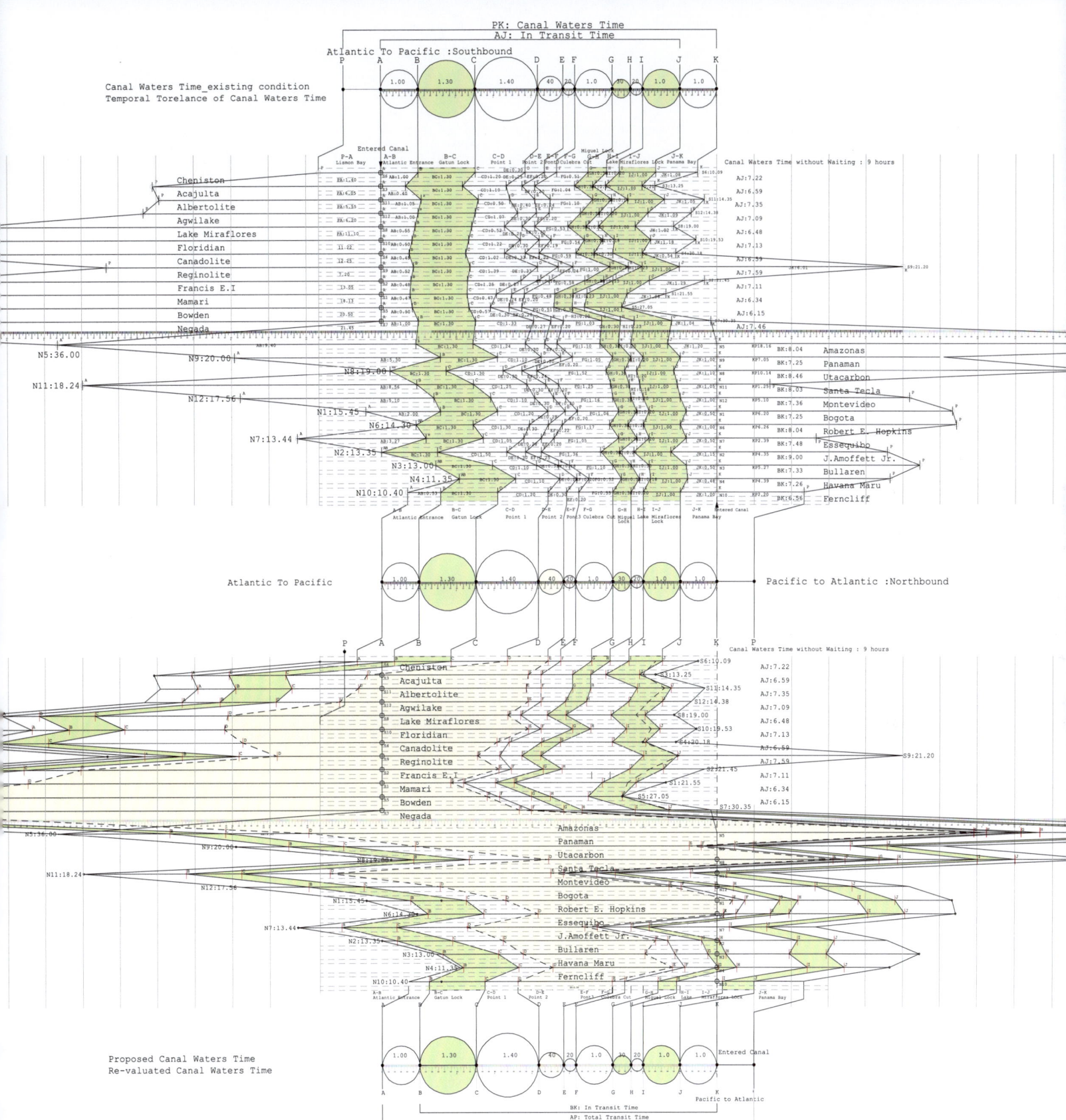

Hypercontext

The 'context' that the architect refers and responds to is always already an artifice. Devised to mediate between the 'real' context out there and the desires and constraints (intellectual and/or physical) of the intervention proposed, it is a highly selective set of spatial, temporal, material and (less so, recently) cultural parameters that somehow are meant to stand for place and potential meaning or belonging. Like the cartographer, the prospector and the field biologist, we architects abstract context for our own very particular purposes. In doing so, we strip it of its full complexity and eliminate its ability to radically intervene in our interventions – on paper at least, and nowhere more so than in the parametricised productions that were ascendant in the middle of the last decade, in the early years of Dip 15. Within the practice and monologic discourse of so-called optimisation, we saw context reduced beyond recognition to a set of three to four determinate, physical parameters, typically sun angle, circulation loading and an internal programmatic schedule, be it for Mumbai, Hackney or the Atacama desert. Reliably excluded from this set was anything indeterminate, as well as anything that could not be equated with useful function, although all kinds of undeclared pleasures were always at play in the glossy, articulated surfaces produced – but that is another story.

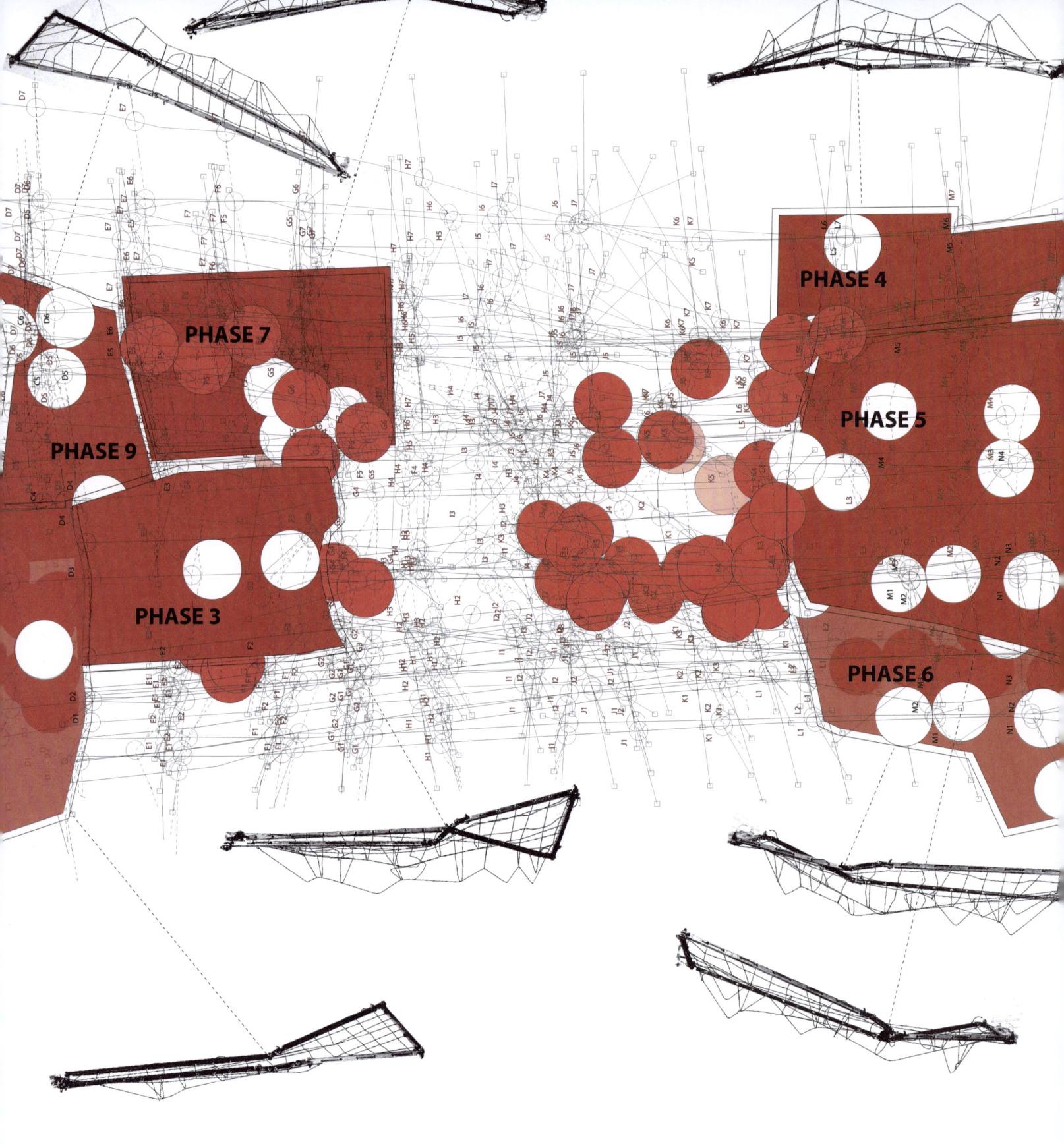

PHASE 4

PHASE 7

PHASE 5

PHASE 9

PHASE 3

PHASE 6

In the *Confessions of St Augustine*, he describes memory as an extraordinary landscape, a convoluted and cavernous terrain that houses information and, when called forth, generates the 'form' that is retrieved knowledge. He reads this terrain in what can only be described as the first fly-through, travelling over and under its surfaces, at will, from any edge and in any direction: 'Behold in the plains, and caves, and caverns of my memory, innumerable and innumerably full of innumerable kinds of things... [O]ver all these do I run; I fly; I dive on this side and that, as far as I can, and there is no end.' * This is landscape as Barthesian hypertext. It is also clearly a (virtual) place, and one that houses many other potential places within its generative matrix. Like Barthes' 'triumphant plural', it always yields itself up differently depending on how you enter and traverse its oneiric cartography. A hypertext is a text written, or in our case drawn, with an awareness of the double artifice of its making, both in its writing (or drawing) and its reading (the architecture it generates in the viewer's mind). Like St Augustine's mnemonic topography it is also multiscalar, non-linear, non-sequential and has no right way up or right way in. This multilinearity and non-sequentiality requires the reader to be no longer an idle consumer but an active producer. As Barthes defined it in 1970 in *S/Z*, 'In this ideal text, the networks [*réseaux*] are many and interact, without any one of them being able to surpass the rest; this text is a galaxy of signifiers, not a structure of signifieds; it has no beginning; it is reversible; we gain access to it by several entrances, none of which can be authoritatively declared

* *Confessions of St Augustine* (revised from translation by EB Pusey (Oxford: John Henry Parker, 1853), X, 17.

It was clear that our redefining of the artifice of context had to do two things: to actively decipher and instrumentalise the indeterminate (that which resists easy quantification, including the cultural and all that follows from it), as well as incorporate what we termed, for want of a better word, the *a-functional*. But how might we inscribe this always-mediating artifice in a way that enabled its own necessarily convoluted architecture to generate or script other architectures? Could we construct this artifice, draw its internal temporal, spatial and material organisation so as to take it to the very cusp of becoming a resolved architectural proposition itself, rendering context and intervention as one?

to be the main one; the codes it mobilises extend *as far as the eye can reach*, they are indeterminable ... the systems of meaning can take over this absolutely plural text, but their number is never closed, based as it is on the infinity of language.' *

Like the context it signifies, hypercontext is never whole, has no pretence to the kind of totality that would, in Barthes' terms, constitute a reversion to the 'paternal eye of the representative model'. This is the same paternal totality that is implicit in the models behind optimisation: for something to be 'optimal', after all, everything must be weighed into judgement, accounted for. In collapsing the determinate with the indeterminate, the functional with the a-functional, our experiments in hypercontextuality implicitly rejected the reductive and strove instead to be a multiplicitous as well as a radical matrix of (sometimes conflicting) specificity.

* Roland Barthes, *S/Z An Essay*, trans Miller (Farrar, Straus and Giroux, New York: 1974), 5–6.

Thus the hypercontext drawing aims to maintain the same open-ended structure of pathways – the perpetually unfinished textuality – that saw the convergence of literary theory and early computing in Barthes' work. 'How can we escape the prison of the four-walled page that relentlessly reappears on the screen?', Ted Nelson asks in his critique of Microsoft and the dominance of its interface legacy. We asked ourselves a similar but not quite parallel question: How can we escape the four-walled prison of the architectural render, of the projective picture, and yet still remain on the page? How can we retrieve the hypertext from the computer and put it down on paper once more, write the truly polysemous drawing? So, like the ticking machine we stole it from, we started to count.

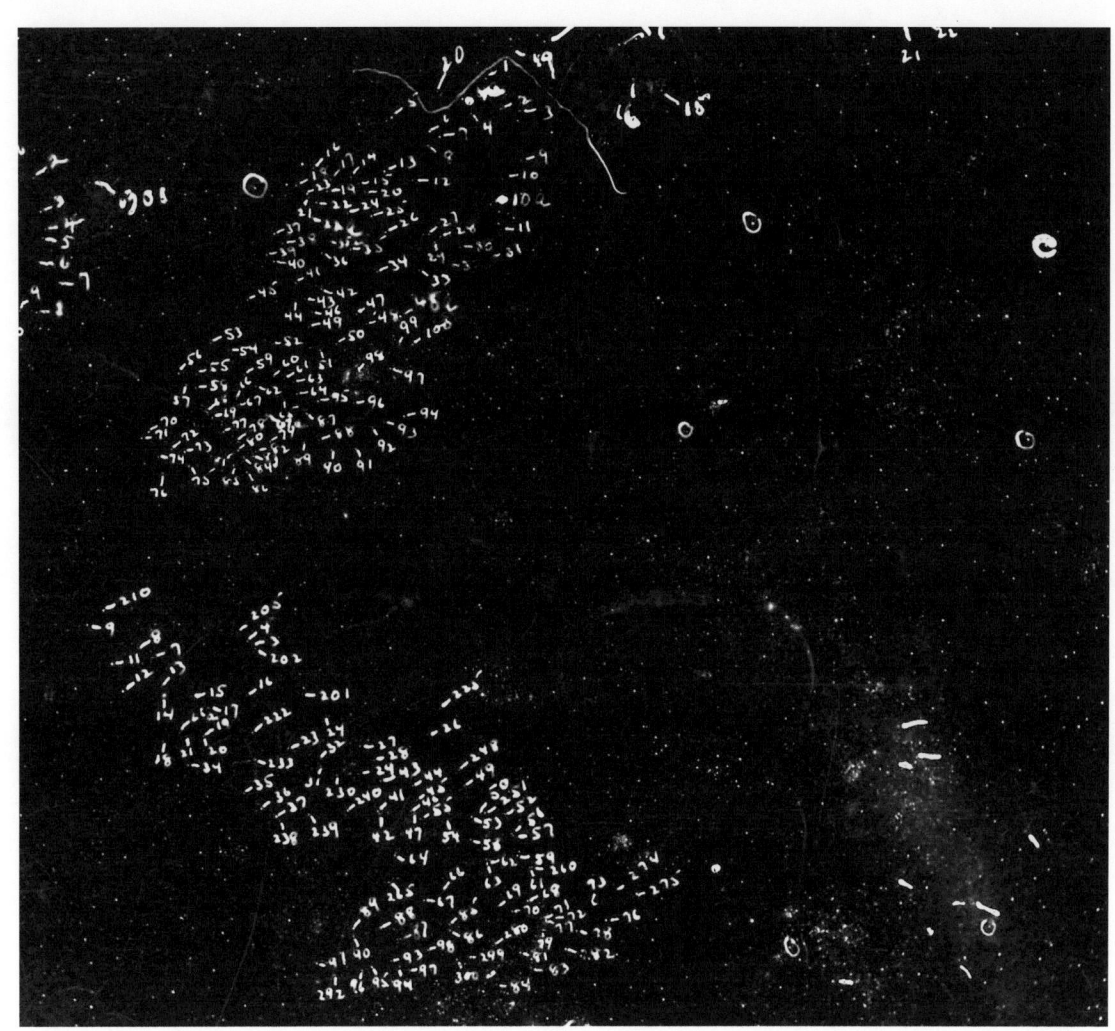

35

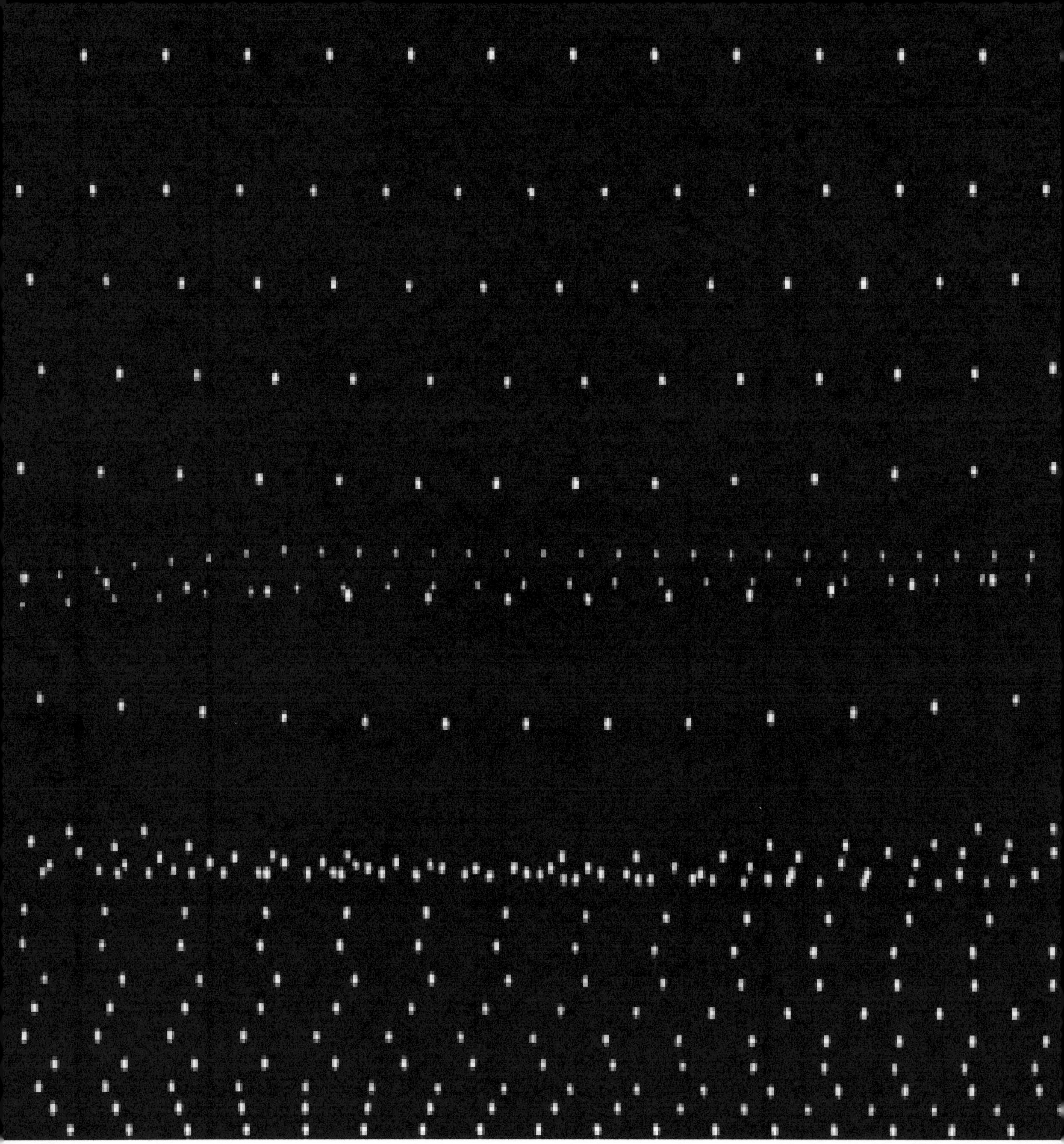

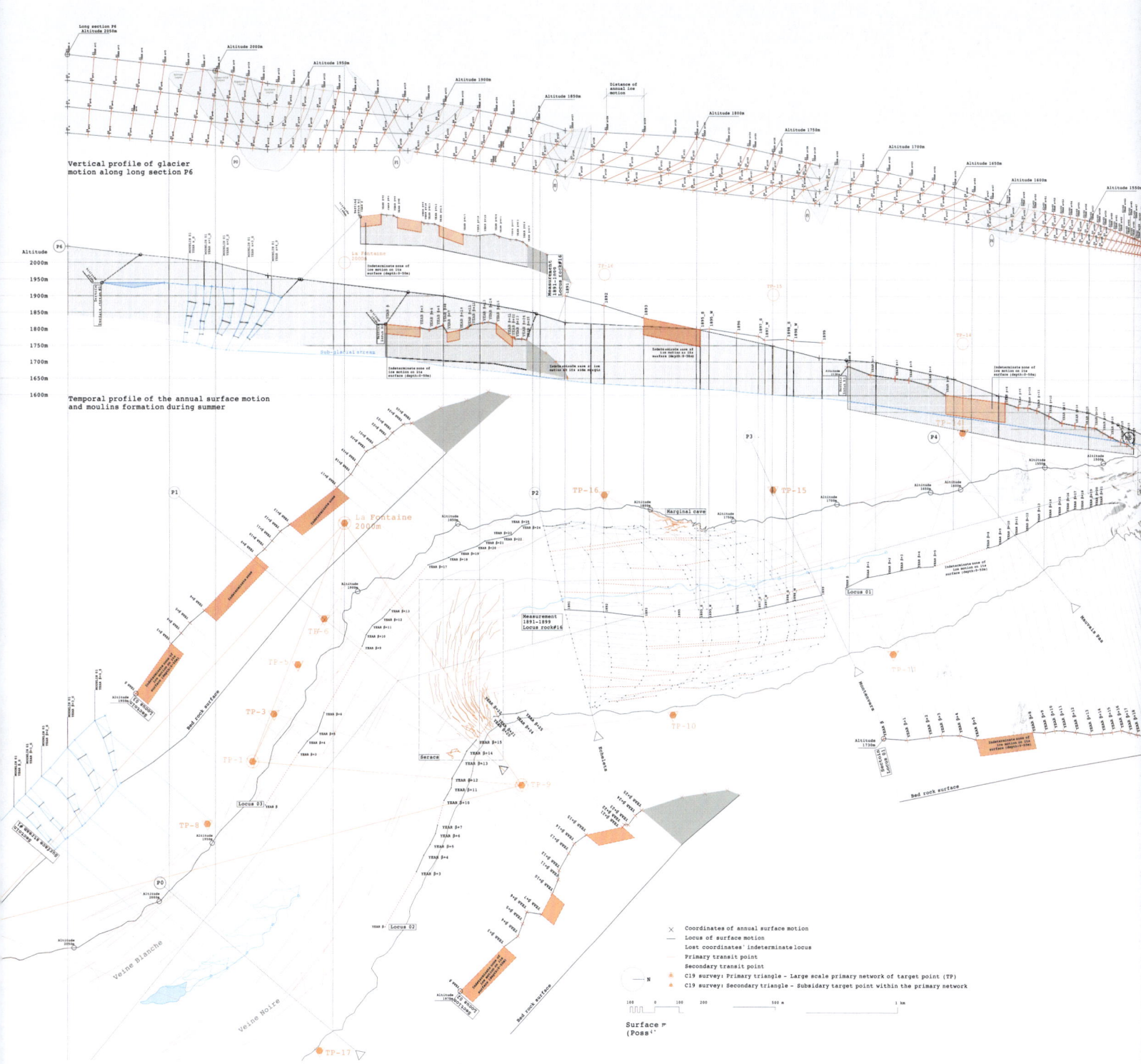

Vertical profile of glacier
motion along long section P6

Temporal profile of the annual surface motion
and moulins formation during summer

La Fontaine
2000m

Bed rock surface

Veine Blanche

Veine Noire

	Coordinates of annual surface motion
✕	Locus of surface motion
	Lost coordinates' indeterminate locus
	Primary transit point
	Secondary transit point
	C19 survey: Primary triangle - Large scale primary network of target point (TP)
	C19 survey: Secondary triangle - Subsidary target point within the primary network

Surface
(Poss

One Potato, Two...

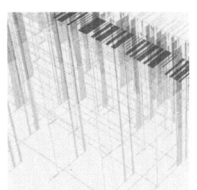

p 13
Fusako Ishikawa

Wittgenstein reminds us that counting is always an experiment. In the middle of his poignantly doubt-ridden crisis on the relations between calculation and counting – the former having a capacity to predict, the latter, to confirm, and the devilish propensity of error to propagate in both – he notes that in counting the answer is nevertheless empirically established each time afresh. The child in Wittgenstein knows this; he draws a five by four grid of circular counters and sets to tallying them up. Row by column. Then column by row. They yield the same result, thus he can *count* the commutative law into being. Or can he? The doubting returns: 'Yes, but only if the pieces don't change... and we don't make some unintelligible mistake, or pieces disappear or get added without our noticing it.' * Counting is a fraught experiment; it is the sublime meeting of pure abstraction and the dumbly material item and, at the same time, the ridiculously infantile business of one potato two. When Babagge mechanised calculation, completing the project of Leibniz before him, the Difference Engine was simply driver cogs counting slave cogs. And, being a material process, resistance was encountered, friction incurred. As Fusako Ishikawa shows in her drawing of the friction distribution in a simple operation in Babagge's machine, *Writing Architecture In the Gap Between The Countable and the Calculated* p 13, the commutative law does not quite stand: counting 2 x 100 requires a lot less work than 100 x 2. Counting is also what architects do. Not just how many bits, but how many steps to the right this bit is from that other bit. And time too: how many more minutes, hours, days, months, years this bit lasts than that bit. The counting machine has now colonised every aspect of architectural production: representation, construction, even the way we think about architecture. Counting is more central than ever.

* Ludwig Wittgenstein, *Remarks on the Foundations of Mathematics*, trans G Anscombe, emphasis in original (Oxford: Blackwell, 1964), III, 17.

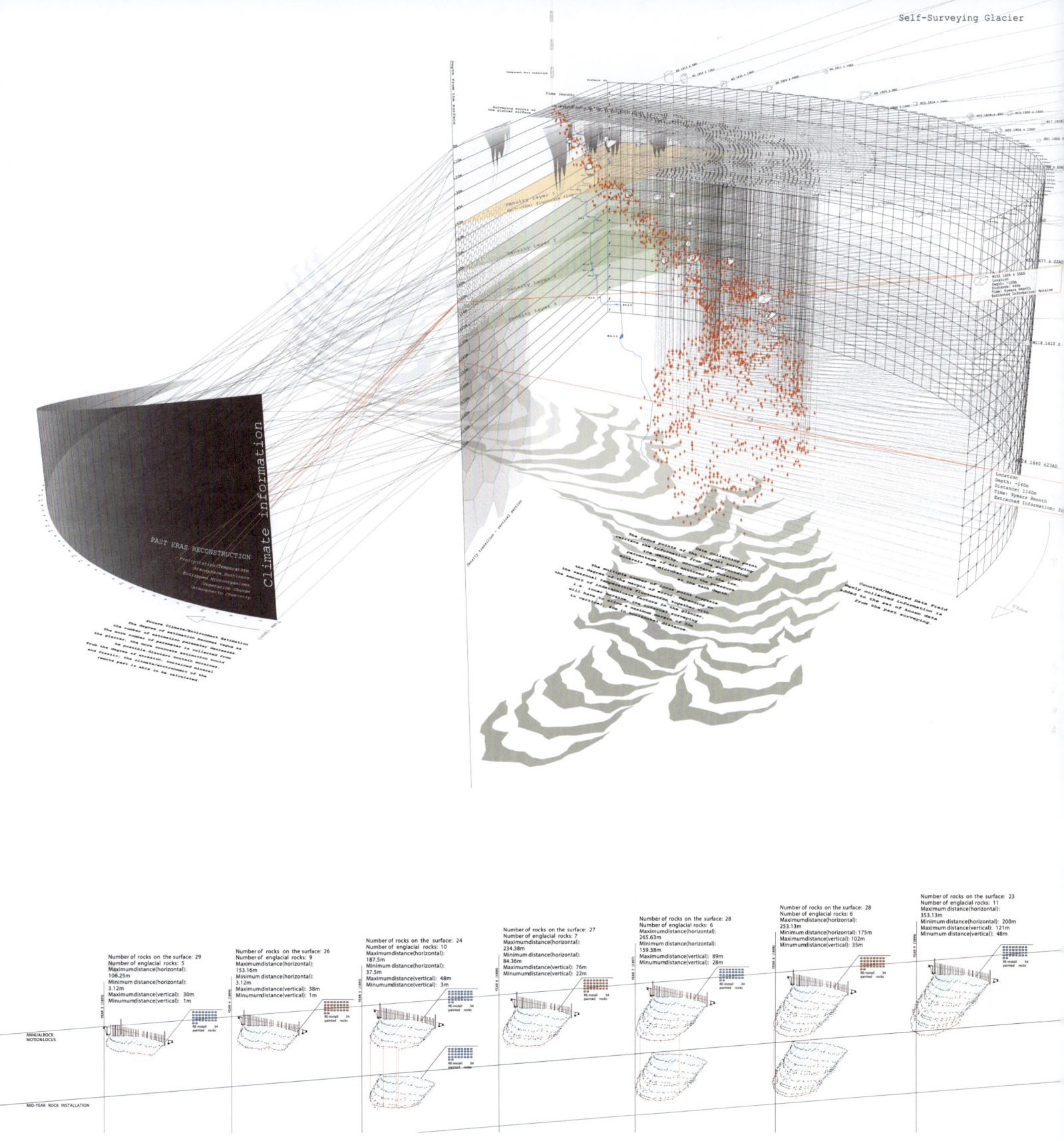

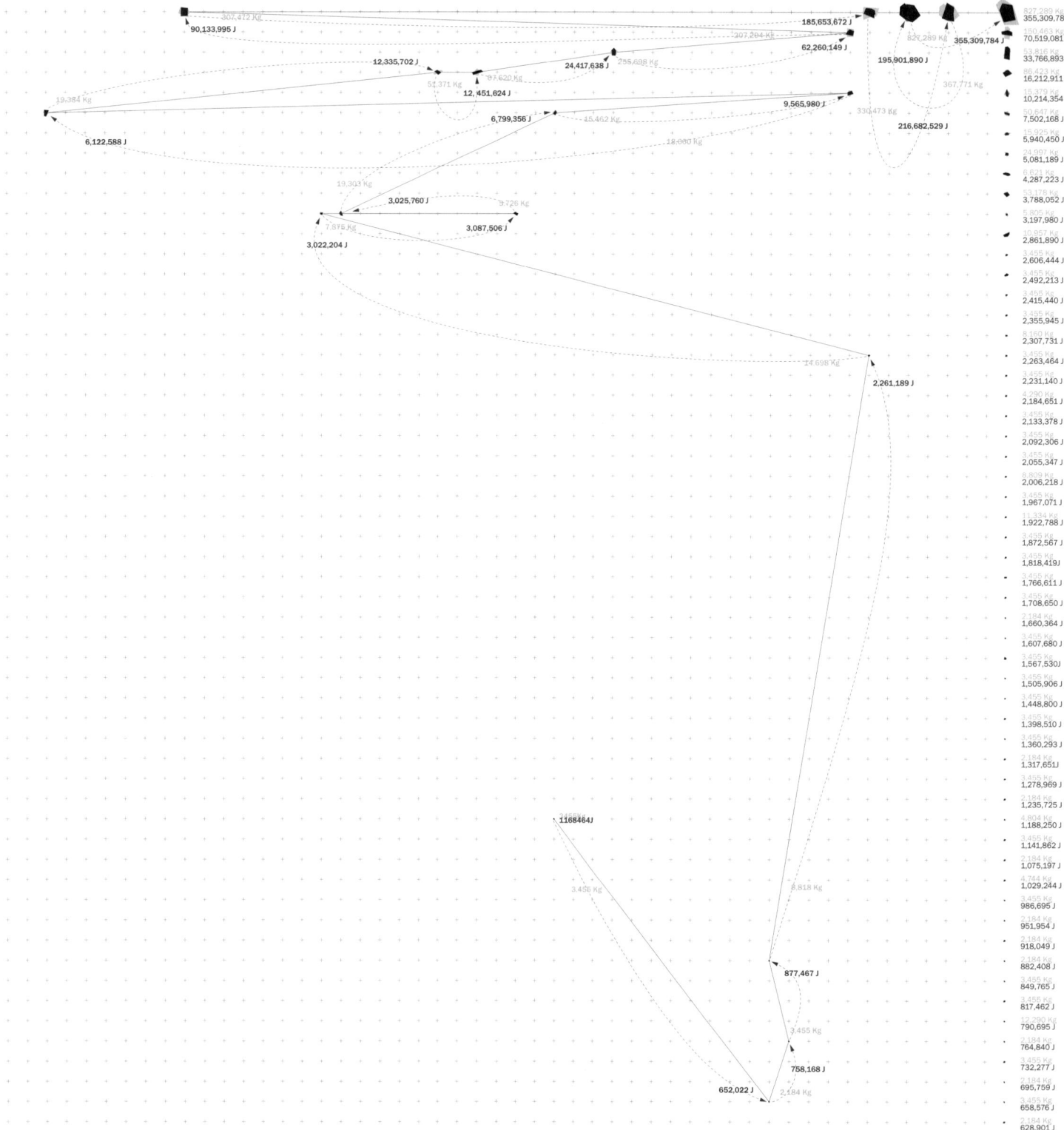

355,309,784 J

185,653,672 J

150,463,624 J
70,519,081 J

827,289 Kg

90,133,995 J

307,204 Kg

62,260,149 J

355,309,784 J

53,816 Kg
33,766,893 J

195,901,890 J

86,423 Kg
16,212,911 J

12,335,702 J

255,698 Kg

24,417,638 J

15,379 Kg
10,214,354 J

51,371 Kg

87,620 Kg

12,451,824 J

367,771 Kg

50,647 Kg
7,502,168 J

9,565,980 J

330,473 Kg

216,682,529 J

15,925 Kg
5,940,450 J

19,384 Kg

45,462 Kg

6,799,356 J

24,097 Kg
5,081,189 J

18,080 Kg

6,122,588 J

6,522 Kg
4,287,223 J

3,878 Kg
3,788,052 J

19,303 Kg

3,025,760 J

9,726 Kg

3,667 Kg
3,197,980 J

3,087,506 J

16,857 Kg
2,861,890 J

7,875 Kg

3,022,204 J

3,455 Kg
2,606,444 J

1,455 Kg
2,492,213 J

3,455 Kg
2,415,440 J

3,455 Kg
2,355,945 J

8,160 Kg
2,307,731 J

3,455 Kg
2,263,464 J

14,698 Kg

3,455 Kg
2,231,140 J

2,261,189 J

4,290 Kg
2,184,651 J

3,455 Kg
2,133,378 J

3,455 Kg
2,092,306 J

3,455 Kg
2,055,347 J

8,809 Kg
2,006,218 J

3,455 Kg
1,967,071 J

1,334 Kg
1,922,788 J

3,455 Kg
1,872,567 J

3,455 Kg
1,818,419 J

3,455 Kg
1,766,611 J

3,455 Kg
1,708,650 J

2,194 Kg
1,660,364 J

3,455 Kg
1,607,680 J

3,455 Kg
1,567,530 J

3,455 Kg
1,505,906 J

3,455 Kg
1,448,800 J

3,455 Kg
1,398,510 J

3,455 Kg
1,360,293 J

2,184 Kg
1,317,651 J

3,455 Kg
1,278,969 J

2,184 Kg
1,235,725 J

1168464 J

4,804 Kg
1,188,250 J

3,455 Kg
1,141,862 J

2,184 Kg
1,075,197 J

3,456 Kg

4,744 Kg
1,029,244 J

8,818 Kg

3,455 Kg
986,695 J

2,184 Kg
951,954 J

2,184 Kg
918,049 J

2,184 Kg
882,408 J

877,467 J

3,455 Kg
849,765 J

3,455 Kg
817,462 J

3,455 Kg

12,290 Kg
790,695 J

2,184 Kg
764,840 J

758,168 J

3,455 Kg
732,277 J

652,022 J

2,184 Kg

2,184 Kg
695,759 J

3,455 Kg
658,576 J

2,184 Kg
628,901 J

Our process of counting started with Ben Mailen slicing up a rough model of the fort in Ceuta using the then newly acquired (and now of course primitive) laser-cutting machine at the AA. The tray of slices sat on the studio table, protruding haphazardly like the keys of a disembowelled piano, and we started to absentmindedly slide them around while talking, to count them with our idle fingers. In/out positions became open/shut, as the 3m-wide Renaissance rubble wall itself became a selective filter, a counting machine. Meanwhile another student, Noam Andrews,

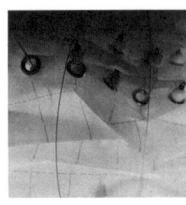

p 31
Noam Andrews

was playing an altogether more complex game, counting and accounting for time and value and weight in his choreographing of a voluptuous facade for the Murallas Reales (royal wall) in Ceuta [*Murailles East, facade detail*, p 31] which transformed the incrementality of the indexical into seamless baroque folds of fatty tissue, all the while colonising the VAT anomalies of this dubious tax haven. By a couple of years later, when Noam was teaching alongside me, counting and the indexicality it engenders had become our *modus operandi*. We used the counting of small things to think about big things — taking lessons from Henrietta Leavitt, one of the human 'computers' employed to count

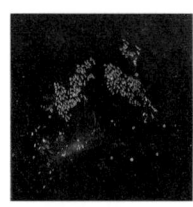

p 35
Henrietta Leavitt

thousands of light points on photographic plates at Harvard College Observatory from the 1890s, and who deduced from this a system that allowed Edwin Hubble to measure the size of the universe.

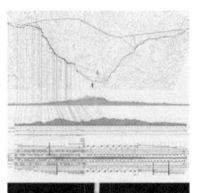

p 63
Theo Wyatt
Petrides

Theo Wyatt Petrides' choreography of artificial stars [*Light Choreography for the Twenty-First Century Grand Tourist's Alpine Passage* p 63, p 36] for the new Gotthard Base tunnel counts its way through the long-lost, winding, sublime Alpine passage of the Grand Tour above, soon to be permanently eclipsed by the 20-minute shortcut of the high-speed train in this Panama Canal of tunnels.

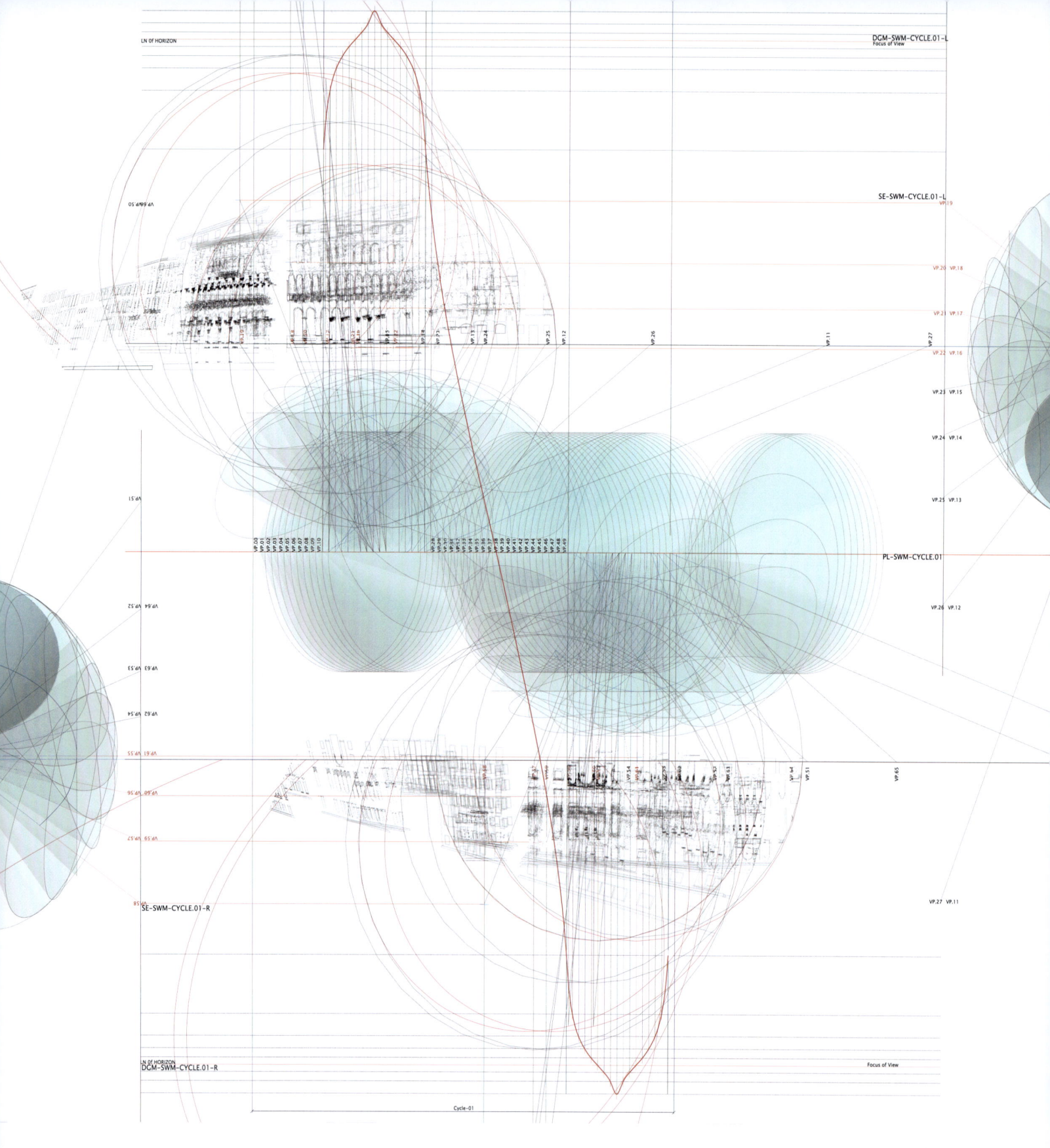

SE-SWM-CYCLE.01-L   VP.19

VP.20 VP.18

VP.21 VP.17

VP.22 VP.16

VP.23 VP.15

VP.24 VP.14

VP.25 VP.13

PL-SWM-CYCLE.01

VP.26 VP.12

SE-SWM-CYCLE.01-R   VP.27 VP.11

After gauging the friction and resistance of Babbage's calculating machine, Ishikawa turned to the counting of a glacier, the Mer de Glace in Chamonix [*Counting the Glacier: Vallot's Survey of the Mer de Glace*, p 37].

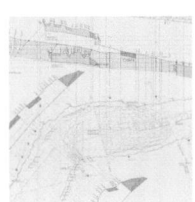

p 37
Fusako Ishikawa

In the nineteenth century Joseph Vallot placed rows of painted and numbered stones across the glacier in order to measure its movement. Similar to Wittgenstein's relations to his counters, Vallot's engagement with the stone-swallowing formlessness of the glacier was defined by the struggles between the surveying (the counting architects do) and the surveyed. Instead of using painted stones to somehow master the inscrutable shifts of the ice, the glacier in Ishikawa's hypercontext in *Glacial Chronograph* p 39 reconfigures what it is to survey, measure and count in the first place. The following year, in *A Small Rock at the Top of the Hill = A Big Rock at the Bottom of the Hill* p 41, Theo Petrides set to counting fallen rocks in the Valley of the Temples in Athens, in an allegory of the futility of restoration and the desire to reconstruct the classical world that drives it.

Sang Hoon Han meanwhile addressed the urban in *Lord Byron's Aquatic Venice: Horizon Zero* p 44, drawing out the poet's strokes as he swam front-crawl down the Grand Canal, breathing to the left, then right, then left. Stroke by stroke he cross-stitched the opposing palazzo facades to form slices (not so very different from those of Mailen's sliced up fort) that examine the shifting relations between panorama and horizon in the new forms of visuality afforded by nineteenth-century technologies. Like Hansel and Gretel's crumbs, the incremental marked our way into difficult terrain. Once entered, things never again seemed quite the same. Wittgenstein had been there before us: 'If you measure a table with a yardstick, are you also measuring the yardstick? If you are measuring the yardstick, then you cannot be measuring the table at the same time.' * Han's drawing asks us: If a table can measure a yardstick could the strokes of an eighteenth-century swimmer notionally straighten the Grand Canal and rewrite the horizon of Venice?

* Ludwig Wittgenstein, *Remarks on the Foundations of Mathematics*, trans G Anscombe (Oxford: Blackwell, 1964), II 74.

45

Histories in the Making — Noam Andrews

It appears to some, but by no means all, that 'history' may have gone out of fashion in the practice of teaching architecture. This of course implies a certain selectivity of gaze, privileging some universities over others, some educators and indeed some traditions of pedagogy over others. But nevertheless, I believe it would not be untrue to claim that, over the last decade, the leading institutions have allowed the teaching of history to become less relevant than it was to the generations of students reared on a healthy diet of modernism.

Perhaps, though, it would be fairer to say that for the ranks of these earlier students, it wasn't that history was intrinsically relevant, but rather that it had *been made* to be relevant as part of the process of becoming an architect. For those students, a trip to Rome was *de rigueur*, and they could turn to Colin Rowe and a well-thumbed copy of *Towards a New Architecture* for an explanation of what was revolutionary about their course of study. History, here, served an integral role in the disciplinary inculcation of architects-to-be into the practices, rituals, belief structures and moral codes of modern architecture. In other words, history, in a purely utilitarian sense, was very useful.

It is not uncommon for pedagogies employing the study of history to be conscripted as agents of the institutional agenda to which they belong. One might even go so far as to say that it is exceptionally rare to find institutions (academies, disciplines, corporations) self-confident enough to promote a course of study that might in any way challenge the values, or validity, of the prevailing constellations and concentrations of institutional power. And so it was with the universities that staked their professional authority in modernism as an aesthetic and ideological paradigm. Twentieth-century architectural pedagogy persistently leveraged the undeniable cultural value of a more or less select group of famous Italian villas and cities (and representations of cities) – Villa Farnese, Villa Madama, the facades of the Grand Canal in Venice, the Nolli Plan – against the average student's expectations of space and inhabitation. By buying into the symbolic, yet non-historicist, disciplinary rationales that linked modernist architecture to Renaissance and Baroque 'precedents', a young architect could feel like he was participating in a reinvention of the Western world's architectural masterpieces, made newly abstract.

The catch was that these same Italian examples had been the source of inspiration for centuries of architectural production, none of it by definition modernist. To accomplish a new symbiosis based upon conceptual analyses of historic forms, without slavishly copying the form itself, semantic coincidences needed to be constructed between elements of historic buildings (which could be visited, drawn and formally analysed by students) and a projective vision of modern living tethered to *pilotis*. While it is not evident that the contours of this discursive approach would provide as stable a footpath for the contemporary architectural imagination, the mythologising of modernism's past worked at the time. Students were taught to invest their burgeoning professional identities in modernist forms and concepts which were intended to be not only new, progressive and revolutionary, but also historically situatable, stable and classic, and thus the beneficiary of architectural traditions that stretched back to the sixteenth century. To put it synoptically, this could only be accomplished by decades-long regimes of pedagogy in which the prestige of the history and practice of modern architecture were mutually self-reinforcing. The wide sweep of survey history courses, beginning from Antiquity and ending at iconic modernist buildings like the Villa Savoye, dovetailed neatly with the demand from teachers of architectural design for modernist staples – bathing pavilions, *brises-soleil* and basswood. The sum total effect of this novel integration of historical and design study was the gradual concretisation of a network of meaning between formal analyses of select historical architectures and a repertoire of modern form and formal operations, such as the famous 'phenomenal transparency'. Furthermore, as the years passed and the modern movement developed its own robust internal history, complete with twentieth-century icons, paradigms and masterpieces, the historical precedents used in architectural education came from within modernism itself. Design exercises tended to follow analyses of modernist buildings in an ouroboros of history and practice. The disciplinary aim was to implant a cognitive framework for the interpretation of architectural form coherent with the equivalencies established by earlier communities of modernist practitioners. And more so, to colonise and transform a student's way of thinking so that their future design work, long after they had left university, would always perpetuate the values they had been taught and the existence of the disciplinary structures which had invented these values.

But nothing lasts forever. How is it that we have come to our present situation, one in which history is no more than a dusty fig leaf straining to provide modesty for a digital body that shows little regard for even the most minimal conventions of academic dress? Does the current near total divergence of research interests between students of architectural history and students of architectural design not point to an intrinsic impoverishment of architecture as it is learned? It would be easy, and perhaps correct, to pin the blame for this on the digital revolution that swept through the academies and washed away traditions of architectural practice, in the process altering what it means to be an architect and establishing co-dependent relationships with new generations of machines. To do so, however, would be to ignore the number of times this same story has been repeated. Whether we talk about the historicism of the École des Beaux-Arts or the 'Texas Rangers', the practice of teaching architecture and the practice of teaching architectural history have a time-honoured track record of going hand in hand: new form, historical justification; historic form reinterpreted in new materials (as in Viollet-le-Duc's 'modern' iron structures inspired by the mid-nineteenth-century Gothic Revival). Far from a unique twentieth-century occurrence, the disruption of the partnership of history and practice by technology is a fundamental *modus operandi* for reordering formal meaning in architectural discourse. It is even more surprising, then, that the engrained patterns of periodic, intra-disciplinary cooperation and estrangement could be so easily forgotten, in a matter of years and a flurry of excitement.

It is credibly claimed that the muscles flexed by computational and parametric software are precisely those underutilised in architecture. Direct links between computer modelling and manufacturing, and between assembly strategy and economic efficiency, exploit redundancies of time and material in the traditional process of architecture-making. Sinuous curves at an architectonic scale and infinite variability of component parts, for example, reveal capacities architecture did not know it had (at least not without expending a lot more effort). It would be hard to fault architectural historians for initially not being able to cope with the rhetorical performance of technical complexity, combined with a bullish apathy towards historical precedent, displayed by practitioners of parametric and computational design in its early years. How exactly could the Barcelona Pavilion, for example, be brought to bear upon the phalanxes of undulating protuberances that streamed from the early twenty-first-century computer? In the internal dynamics of the discipline, it was a practice-oriented paradigm that diverged, suddenly and sharply, from the theories of its modernist and postmodernist predecessors, discarding the semantic apparatus of architecture which had been cyclically built, and rebuilt, over hundreds of years. The teaching of architectural history found it hard to keep up. It was not that the Villa Madama was any less beautiful; rather, it was that the paradigmatic building samples historically used to teach architecture no longer seemed to speak to how practitioners at leading universities sought to teach contemporary architecture.

But it has to be asked whether the rapid evolution of software and hardware technology is in and of itself unhealthy for the discipline of architecture. Perhaps counter-intuitively, it seems that the act of pushing the boundaries of architectural practice into a realm with little connection to the Italian stalwarts of modernism has breathed new life into the ways in which history can be used to augment, strengthen, ground and contextualise the teaching of architecture. Surely design is impoverished by its current schism from historical discourse, but would it be such a bad thing to lovingly set aside the icons of architectural worship for a chance to reinvent a critical space for history, one that is more directly relevant to the teaching of contemporary practice?

In my estimation, this volume of selected work from Diploma Unit 15 is testament to the productivity, pleasure and risk-taking of reintegrating history into contemporary methods of producing, and indeed teaching, architecture. The work must also be seen as supporting a very particular reading and construction of history that stands in direct contrast to recent attempts by theorists and historians to absorb the formal languages of digital design into the historical lexicon of architecture – as in the use of the word 'ornament' to discuss the articulated skin of a parametric surface. Equally, it goes against the trend of using a parametric vocabulary to anachronistically describe the formal properties of Antique architectures. One cannot help but wonder whether reinscribing contemporary practice within categories established by a traditional architectural history is truly the most productive approach to addressing the aporia of our current moment.

One possibility to consider, quite simply, is that the histories contemporary architecture *needs* do not fall, strictly speaking, under the remit of traditional architectural history. There may be other confluences of historical events that would speak louder to students educated under the current pedagogical regimes. We might think of this as an oblique history of architecture, perhaps architectonic in substance, but substantially located within the discourses of other historical disciplines. The *Building Geometry* exhibition at the Graduate School of Design at Harvard University, which I co-curated in January 2012, was one such attempt to use the exhibition format as an opportunity to insert into a school of architecture material drawn from the history of mathematics,

in this case nineteenth-century French and German mathematical models. At one level the models – products of the tenures of Gaspard Monge (1746–1818) at the École Polytechnique and of Felix Klein (1849–1925) at the University of Göttingen – belonged to a historical moment in which students were taught abstract formal knowledge, called Synthetic or Descriptive Geometry, through material artefacts. Championed under the directorships of Monge and Klein, the models also embodied an institutionally sanctioned intellectual, and indeed aesthetic, programme for geometry.

To produce the Klein models, numerous parameters needed to be fixed in order to generate values revealing the characteristic 'singularities' of mathematically defined, non-Euclidean surfaces, which were then translated into series of uncannily modern plaster sculptures. Representing equations by the singularities they could produce was by no means self-evident, and tied directly into Klein's theories on geometrical classification. Klein taught his students that apprehending these surfaces in physical form was fundamental to 'knowing' a surface, reflecting his conviction that *räumliches Anschauungsvermögen*, translated as the ability to spatially visualise, was key to the evaluation and doing of mathematics. On the other hand, the French models, actually produced by the famous Pixii workshop for Monge's disciple Théodore Olivier (1793–1853), were expensive brass and mahogany affairs. Consisting of weighted silk strings hanging from frames, the models were operable and described groups of geometrical transformations deemed to be otherwise difficult to visualise. Many of Monge's students had different professional goals to Klein's, coming to the Polytechnique not so much to work with higher level mathematics as to be trained as members of a newly emerging professional class of architects, engineers, stonecutters or carpenters. The Descriptive Geometry taught by Monge was very much tailored to them; the product of a post-Revolutionary ethos in which 'practical' mathematics was deemed to reinforce qualities of judgement and reflection necessary for a worker's productive contribution to society. Here we find that by tapping into wider discourse networks, histories may be revealed which more directly tackle the preoccupations and condition of contemporary architecture, in this case the links between a practice of making and the exploration of surface geometry.

On another level the mathematical models, with their prescient formal qualities and ambivalence to the perspectival gaze, appear to anticipate the forms and geometries generated by twenty-first-century computer software. While these qualities are not nearly as interesting to

p50
Théodore Olivier,
*geometric string figure
of intersecting cones*

historians of mathematics as they might be to practitioners of architecture, *Building Geometry* aimed to use the models' formal similarity to confront architecture students with an alternative pre-history to their current studio projects. In so doing, the intention was to inject a modicum of institutional critique into a student culture dispossessed of some of its nerve. If the nineteenth-century mathematical models could be accepted by architecture students as products of ideologically loaded disciplinary and pedagogical initiatives, perhaps they might also not deem their projects exempt from the implicit ideological agenda of the institution in which they were produced. My hope was that students might use this obliquely architectonic history as an the opportunity to look critically at the process of their own professionalisation, and to see their education as participating in the same types of disciplinary politics that have always marked academic training.

The histories addressed by Diploma 15 were those scattered along the Grand Tour, as embodied in the trail of must-see buildings and ruins that had enticed pleasure- and edification-seeking gentlemen of means to the sweat-soaked streets of Italy in the eighteenth century. And although it would be a misrepresentation to say that historical engagement was the driving force behind the unit work at its inception (the unit began by using evolutionary paradigms of island biogeography in order to create architectural adaptations to economic and political islands), by 2008 its focus had shifted to the 'non-physical', cultural contexts of 'Antiquity' and 'The Future' that had coevolved with the Grand Tour sites. At that time in the Architectural Association, Diploma 15 fought a battle defending the right to have 'context' sit at the same table as other generators of architectural proposals – form, technology and programme. And by gradually broadening the term's remit to include larger cultural contexts, the unit allowed itself to slip away from relying on a 'scientific' conceit and moved towards the development of 'hypercontexts' – amalgams of linked information that in and of themselves gestured, to greater and lesser extent, in the direction of architectural proposals. In a way this shift from physical site to cultural site made the task for the students doubly challenging: now their projects had to convincingly address the constraints of a cultural history as well as those of a physical place. Bringing the collection and analysis of historical information on Naples to bear upon the politics of contemporary Naples, say, became very much the core conceptual move of many of the better Diploma 15 projects.

But thinking back on it now, what appears to have been truly at stake, in some ways, was less the visibility of context as a critical tool in the architect's toolkit (although this is certainly an important issue) than the idea of what architectural education had been and could still be, and the possibilities of history as a resource for a vibrant, creative practice. It should go without saying that the history under discussion had been vetted and tacitly deemed to be in accordance with the pedagogical values the AA wanted to endorse – a stroke of good fortune that I attribute partly to the quality of the base material and partly to a growing sense in architectural academia that the prevailing technological paradigms had not quite panned out the way everyone had hoped. As students and teachers, we were given free rein to retrace (and reinterpret) the familiar journeys to the haunting beauty of Tivoli, the lunar-splendour of the *mer de glace*, the sun-drenched vision of Agrigento and the solemnity of Herculaneum. We scaled glacial walls, entreated one student to re-enact Lord Byron's habit of diving into Venice's Grand Canal, and raced around the Lingotto in Turin. It was romantic, in a cultural sense; it was most definitely physical, compressing into two weeks what had taken Goethe two years; and I believe it was educational. Far removed from the mid-twentieth-century modernist pilgrimages, with their stress on learning abstract formal concepts from Renaissance and Baroque buildings, the tours brought us face to face with the key sites around which some of Western civilisation's richest cultural narratives had been repetitively constructed. By cultivating an awareness of the historicism of these narratives, students learned about the historical contingency of our own contemporary visions of history. They also learned to recognise the integral role played by media in the construction of cultural values, in other words, how the many images produced of Antique sites or nineteenth-century technology did not represent so much what the artist had actually seen as the cultural framework within which he was working (as per Gombrich's understanding of style). When combined in architectural proposals, these lessons produced a powerful cocktail of cultural self-consciousness. By playing with and against type, students could selectively appeal to our current notions of history while simultaneously revealing the constructedness of these notions.

The fact remains that this productive engagement with history had to happen primarily within the space of visual representation, and not within the typical academic format for treating historical topics, the space of the essay. This crucial change in format, from an essay accompanied by several images to an image-based portfolio accompanied by several statements, had repercussions for the range of topics that could be addressed. As a collection of historical images is rarely the same thing as an architecture project, the students were challenged to produce drawings which would not only do justice to the complexity of the historical material and the results

Animalium signantur litere A. adjungitur hisce Scala Geometrica cujus ope, quisque voluerit partium singularum proportiones elicere queat. Ut ex hujus ARCÆ dispositione Athei increduli discant non fuisse adeo incapacem ARCAM, Ut non cu

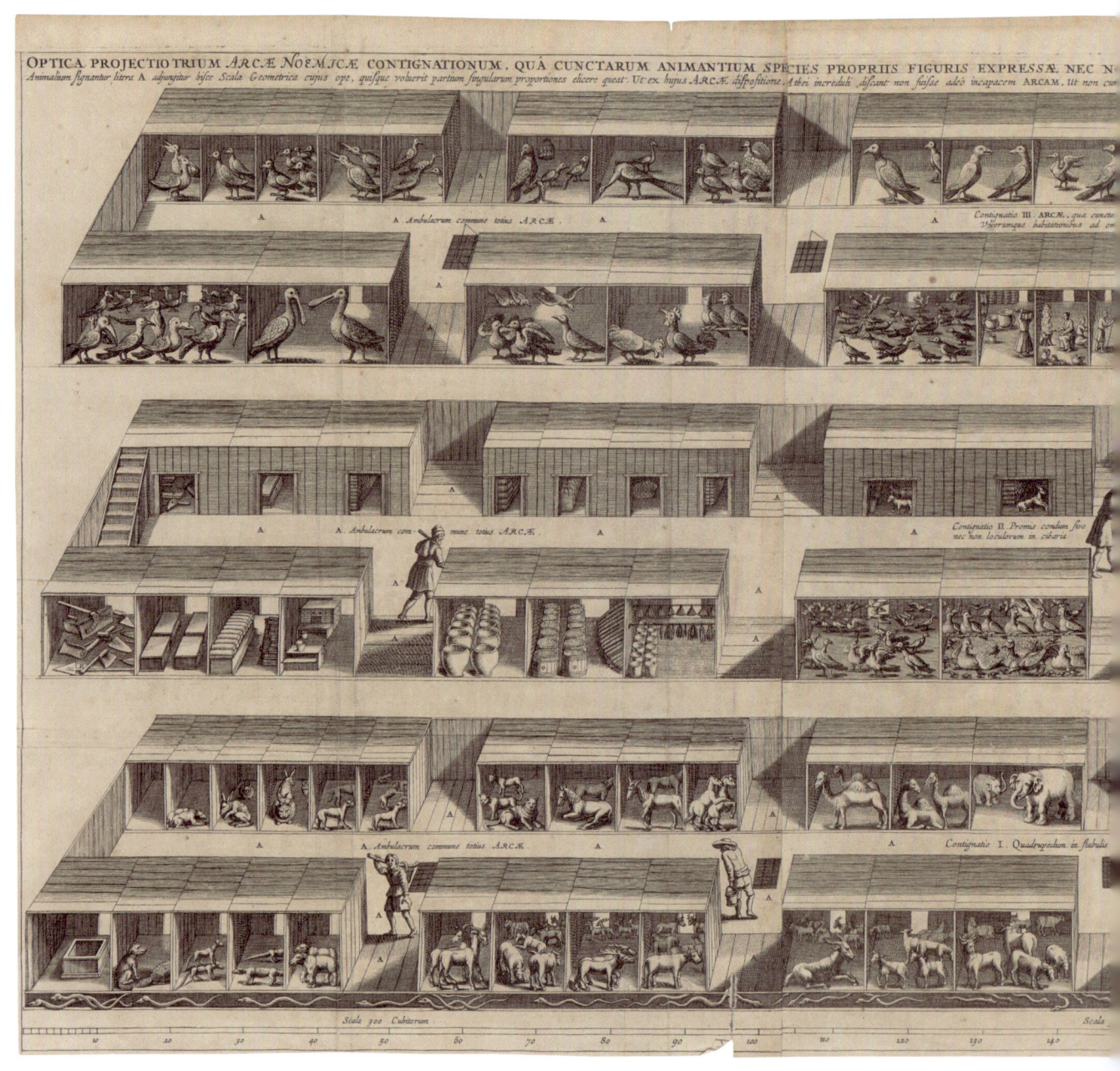

A. Ambulacrum commune totius ARCÆ.

Contignatio III. ARCÆ, qua cuncta
Visorumque habitationibus ad o

A. Ambulacrum commune totius ARCÆ.

Contignatio II. Proma condum suo
nec hor. loculorum in cibaria

A. Ambulacrum commune totius ARCÆ.

Contignatio I. Quadrupedum in stabulis

Scala 300 Cubitorum.

Scala

10   20   30   40   50   60   70   80   90   100   110   120   130   140

54

UNDEM STABULA ET MANSIONES EX UTRAQUE ARCÆ PARTE ORDINE DISPOSITÆ, SPECTANTUR AMBULACRA IN ADMINISTRATIONEM

stium quas in Orbe Terrarum reperiuntur species commodè continere potuerit, imo complura adhuc superfunt Stabula, quæ malè de ARCÆ sentientium ipsis Bestys adnumeratorum habitationi reservantur.

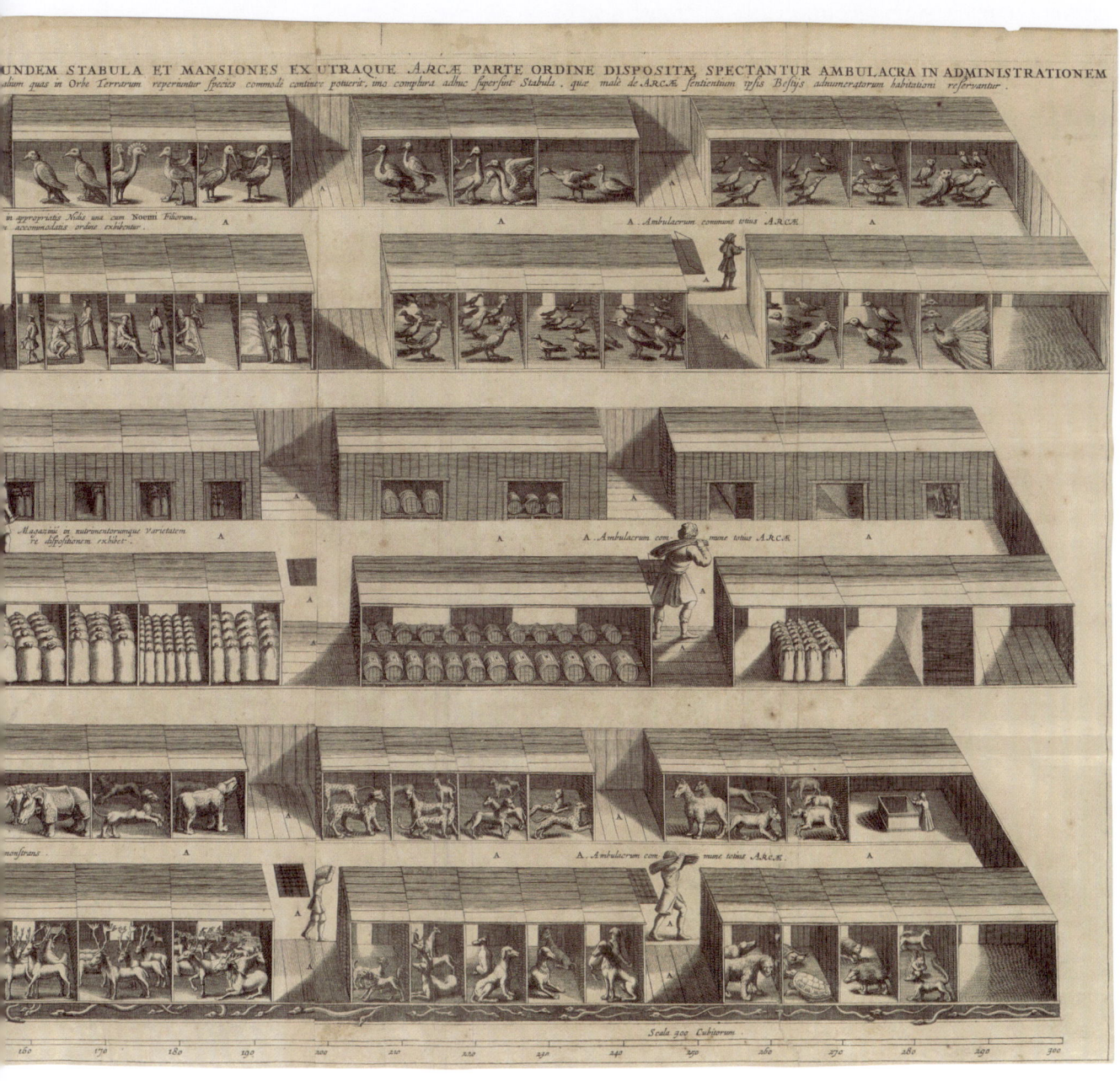

Scala 300 Cubitorum

160   170   180   190   200   210   220   230   240   250   260   270   280   290   300

of their research, but would also perform the translation of the most salient issues into a thesis which could then be 'tested' in architectonic form. While there are certainly many ways, in theory, to accomplish this, in practice, working literally with 'what one saw' resulted in overly figural drawings that were trapped in an uncomfortable relationship to their original historical material. It seemed that reproducing a historical image had to be done carefully and with subtlety, as its presence could overwhelm a drawing and keep it tethered to a textbook-like feeling that shut down creative speculation. The power of the image had to be curated effectively, or there was nowhere to go.

The alternative was to keep the historical material separate, and hold it in balance with the large speculative drawings produced by Diploma 15, many of which have been reproduced in this volume. These drawings resulted from a search for historical information that could be extracted and plotted on the page, a way of sidestepping the parlour games of postmodernism by not making the connection to history hinge upon formal similarity or visual cues. I am very much aware that the use of the term information appeals to a notion of scientific objectivity that has been effectively historicised in recent years. But to use the term information, or even data, served two important discursive purposes. First, it challenged the primacy of the meagre dataset deemed appropriate for use in architecture by a 'parametric discourse' fixated on environmental factors. And secondly, 'information' accomplished the task of distilling a complex of historical events into a conceptual quantity which could be worked over on paper. There is a sense in which many of the Diploma 15 drawings operate through a tenacious literalism, asking explicative questions of historical constructs in order to illustrate how these constructs might actually work and inform new proposals.

The Jesuit Athanasius Kircher's (1602–1680) treatise *Arca Noë* (1675) is a good historical precedent for this kind of pragmatic reasoning. Taking the biblical story of Noah's ark as self-evident, Kircher sought to figure out exactly how big the ark would have had to have been to accommodate the entire animal kingdom, the order in which animals would have been led onto the ship, and how they could be stored on board so that they would not eat each other. Rather than getting flustered by the existential questions, Kircher kept asking practical ones. And by asking practical questions, he came up with a vision of the past alongside several exquisite illustrations. Similarly, Yo Murata's investigation of Juan van der Hamen's (1596–1631) *Still-Life with Flowers* (1627) engaged with the still-life painting as a meditation on death and the passage of time, in the guise of an impossible

————————— p 54
Athanasius Kircher

————————— p 57
Juan van der Hamen

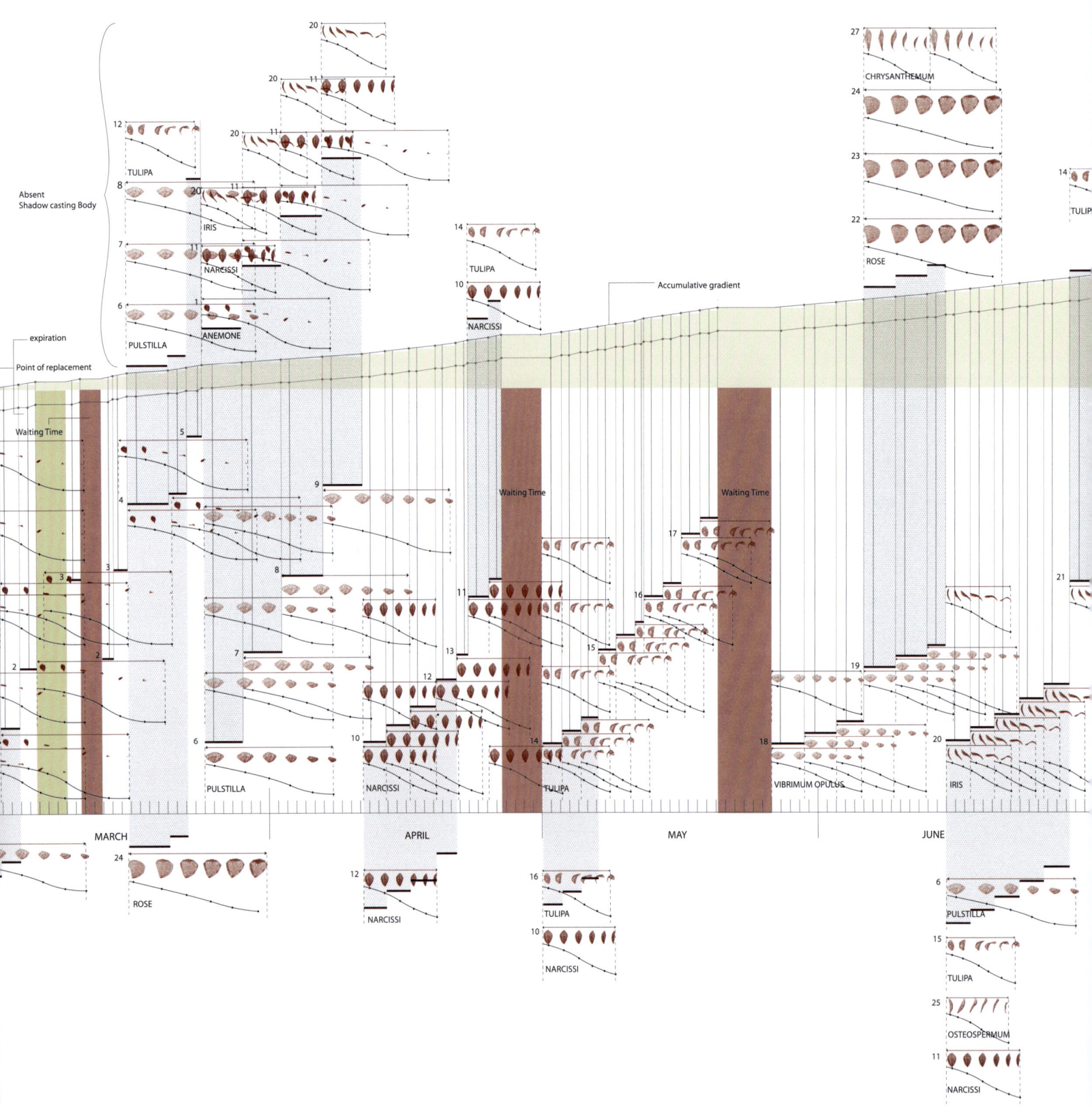

Absent
Shadow casting Body

expiration

Point of replacement

Waiting Time

TULIPA

IRIS

NARCISSI

PULSTILLA

ANEMONE

TULIPA

NARCISSI

Accumulative gradient

CHRYSANTHEMUM

ROSE

TULIPA

Waiting Time

Waiting Time

PULSTILLA

NARCISSI

TULIPA

VIBRIMUM OPULUS

IRIS

MARCH

ROSE

APRIL

NARCISSI

MAY

TULIPA

NARCISSI

JUNE

PULSTILLA

TULIPA

OSTEOSPERMUM

NARCISSI

58

arrangement of flowers never able to bloom together. Nevertheless, she concluded that it was still possible to determine the season when each flower would bloom, the fictive shadows their figures would cast, as well as represent the ways that their leaves and petals would theoretically wilt. Yo Murata's drawings on this subject elucidate the artifice of the painting even as they hint at the optimal times for harvesting the flowers needed to complete the painting. And by having proceeded methodically, Murata's work on van der Hamen allowed her to establish a convincing intellectual framework and graphic language for her subsequent architectural proposal (a cemetery) predicated upon multiple rates of decomposition and decay.

As with Yo Murata, the work of Marilia Spanou and Theo Wyatt Petrides illustrates the playful possibilities of using historical material as a source of inspiration, exploring two very different crossings of the Alps, namely Hannibal's famous journey in 218 BC during the Second Punic War and the picturesque route of the average eighteenth-century gentleman respectively. In the case of Theo Wyatt Petrides, his research translated neatly into a proposal for a permanent light installation in the Gotthard Base tunnel – the immense infrastructural project connecting Germany and Italy through a tunnel burrowed under the Alps. Having conducted site visits and analyses of eighteenth- and nineteenth-century paintings of the Alpine crossing, most notably by JMW Turner (1775–1851), his installation re-enacted the visuality of the overlapping vistas and changes of field depth experienced by a passenger on a bumpy carriage ride along narrow Alpine paths. Translated into a multimedia extravaganza on the walls of the new tunnel, the choreography of Theo Wyatt Petrides' proposal was penned like a musical score, corresponding to a sped-up version of the sights that would now be lost forever with the opening of the tunnel.

Marilia Spanou tackled the indeterminacy of Hannibal's crossing by comparing the various routes theorised by historians, including one theory attributed to Napoleon. In drawing the 'spatial and temporal conflict' of these theories, and cross-referencing them with GIS data, she was able to speculate upon the location of various known events, such as when 'horses and mules fell off the edge with their loads' or when Hannibal's men were 'attacked by the Allobroges'. But rather than attempting to come up with the most accurate theory, Spanou's drawings hold all of the theories in tension, plotting them over each other and mapping degrees of uncertainty, including the spatial dislocation of events (from one theory to the next) and the range of geographical areas which could have been covered during the night and day (between points of known information). Working masterfully to create a graphic language capable of translating

p 58
Yo Murata

p 62
JMW Turner

p 36, 63
Theo Wyatt Petrides

p 65
Marilia Spanou

textual sources, she illustrates how historical material, if approached with a fastidious attention to detail, can produce startlingly original graphic results, even by spatialising the impossibility of conclusively answering historical questions.

Like many of the projects in this volume, the innovation in Marilia Spanou's work occurs in the drawings. The space of representation is the primary site of conceptual development, because it is here that history may be possibly materialised in a visual form with enough generative potential for further design work. This process is repetitive and laborious; moving from textual sources to the invention of a novel graphic language is never easy. Building up enough representational momentum to produce the density of information necessary to justify the existence of a large-scale drawing is similarly painful. A flexible idea of what a drawing (based on Hannibal) might look like has to be maintained while developing a rigorous system of logic in order to extract a narrow set of information from the texts or other original sources. This happens in the space and time of production, without complete knowledge of the finished product, and with a trust that the results will be worth the wait. More akin to works of art than two-dimensional printouts from a digital model, Marilia Spanou's Hannibal drawings could not possibly have been automatically generated. They refuse the emptying out of visual signification that the increasing integration of technology often produces. As evidenced in these and other standout Diploma 15 drawings, like those of Sayaka Namba and Angelo Sanghoon Han, representation preserves its ability to concretise multiple processes; to combine objects of different scales in the same space; to bring together different sets of information. These visual configurations, themselves necessarily in dialogue with the additional drawings making up the architecture project, are 'good to think with', demanding the active engagement of the viewer to correlate relations between graphic symbols, and between graphic symbol and historical referent. As such, they inherently challenge the flaccidity of the current visual culture in architecture and the intellectual complacency that results from an over-reliance on pressing '⌘P'.

p 17–18
Sayaka Namba

p 10–11, 77
Angelo Sanghoon Han

The task at hand, as I see it, has been to ask what it is that 'history' can continue to provide for the evolving practice of educating architects in an age which claims little connection to the ghosts of architecture's past. One strategy, as previously mentioned, is to persist in using traditional architectural terminology to render computational or parametric architecture more familiar. The fact that this strategy maintains the cultural prestige of these theorists and historians, and the relevance of their disciplinary expertise, should not obscure the fact that architectural practitioners themselves also benefit from this endowment of cultural capital. However a more useful strategy to deal with the productive disruptions wrought by technology is to find histories that speak more clearly to our contemporary condition, irrespective of their disciplinary moorings. Here, it is the responsibility of the architect-educator to identify thematic fault lines in contemporary architectural discourse and begin the work of placing them in dialogue with earlier moments of technological advancement and its impact on disciplinary norms and visual cultures. Finally, the work of Diploma 15 is suggestive of yet another approach that draws on the richness of historical material as a source of inspiration for contemporary design and as a strategy for addressing the complexities of site and context. Selectively adopting a historicism that makes use of historical visual and textual cues in the paper space of a project even as it extracts abstracted 'operative themes' from historical material, Diploma 15's nuanced strategy gestures to a fruitful rapprochement between architecture and wider bodies of culture.

Nevertheless, however productive an active engagement with history may be for teaching architectural design, it is necessary to continue to ask tough questions of the nature of this engagement. The use of historical information to produce the self-conscious complexity characteristic of many of the Diploma 15 drawings is very much a response to a prevailing aesthetic paradigm and the use of contemporary technologies. Diderot and d'Alembert also attempted to map information in their *Encyclopédie* by configuring diverse figural and abstract forms, and the *Encyclopédie* looks nothing like these drawings. To own up to the fact that the method of consciously incorporating historical material into architectural representation is culturally contingent, is to acknowledge the impact that aesthetic paradigms have upon the production of 'successful' representational forms. It stands to reason that, if applied correctly, history can put pressure upon the present. But the histories chosen, and the graphic methods of interacting with them, speak volumes about our time.

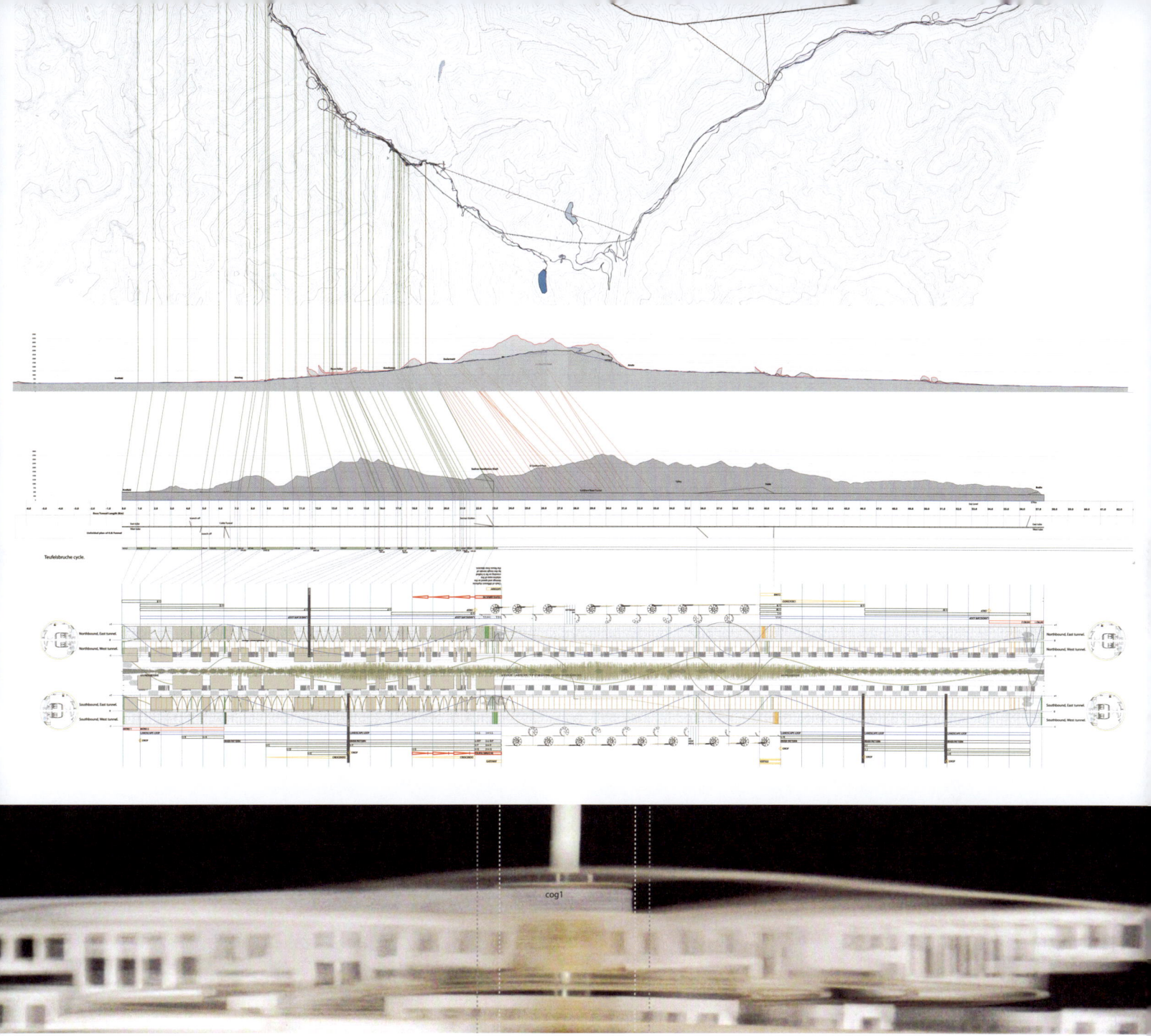

Teufelsbruche cycle.

cog1

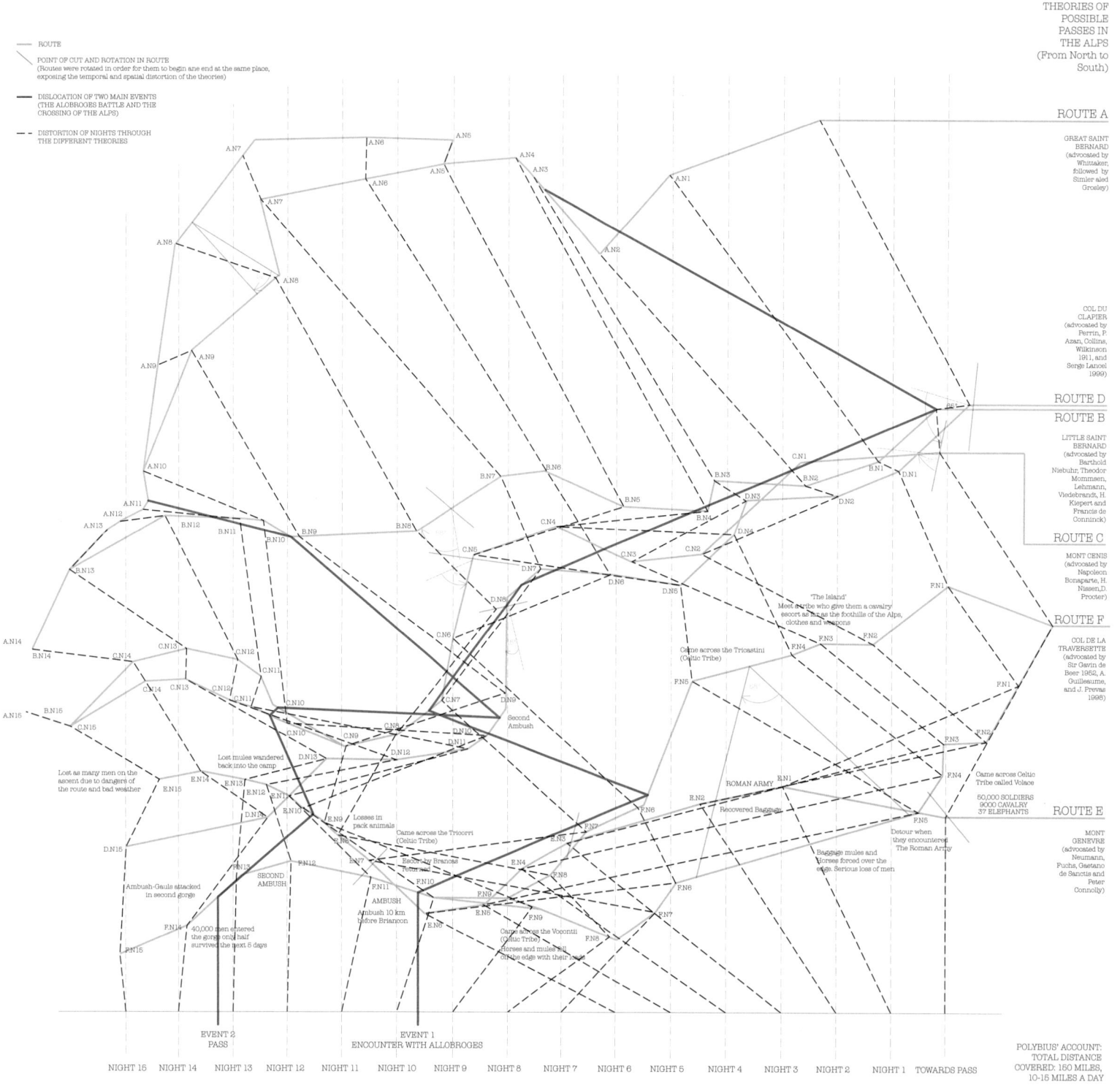

THEORIES OF POSSIBLE PASSES IN THE ALPS (From North to South)

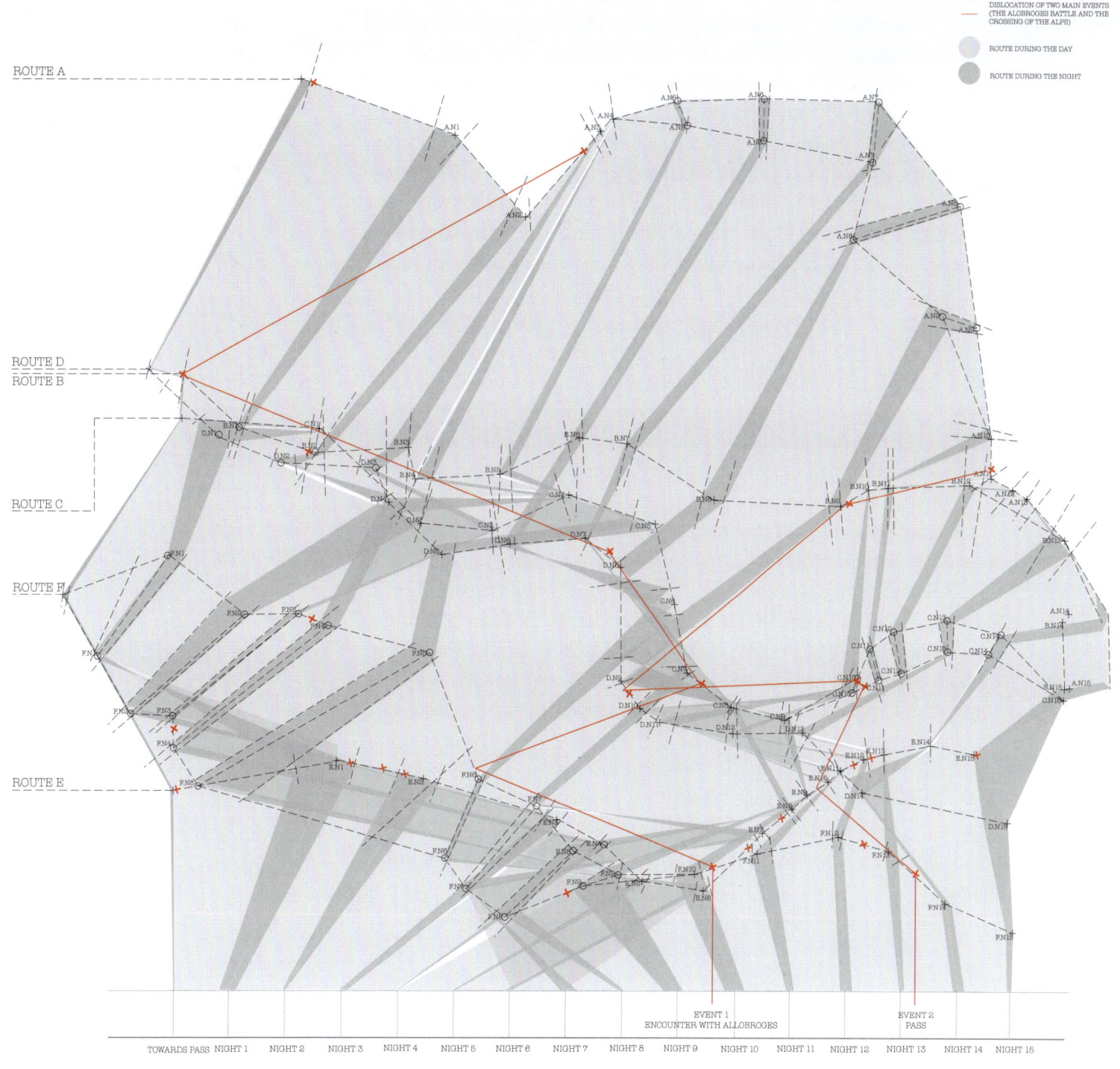

DISLOCATION OF TWO MAIN EVENTS
(THE ALOBROGES BATTLE AND THE
CROSSING OF THE ALPS)

ROUTE DURING THE DAY

ROUTE DURING THE NIGHT

ROUTE A

ROUTE D
ROUTE B

ROUTE C

ROUTE F

ROUTE E

EVENT 1
ENCOUNTER WITH ALLOBROGES

EVENT 2
PASS

TOWARDS PASS NIGHT 1   NIGHT 2   NIGHT 3   NIGHT 4   NIGHT 5   NIGHT 6   NIGHT 7   NIGHT 8   NIGHT 9   NIGHT 10   NIGHT 11   NIGHT 12   NIGHT 13   NIGHT 14   NIGHT 15

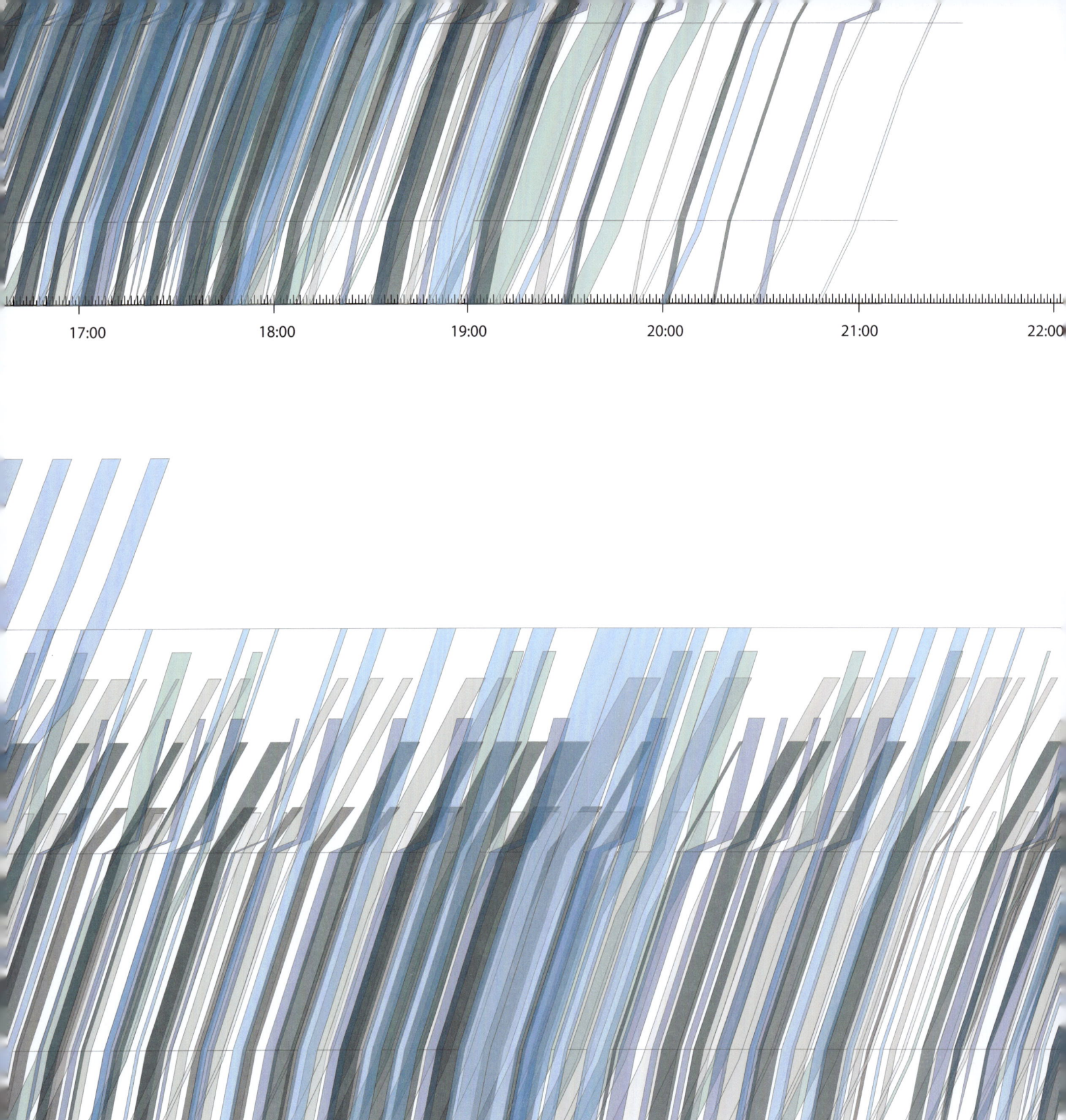

17:00   18:00   19:00   20:00   21:00   22:00

The Big Drawing, or How Big is the Table?

It follows that any drawing carrying so many iterative marks will be big. We measured the limits of this bigness by a table, or to be precise by '*the tables*' that have inspired the peculiar name of the AA's final examination, where students present their portfolios on top of the aforementioned four-legged beasts in the AA Library. These tables are fortunately quite big (228 x 105 cm), but still our drawings would hang over the edges, draping the laps of the bemused examiners. Exceeding anything that was convenient or corporate, their sheer size would engulf our flailing arms as we attempted to aid the students in a smooth rendition of their portfolio. Occasionally the drawing exceeded itself in other ways and became three-dimensional, a model, but always one to be read as a drawing, or as a set of drawings joined in space – as was the case with Derin Ozken's *Three Regimes, Fifty-One Typological Transformations and One Hundred and Twenty-Seven Years: The Unravelling*

p 21
Derin Ozken

of Typological Loyalty <u>p 12</u>, <u>21</u>. The notative impulse was always present: the drawings were never the seamless excretions of rapid prototyping, but rather the time-consuming assemblage of a myriad of components, and often bits of string that somehow wanted to simply be a very fine, drawn line. This, most clearly, in Noam Andrews' hypercontext model [*Murailles East, Structure and Facade Detail*, <u>p 31</u>, <u>67</u>], where 3D drawing became a machine to generate 2D drawings.

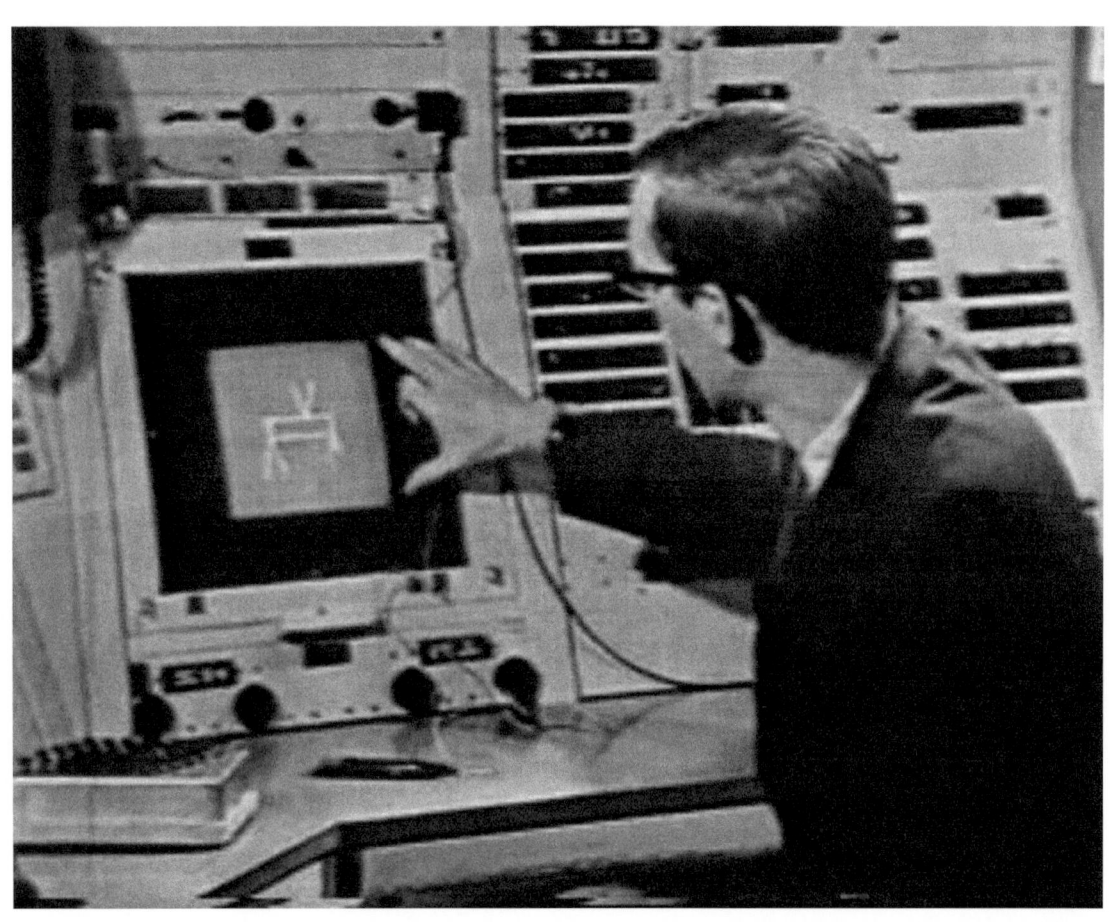

Sketchpad software (now widely recognised as the progenitor of the design software that incubates all architecture today). Sutherland instructed his TV audience to picture a piece of paper, two miles wide, behind the window, bearing a drawing measuring a quarter of a mile across. * Trapped inside the computer, Sutherland's drawing is read through a scope, giving the ability to focus on 'any portion of the page desired at any degree of magnification'. By contrast, our digital drawings are stranded outside the computer, scopeless and unwieldy. If you are close enough to read them, you can't see the whole; if you step far back enough to see the whole, the frailty of their hatchings eludes you. Unlike the anamorphic, multiscalarity has no true viewing point. There can only be one conclusion for these drawings that fail as drawings. They are drawings not to be looked at but to be read.

More like bedsheets than drawings, these drawings spoke of other scalar loyalties as they invoked the span of a drawing body — of early 1950s Matisse, with his stubby brush taped to the end of a long broom handle, sweeping trails of acrobat's contours. Except our broom handle was the plotter's arm and the hypercontext drawings were, for the most part, devoid of figure, their surface etched instead with the incremental bites of the boustrophedon-like printing head. 'Scope' and 'magnifying glass' and 'window' were the words Ivan Sutherland used in 1963 to describe the interface of his pioneering

* See *MIT Science Reporter: Computer Sketchpad*, John Fitch, dir. Russell Morash, WGBH-TV, Boston, 1963. Also Ivan Edward Sutherland *Sketchpad: A Man-machine Graphical Communication System*, PhD dissertation submitted in 1963 to Massachusetts Institute of Technology, published by University of Cambridge Computer Laboratory, 2003, 64.

Mary Beard and Francesca Hughes
in Conversation

*Newnham College, Cambridge, a don's study, the sound of a clock
ticking on the mantelpiece and of furniture being dragged around.*

Francesca Hughes Now I want to…
[starts dragging a table across the room]

> *Mary Beard* What do you want to do?
> *[pulling two chairs up to the table]*

FH What I want to do is to start by putting some images
on the table. One is…

> *MB* Ooh!

FH Yes, they're good ones. One is Claude Lorrain's *Seaport with
the Embarkation of the Queen of Sheba* of 1648 and the other is
Turner's homage to Claude Lorrain, *Dido building Carthage*,
done 160-odd years later. I thought we could talk around these
images and use them to set up the idea of Antiquity as a *context*
for invention. More specifically I wanted to ask why on earth,
a century and a half later, Turner was doing this copy of Lorrain
copying Antiquity?

    Copying is of course the central medium for the fabrication
of the artifice of Antiquity, allowing each era to remake
antiquity into whatever they need it to be. One of the students
in the unit, Angelo, performed a kind of spatial forensics on the
two paintings and discovered that the painting by Lorrain has
a very simple perspective, a single vanishing point, whereas in
the Turner each fragment of Antiquity, each piece of architecture,
has its *own* vanishing point, and they're all in different locations.
So Turner, in paying homage to Lorrain through the medium
of Antiquity, is also conducting some kind of radical spatial
invention – long before cubism, he's setting up a multiplicitous
spatiality. Angelo concluded in his *Perspectival Forensic Study*
that this invites one to think either that the subject is moving

——————————— p 72
Claude Lorrain

——————————— p 73
JMW Turner

——————————— p 10–11, 77
Angelo Sanghoon Han

74

around, is a roving eye, so the vanishing point is moving. *Or that the subject is actually a crowd – a crowd of people looking at the painting – and so the multiplicity is echoed in the audience. Or that Turner is somehow really declaring that these are fragments, they're on their own, they're un-whole, and therefore he cannot install the wholeness of a single-point perspective. And it struck me that this might be a good way to put to you what your work is: the 'making', as you refer to it, that you must do when working with this artifice of Antiquity, and the kind of self-consciousness of the copying that's embedded in that.*

MB Yeah, what's interesting to me, in terms of the analysis of the painting to start with, is both what you say, but also the way it reflects upon the iconographic subject. What strikes me first of all is that you have a city here – Dido is building the city of Carthage, but the unfinished Carthage is indistinguishable from the ruined Carthage. So in a sense the 'project' is always already ruined. The ruin is both a beginning and an end, both a death and a start, and you can't actually tell the difference between the two. And of course the other thing is that it's a tragedy, isn't it? Because along with the iconography this is a reading of Virgil: Dido is never going to build Carthage. You've got all that sense of fragmentation and a kind of multiplicity of viewpoints on the scene, but it's a scene anyway that Dido is never going to finish. So it's an image of a city, it's an image of fragmentation, of starting, of finishing. And we're coming upon this both too early and too late – which is really in a sense what Classics is all about. You're never quite there soon enough, but you're always there too early.

FH Too early how?

MB The fragment is potentially incomplete in two ways. I mean Turner is asking you the question (and probably Claude Lorrain is too, to some extent): is it not yet finished, or is it ruined? Have we finished the project of antiquity, and are therefore seeing it in its *decadence*, literally having 'fallen down', or is there somehow still a possibility of completion? As with Fuseli's foot [a reference to *The Artist Moved to Despair by the Grandeur of Antique Fragments* by Henry Fuseli, 1778–79], you can't tell the difference

p78
Henry Fuseli

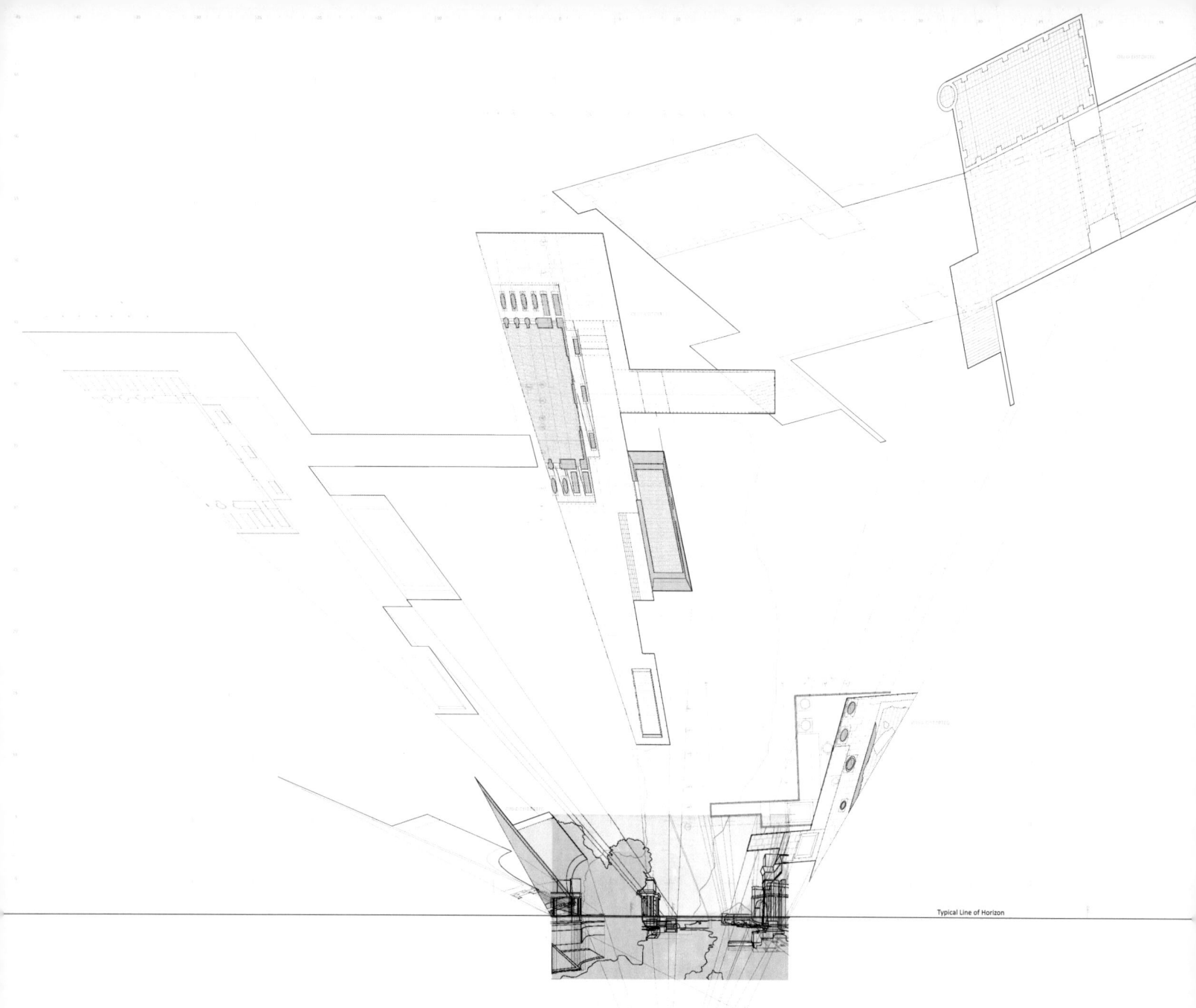

Typical Line of Horizon

VPnt-Default

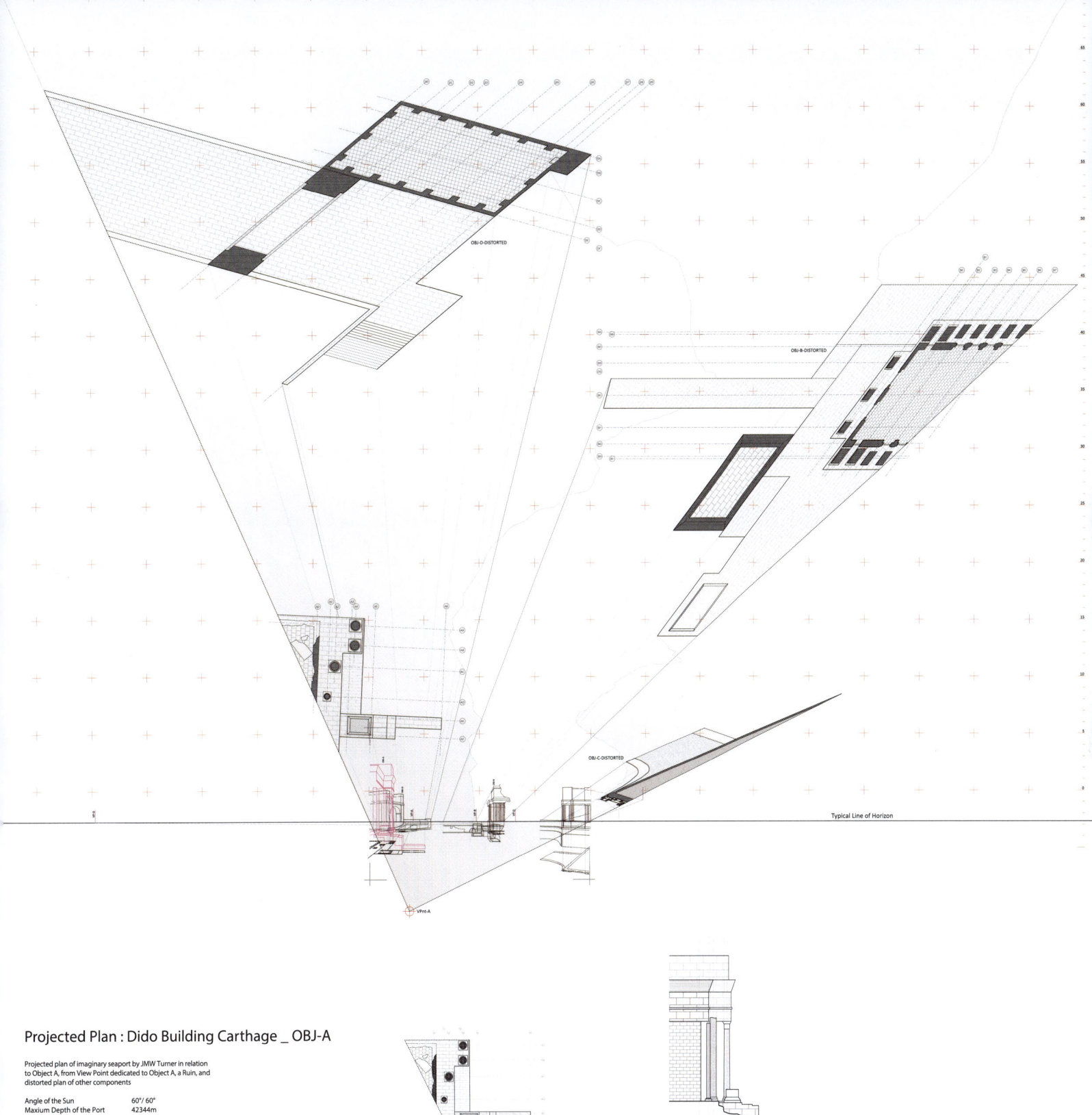

OBJ-D-DISTORTED

OBJ-B-DISTORTED

OBJ-C-DISTORTED

Typical Line of Horizon

VPnt-A

Projected Plan : Dido Building Carthage _ OBJ-A

Projected plan of imaginary seaport by JMW Turner in relation
to Object A, from View Point dedicated to Object A, a Ruin, and
distorted plan of other components

Angle of the Sun   60°/ 60°
Maxium Depth of the Port   42344m

– Weight of composition is shifted to the east
– OBJ-B, OBJ-C, OBJ-D are stretched generally in vertical direction

PL-OBJ-A

SE-OBJ-A-01

78

between a fragment that isn't finished yet and a fragment that has fallen down. And poor old Dido, she'll never finish this city – she has to end up on the bloody pyre, you know, because she is the person who allows Rome to happen, who makes Rome. So it's a terribly loaded image.

FH Is that why Turner changes it from Sheba to Dido?

MB I don't know, but it's not like, 'There's our Sheba, off she goes!' Dido's never going to leave, she's going to be on the pyre here. And she is the victim of a man, Aeneas, who will build this city – or something that looks just like it – somewhere else, and that somewhere else is going to be Rome.

FH This fragment can only be completed somewhere else, in another kind of stone, another time, another place. So is that then the project of Antique scholarship?

MB Well there's more than one project of Antique scholarship, isn't there? And I think that it is built on some of the paradoxes you see here. In part it's about recuperation and return. And anybody who did Classics, or looked at classical literature or classical history or classical archaeology, would be telling you a lie if they said they'd never thought: 'What was it really like?' or 'How could I complete that?' 'What was it like then?' – you can put it as if it was a very simple question to ask, but it is of course a terribly difficult question, because you are saying: 'What would be the conditions under which I could know what it was like? What would I need to know in order to hear Virgil for the first time, like somebody heard it in the age of Augustus?' And an awful lot of apparently rather cheesy nineteenth-century classical painting was playing with those ideas. Alma Tadema, for example – as recent work shows – is obviously much more complicated than he has traditionally been taken to be. So there is that, but then there's also the sense that Antiquity is an uncompleted project. You know, what *are* we doing when we read Plato? Actually, we're not just looking back, we're not just trying to 'decode' Plato, we're trying to *do* philosophy as a project, and doing philosophy within the modern world is, as philosophers always tell you, about the project of completing

Plato. And so you've got something that is retrospective, something that is prospective, and then of course you've got everything that happens in between, which is what makes it so rich. Turner's painting is a very good example of that. It's not doing either of those operations in a way that is unmediated by all the other kinds of ways that question has been asked and answered. So, in completing the project of Plato, you might say, prospectively, one is in dialogue not only with Plato but with everybody else since Plato who has read and thought about completing Plato's project. So it's a kind of really intricate palimpsest. And at the same time, in trying to recapture what it might have been like to be there – you know, to be in Carthage when Dido was building it – you're also engaged with a discussion about and with all the other painters and writers and musicians who have asked that question before you. So in a way, the kind of cheesy thing to say is that Classics *is* about Western culture, because Western culture has defined itself in relation to a classical tradition, whether by the incorporation or the rejection of it.

FH That palimpsest in a sense is the artifice that is the context of this ongoing reconstruction.

MB Because we can't get back there. I think that no classicist can ignore that question, but we also at the same time know that it is an impossible project. But then, so is completing the classical project, so it's actually bringing you right up, face to face, with the impossibility of Western humanist culture.

FH I came across, I think on YouTube, your account of going aged five to the British Museum, of the cabinet being opened, and you being handed a very, very old piece of bread as a wonderful example of some kind of unmediated contact with the Antique. One knows this poor old piece of bread is no longer just a piece of bread, but is loaded with ridiculous significance and baggage. But what that sets up is this very dynamic relationship of simultaneously believing in and wanting unmediated contact and yet taking pleasure in the artifice…

MB Yes, that's right, and I think one way of looking at that close encounter would be to just see it as a naïve, unmediated encounter with Antiquity. And, of course, in one way that's how I've mythologised it. But while not many five-year-olds are good at museology, I think in some ways they've got quite a good sense of it, and what's important about the story is not just the bread, but also the institution, the case and the guy who is going to open it for you – the hierarchical set of relationships that enable you to get close (or not) to that object. And so if you put the average five-year-old in that situation and asked them the right questions, you would already be able, I think, to catch that sense of ambivalence between the fantasy of the unmediated contact and the pleasure in the artifice – which was the key, and the case, and the man.

FH Well five-year-olds are very clever things, and I wonder to what extent your relations to Antiquity have actually changed since then? There is still the pleasure of opening up cabinets and getting into locked up stuff, which is kind of the Angela Carter moment. But there's also, as you've pointed out yourself, this heuristic desire to get your hands on it.

MB Yeah! The problem is… *[laughing]*… when anybody tells that kind of story about themselves we all know that it has been repeatedly mythologised, turned into a founding, aetiological myth. So in some ways the fact that you remember that kind of story has its own power. Because of course as the story gets told and retold it becomes an artifice itself, doesn't it? Just as classical scholarship is. Why do some of us work on the History of Classical Scholarship? Because the subject has become a subject in itself already.

FH So to what degree does this kind of artifice-engine rely on the fact that the subject-matter is in a state of utter fragmentation, always requiring a kind of join-the-dots operation. There's never so much knowledge that it rules out the possibility of invention or the fabrication of artifice, and never so little that you simply can't join the dots. Although, that said, when one thinks about Anne Carson's translation of the Sappho fragments [*If Not, Winter: Fragments of Sappho*], she is working with the absolute

p 82
Anne Carson

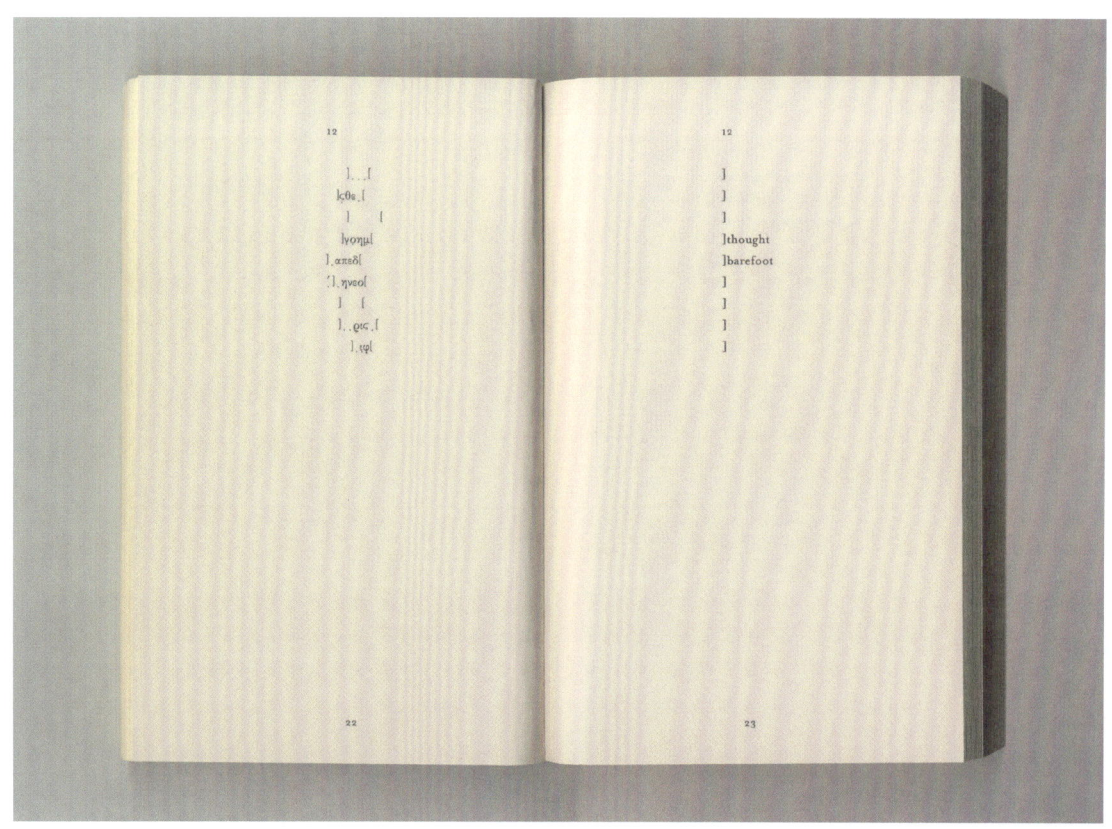

minimum of material, and rather than trying to fill in the gaps she uses square brackets to stand for selected absences on the page…

MB Yes! And what's interesting about Carson is that she's drawing (because she's a classicist) from the very traditions of academic papyrology. What do you do when you edit a papyrus? You use precisely those square brackets: that's the convention of textual representation. I suppose that is the other side to what I was just saying, in that she's representing Sappho using the very tools of the trade – the conventions of the academy and academic Classics – that normally attempt to represent the text as an object of Antiquity.

p 85
Fragment of mural from Herculaneum

FH That's interesting. So on the one hand you have this fragmented subject-matter that requires a degree of invention to happen, the kind of join-the-dots approach that you find, say, in Piranesi's *Campo Marzio*, or Marguerite Yourcenar's *Memoirs of Hadrian*…

MB Yes, Yourcenar is a good example…

FH … and then on the other hand you have this quite unstable dynamic mechanism, shuttling between the desire for unmediated contact with Antiquity and taking absolute pleasure in the fact that it's unattainable, so you might as well invent it anyhow. So how do these two work together – this dynamic relationship and the kind of fragmentary constitution of the subject-matter? How do they come into play together? Because they're both, from the point of view of an architect, incredibly architectural conditions. Architects weave endless fictions about why their building is the way it is, via the idea of the concept sketch, or the ridiculous post-rationalisation that happens, and yet architecture also has to be tediously pragmatic in other respects. And architecture always is a fragment: it's the product of a society, but always just a piece of debris from that society. So within your own work, let's say, how do you see the relationship between this dynamic to-and-fro-ing of understanding and the kind of fragments it has to tackle?

MB I think that's very hard to answer. Partly because by and large, in theorising the subject, those two questions tend to be treated in parallel rather than in intersection.

FH And why is that?

MB It's easier that way, isn't it? The question you ask is quite difficult. I think it must be right that the fragmentary nature of our encounters with the classical past makes the paradox that you're talking about – between unmediated access and completion and the impossibility of the project – more undeniable, more evident. It goes without saying that the study of any period of history is inevitably based on that paradox. Classicists are probably better at enjoying that because the fragmentary nature of the material and the particular nature of the fragments themselves – compared with, say, Egyptology – means they can't avoid that particular problematic question. But classicists can't avoid that particular problematic question because the centrality of the fragment (which goes beyond the material fragment, as all ancient literature is fragmentary) really rubs your nose in that particular set of historical debates. I think that Classics copes with it better than, for example, many people working on the nineteenth century, who actually have a much less problematising version of what it is to tell a historical story, because they can kid themselves much easier. And it's actually much richer than Egypt because of the particular concatenation of text and image and materiality – and the particular length and depth of tradition of the engagement, and the multinational engagement. Because we're also about fragments of study, you know?

FH Yes! In Marilia's drawing of the fragmentary evidence of Hannibal's passage through the Alps, she was looking at the various accounts – Livy, Polybius and so on – and their collective extremely fragmentary knowledge about the various theories of the exact route through various passes...

———————————————— p 65
Marilia Spanou

MB Yeah, I remember it… And none of them had ever seen a bloody Alp in their lives!

Mont Blanc
Courmayeur
La Salle
Saint-Pierre
Ugine
Albertville
Col de Petite Saint Bernard
Grignon
Bourg-Saint-Maurice
La Bathie
Saint-Pierre-d'Abigny
Aime
Chambery
Montmelian
Moutiers
Col de Mont Cenis
Voiron
Susa
Bussoleno
Grenoble
Saint-Martin-d'Heres
Echirolles
N45E006
Oulx
N45E007
Saint Chaffrey
Montgenevre
La Mure
Briancon
L'Argentiere-la-Bessee
Mont Viso
Guillestre
Embrun
La Batie-Neuve
Chorges
Veynes
Lac-de Serre-Poncon
Serres
Monte Oronaye
Barcelonnette
Laragne-Monteglin
Seyne
Demon
Sisteron
Digne-les-Bains
Chateau-Arnoux-Saint-Auban
N44E006
N44E007

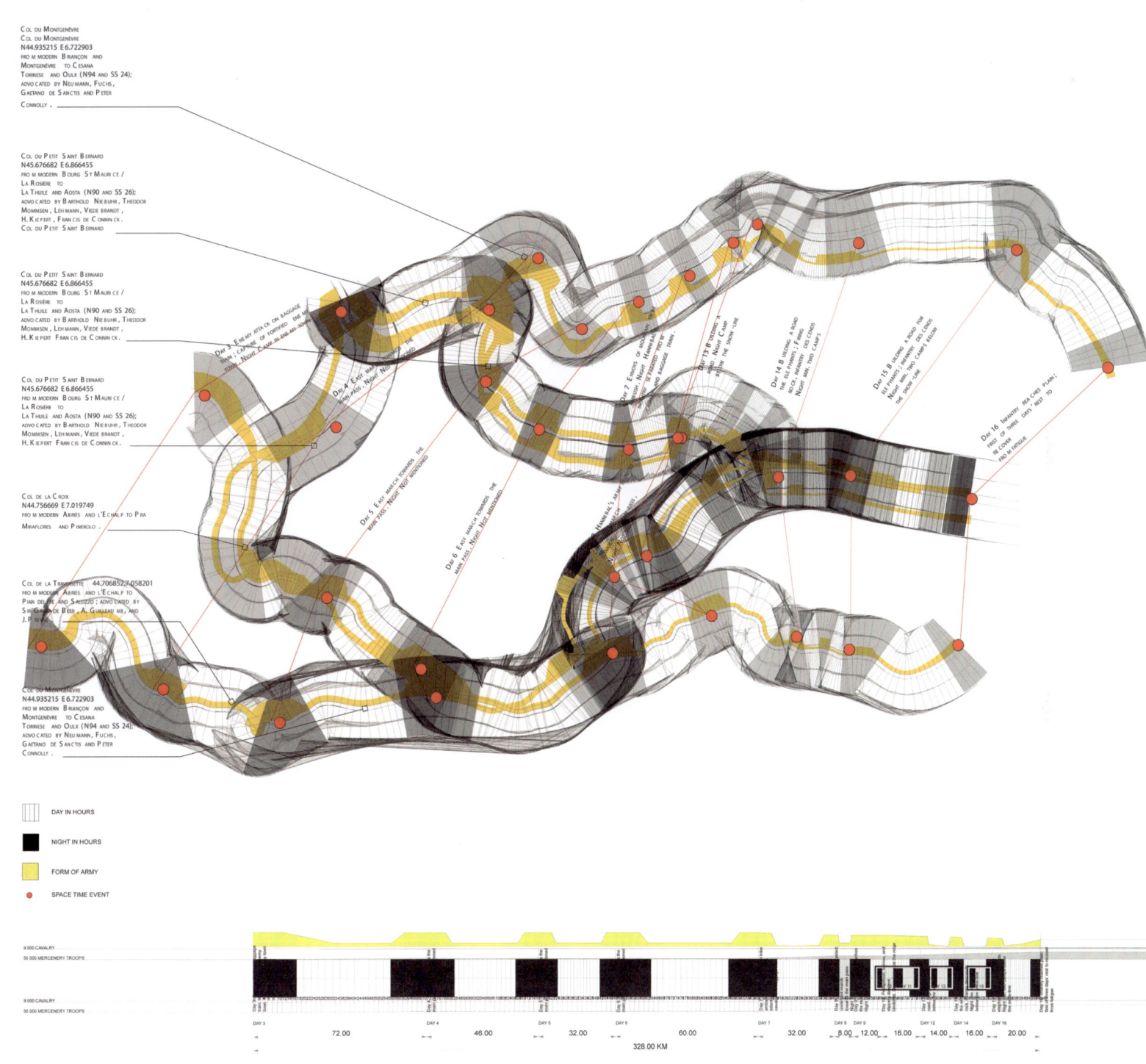

Col du Montgenèvre
Col du Montgenèvre
N44.935215 E6.722903
from modern Briançon and
Montgenèvre to Cesana
Torinese and Oulx (N94 and SS 24);
advocated by Neumann, Fuchs,
Gaetano de Sanctis and Peter
Connolly.

Col du Petit Saint Bernard
N45.676682 E6.866455
from modern Bourg St Maurice /
La Rosère to
La Thuile and Aosta (N90 and SS 26);
advocated by Barthold Niebuhr, Theodor
Mommsen, Lehmann, Viedebrandt,
H. Kiepert, Francis de Coninck.
Col du Petit Saint Bernard

Col du Petit Saint Bernard
N45.676682 E6.866455
from modern Bourg St Maurice /
La Rosère to
La Thuile and Aosta (N90 and SS 26);
advocated by Barthold Niebuhr, Theodor
Mommsen, Lehmann, Viedebrandt,
H. Kiepert Francis de Coninck.

Col du Petit Saint Bernard
N45.676682 E6.866455
from modern Bourg St Maurice /
La Rosère to
La Thuile and Aosta (N90 and SS 26);
advocated by Barthold Niebuhr, Theodor
Mommsen, Lehmann, Viedebrandt,
H. Kiepert Francis de Coninck.

Col de la Croix
N44.756669 E7.019749
from modern Abriès and L'Echalp to Pra
Miraflores and Pinerolo.

Col de la Traversette 44.706852;7.058201
from modern Abriès and L'Echalp to
Pian del Re and Saluzzo; advocated by
Sir Gavin de Beer, A. Guillaume, and
J. P. Novis

Col du Montgenèvre
N44.935215 E6.722903
from modern Briançon and
Montgenèvre to Cesana
Torinese and Oulx (N94 and SS 24);
advocated by Neumann, Fuchs,
Gaetano de Sanctis and Peter
Connolly.

DAY IN HOURS

NIGHT IN HOURS

FORM OF ARMY

SPACE TIME EVENT

9 000 CAVALRY
50 000 MERCENERY TROOPS

9 000 CAVALRY
50 000 MERCENERY TROOPS

72.00   46.00   32.00   60.00   32.00   8.00 12.00 16.00 14.00 16.00 20.00

328.00 KM

STRABO A.D. 24.

CASAUBON 1609

CHEVALIER DE FOLARD, 1729

WHITAKER - SOME TIME BEFORE CRAMER

CRAMER, 1820

CECIL TORR 1924

SIR GAVIN DE BEER 1952

F.W. WALBANK 1956

LAZENBY 1978

ERNLE BRADFORD 1981

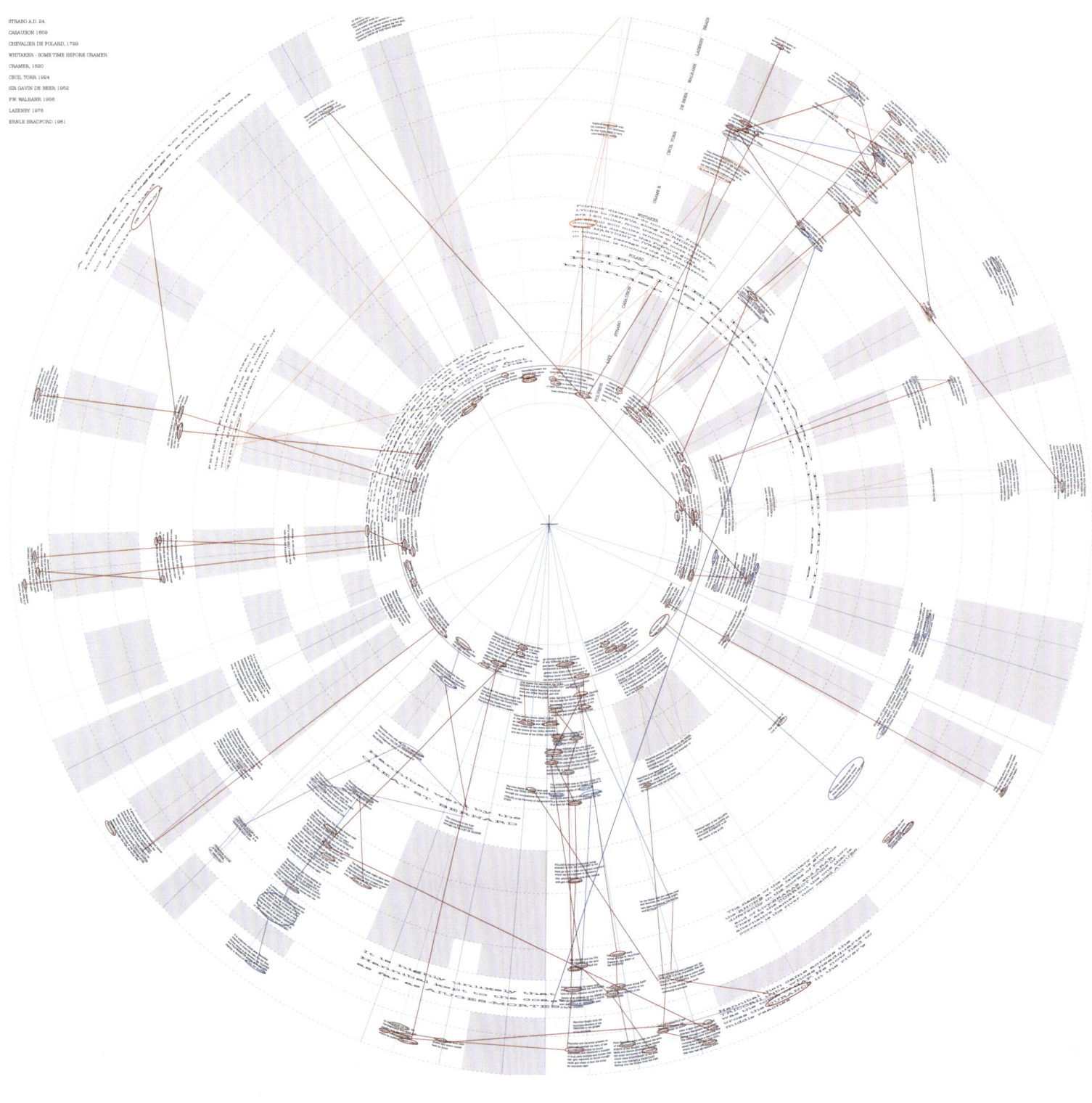

FH OK *[laughing]*, none of them had ever seen an Alp in their lives. But if you assemble them together, using Livy's marching day as a kind of space–time unit, the artifice that you end up with – the compound of the various potential routes and accounts – produces some strange anomalies of its own. So you get a couple of hours of night in the middle of the day: day becomes kind of striated with night. And this is Karl's drawing, which again looked at the different routes and actually changed the landscape of the Alps into a series of Bridget Riley-like marching days. You have areas where Karl can be quite precise about where Hannibal was, and areas of incredible indeterminacy. I guess what emerges from this is a sense that working with fragments throws up a very patchy landscape – whether this is a physical or a textual landscape. And Marilia's second drawing [*The Ruin of the Narrative*] looks at the textual body, the accounts of Hannibal's passage from Polybius and Livy all the way through to Bradford's work on it in 1981. She looks at how the mistranslation of different rivers (the Durance, for example), combined with an excessive artistic licence, ultimately makes a ruin of the text.

p 91
Karl Kjelstrup-Johnson

p 86, 87
Karl Kjelstrup-Johnson

p 88
Marilia Spanou

MB What I think is interesting about this, from my point of view, is that it has turned what is a fruitless but seductive, mad, academic project into something whose foundations you can see to be interesting. If a student came to me and said: 'Do you know what I'm going to work on? I'm going to work on how Hannibal crossed the Alps', I would say: 'Oh for god's sake, what do you think you're doing?' But these students have in some ways shown that the *very sense of the impossibility of answering the question* is a subject that can be explored.

FH Absolutely.

MB It has turned an impossible question into a subject in its own right, which I think is very smart.

FH In terms of mining that indeterminacy for invention?

MB Yes, in various ways it's both mining that indeterminacy but also saying: how would you represent that mad project, how can you see what that is?

FH And is that so very different from what you do? Because you're always working with indeterminacy, and there must be an incredible self-consciousness that goes with that.

MB Yes, but come on, you have a different rhetoric in operation here. Any classicist is going to have two ways of thinking about this. One is to say: 'Look, what questions do you want to ask about Hannibal?' And we would probably stand rather distant from this and say: 'Forget the fucking route, what is it that Livy is trying to say? What is the story about the vinegar and rocks all about?' So we would try to reformulate it so that we didn't have to think about how Hannibal actually crossed the Alps. Now of course you can follow a different trajectory, you can say: 'No, look, the idea of how Hannibal crossed the Alps is such a seductive one that we have to think about its different potential answers, even though we simultaneously know there is no answer.' Now why I like this is because it *says* something about that question. Classics, like any academic subject, operates simultaneously by enjoying and celebrating the questions and the answers of the past in these terms, and also simultaneously rejecting them. There's a pull in both ways.

FH So in a sense you're declining to comment on the self-consciousness in your practice? And it might be your practice as opposed to the practice of other classicists.

MB I think the point is that you can't always be commenting on your own practice. And the sophistication of the subject demands that those two things go hand in hand but are also in tension. There's a degree of solipsism into which one should not necessarily always fall [wryly]. To give a different example (but I think you can see the same resonance in it, really): what is the great buzzword amongst most humanities subjects? 'Interdisciplinarity'! And yet of course interdisciplinarity depends on there being disciplinary boundaries; it is actually parasitic upon the very boundaries it chooses to transcend. And so that sense of self-consciousness about the history of the subject is parasitic on a different set of non-self-conscious approaches.

FH Yes. And one doesn't want just to be a parasite!

MB You know, as you sometimes say to students who get very bound up with the self-reflexive nature of the subject, in the end it has got to be *about* something. But I think the difficulty in my practice is that it has actually got to be *more* than being 'about something'. And how you deal with that on a day-to-day basis is normally to say: 'Oh, for god's sake, don't work on Hannibal crossing the Alps.'

FH *[laughs]* We'll leave Hannibal behind … I don't know if you remember, but we looked at how the kind of serial reinvention of Antiquity has operated through what seemed to us key types, key vehicles: the alpine passage being one of them, the copy, the collection being another, and the ruin another. It would be good to spend some time discussing the relationship between the textual ruin and the physical ruin, because it touches on a very acute point in the economies of architectural culture whereby the ruin, or the image, of the building is worth so much more than the textual or spoken word. If a picture is normally worth a thousand words, then for the architect it's worth a million words. On the other hand, what seems to be the set up in a lot of classical scholarship is the equivalency between the physical ruin and the textual ruin – the possibility of a more democratic relationship between the physical and the textual. And a physical ruin that became central to Marilia, who constructed the textual ruin in Hannibal's crossing, is Hadrian's Villa, where she looked at the absolute mess of the interpretation of the circulation.

p 96
Marilia Spanou

MB Yes! How interesting.

FH I mean, it's quite amazing, we still don't know where the bloody front door is.

MB No, we still don't, and the history of its interpretation over the last 100 years is absolutely extraordinary. It has become a kind of template onto which people have projected their own changing vision of what the classical world somehow is about. So that in the 1930s every blasted building was thought to be a library, and in the 1990s every blasted building was a dining

p 94
Giovanni Battista
Piranesi & Francesco
Piranesi, *Pianta delle
Fabriche esistenti nella
Villa Adriana*

room. It is one of the most … not just misunderstood but utterly *un*-understood buildings. It is therefore extremely interesting, because it is a playground for deciding what you think the ancient world was about.

FH Right, so it's the ultimate artifice-machine in terms of a ruin, in terms of a fragment.

MB Yes, I think so. It's better, really, than the Palatine Palace for that. Partly because of its distance from Rome, partly because it's Tivoli, it's something you go to, you don't just come across it when wandering around the *centro storico* of Rome. And partly because, as you say, it's not clear what it is. Is it a town? Where's the front door? In a way it has become a rather unrecognised metaphor for the ancient world.

FH And what's happening with Hadrian's Villa now? Apart from there being no money and no work?

MB If you want the real truth about whether Hadrian's Villa scholarship is going anywhere in nitty gritty archaeological terms, I don't think it is. It's partly because (and I suspect this is where our two visions of Classics – recuperation vs celebration of artifice – are going to find themselves in tension) there is a sense in which the archaeological project is driven by discovering precisely where something like the front door is, when actually we are never going to know where the front door is. And I think in the late twentieth century there were patches of rather more radically interesting sorts of scholarship about it, bringing together what little we know about the place from extremely, blissfully unreliable literary sources.

FH Pirro Ligorio?

MB I mean ancient literary sources, there's *Historia Augusta*, which gives us our only pre-medieval version of it. But you start to see (and this is why it's really a template for the classical world) – that actually what Hadrian is doing here is representing the empire to himself at home. So it is on the one hand a palace, a villa, a place where Hadrian was when he wasn't all over the

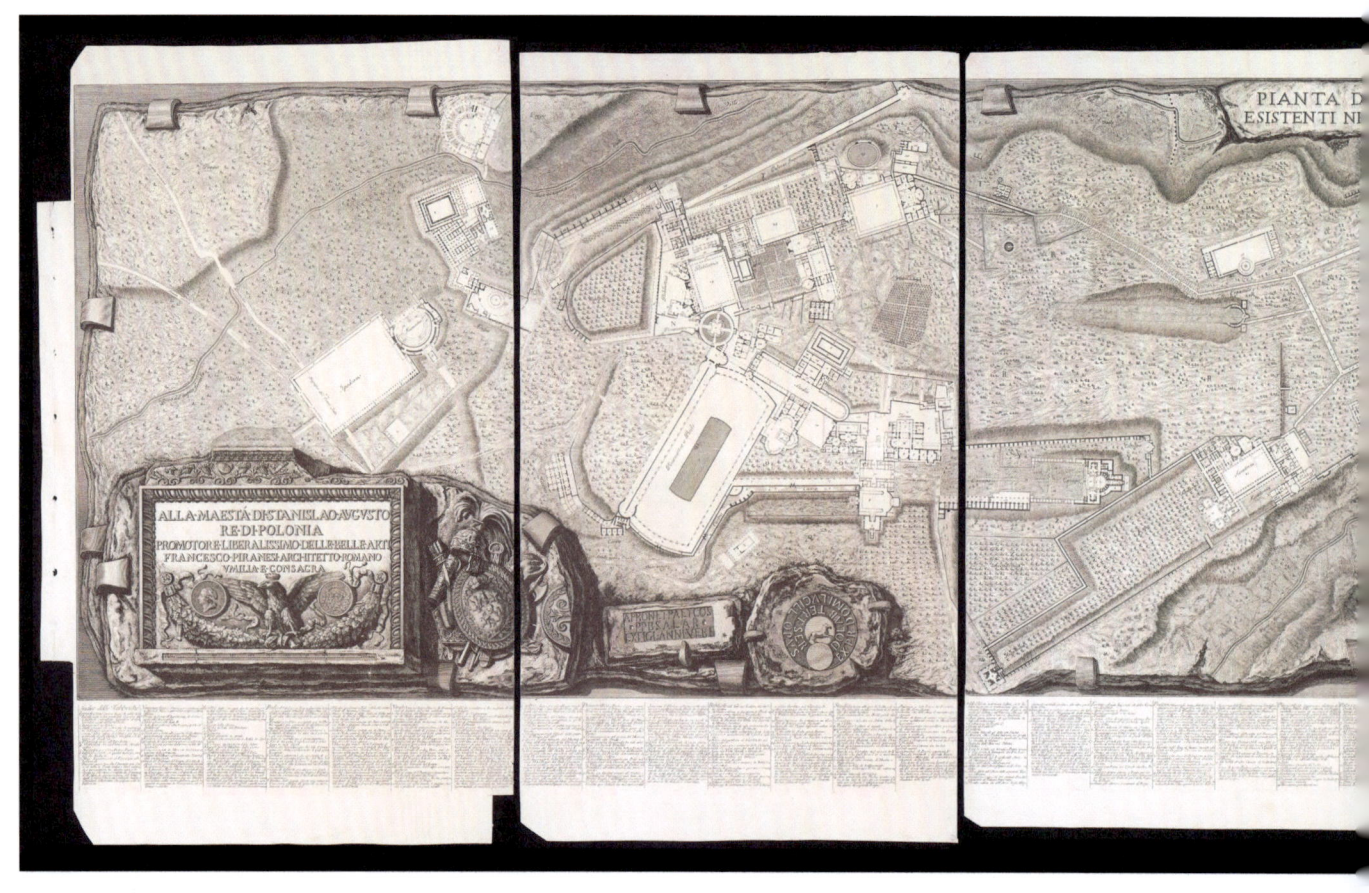

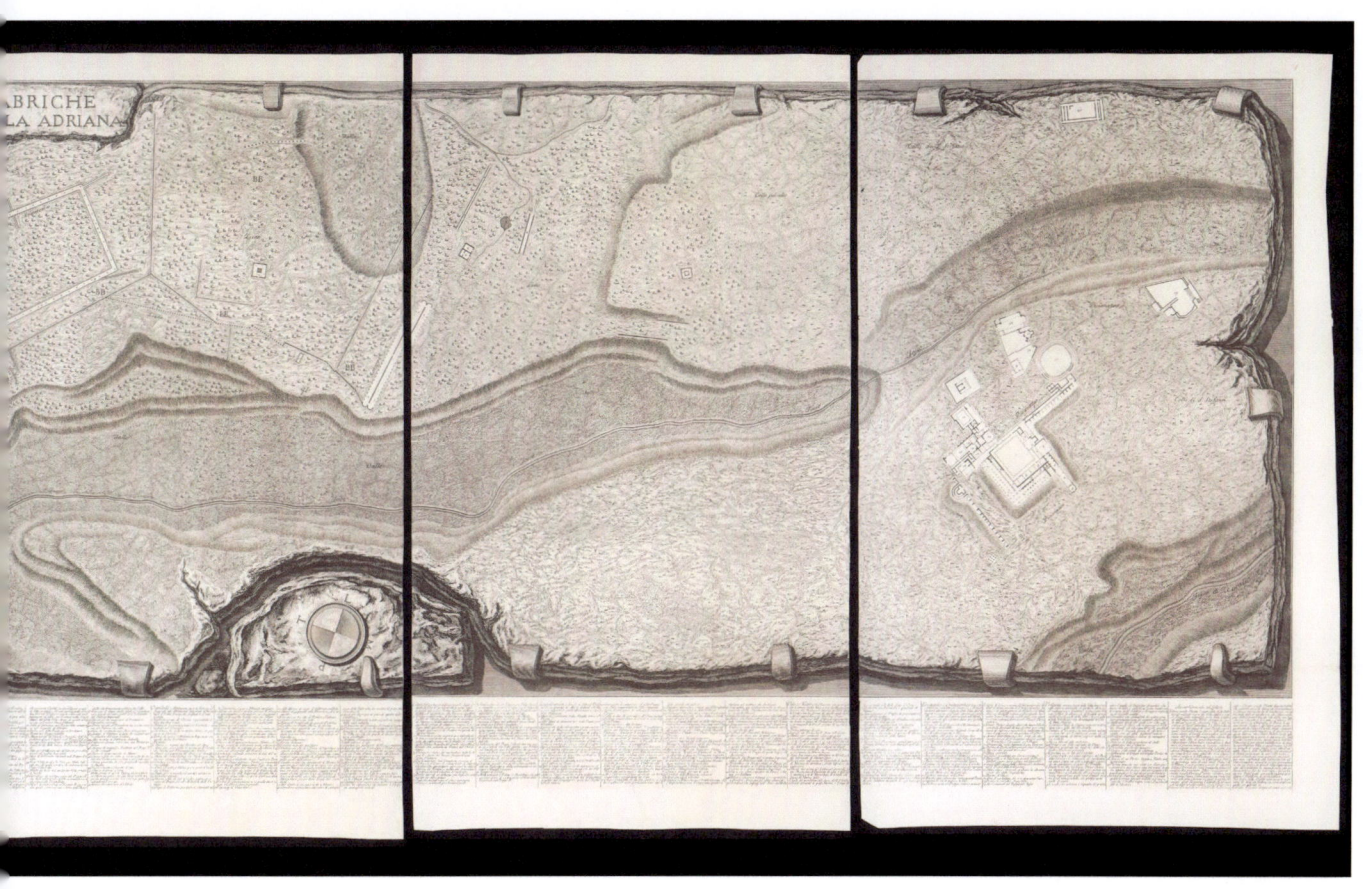

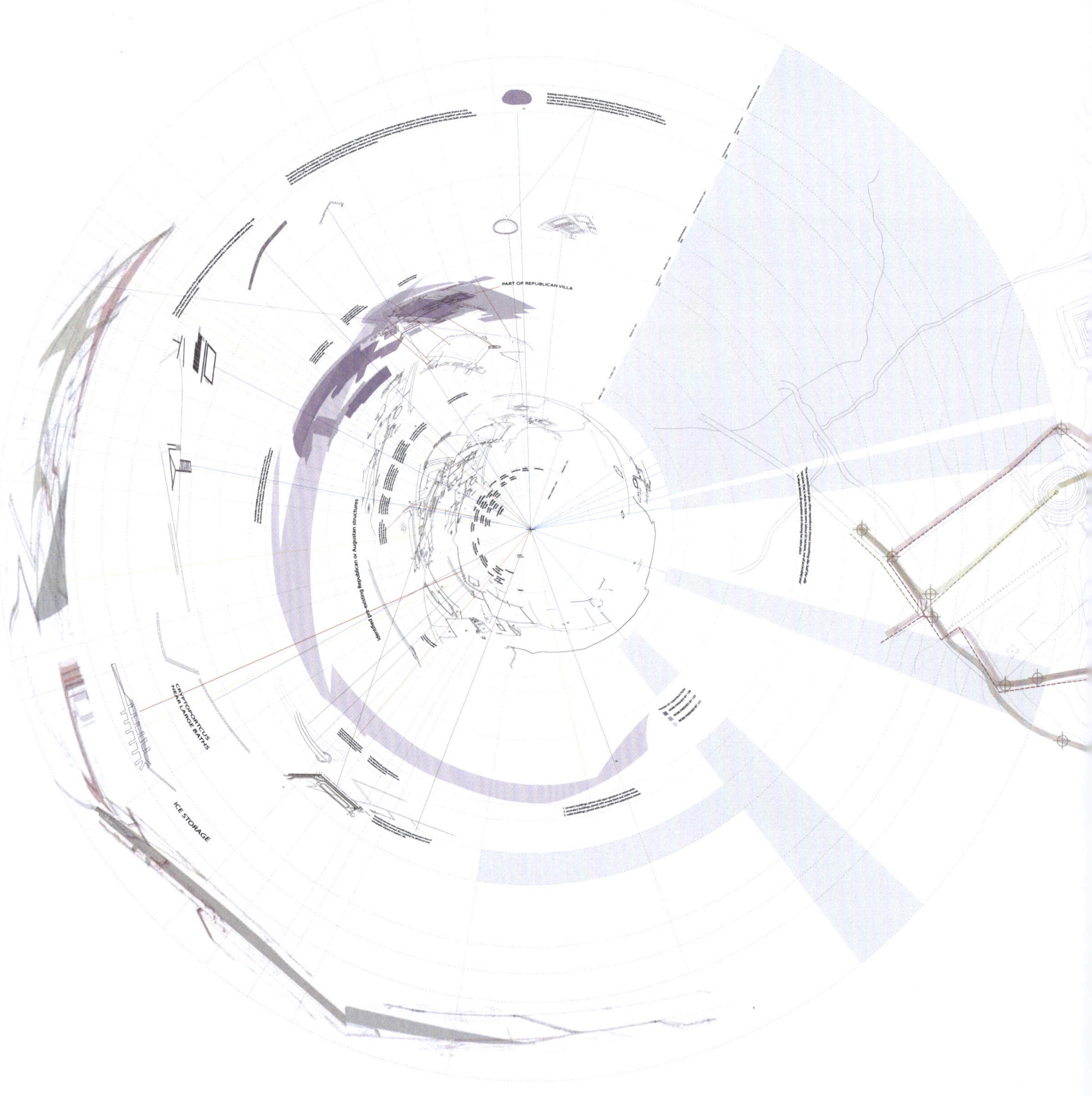

PART OF REPUBLICAN VILLA

Identified Republican or Augustan structures

CRYPTOPORTICUS
NEAR LARGE BATHS

ICE STORAGE

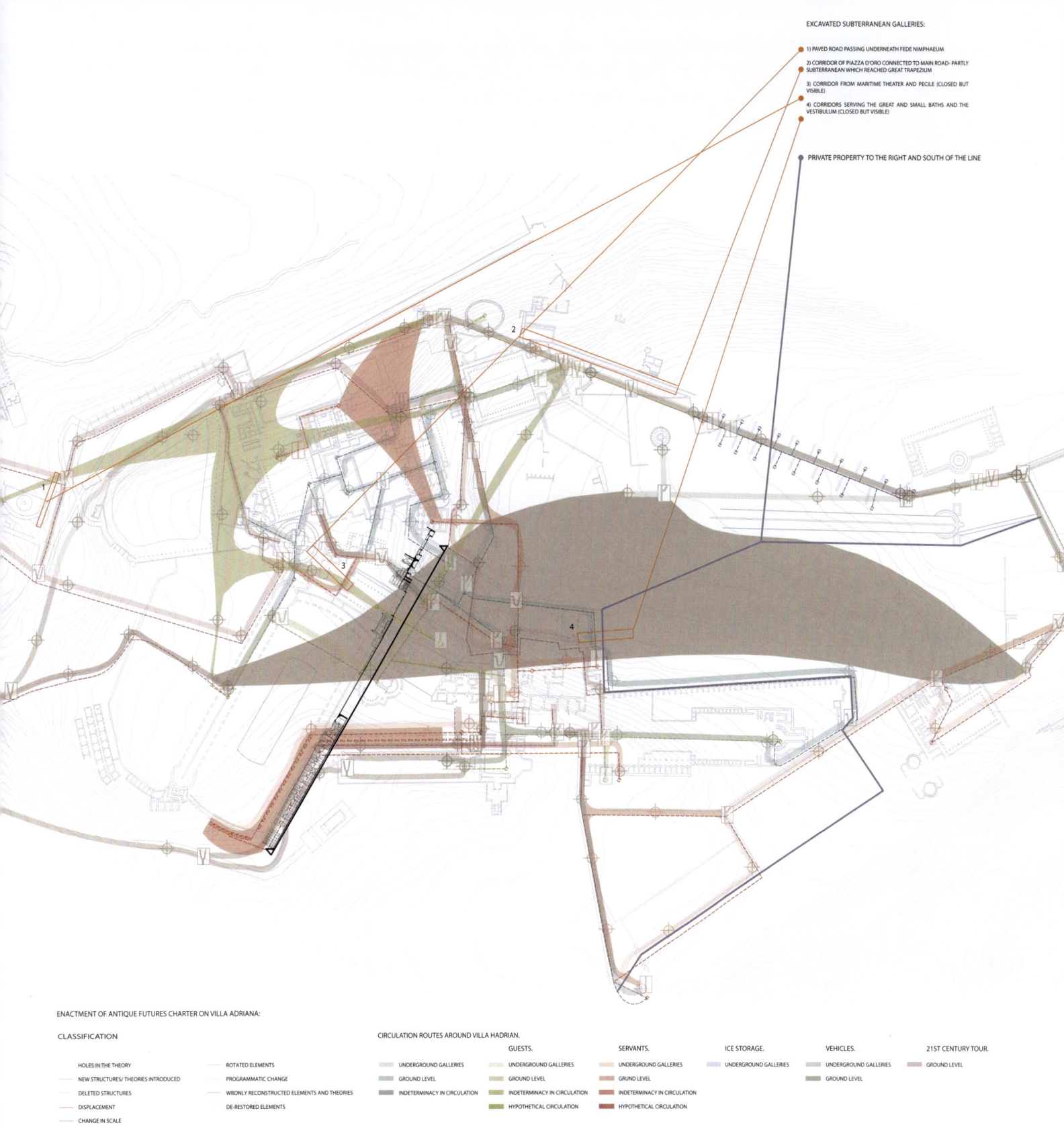

EXCAVATED SUBTERRANEAN GALLERIES:

1) PAVED ROAD PASSING UNDERNEATH FEDE NIMPHAEUM

2) CORRIDOR OF PIAZZA D'ORO CONNECTED TO MAIN ROAD- PARTLY SUBTERRANEAN WHICH REACHED GREAT TRAPEZIUM

3) CORRIDOR FROM MARITIME THEATER AND PECILE (CLOSED BUT VISIBLE)

4) CORRIDORS SERVING THE GREAT AND SMALL BATHS AND THE VESTIBULUM (CLOSED BUT VISIBLE)

PRIVATE PROPERTY TO THE RIGHT AND SOUTH OF THE LINE

ENACTMENT OF ANTIQUE FUTURES CHARTER ON VILLA ADRIANA:

CLASSIFICATION

HOLES IN THE THEORY   ROTATED ELEMENTS

NEW STRUCTURES/ THEORIES INTRODUCED   PROGRAMMATIC CHANGE

DELETED STRUCTURES   WRONLY RECONSTRUCTED ELEMENTS AND THEORIES

DISPLACEMENT   DE-RESTORED ELEMENTS

CHANGE IN SCALE

CIRCULATION ROUTES AROUND VILLA HADRIAN.

	GUESTS.	SERVANTS.	ICE STORAGE.	VEHICLES.	21ST CENTURY TOUR.
UNDERGROUND GALLERIES	UNDERGROUND GALLERIES	UNDERGROUND GALLERIES	UNDERGROUND GALLERIES	UNDERGROUND GALLERIES	GROUND LEVEL
GROUND LEVEL	GROUND LEVEL	GRUND LEVEL		GROUND LEVEL	
INDETERMINACY IN CIRCULATION	INDETERMINACY IN CIRCULATION	INDETERMINACY IN CIRCULATION			
	HYPOTHETICAL CIRCULATION	HYPOTHETICAL CIRCULATION			

97

blasted empire, because of course the joke is the greatest palace of all was built by the guy who was never in Rome. But then what you have is a sense of him recreating the empire at its very centre. And that's a really radical project. It's spatially very interesting.

FH Yes, and in terms of scale, in terms of all kinds of things.

MB Yeah, and there are some wonderful jokes about it. If you think of the Aphrodite of Knidos statue, one of the most famous statues of Antiquity that survives only in copy – 'version' I should say, perhaps not copy – there has been quite a lot of work wanting to explore its original context, partly using a second-century AD text which, amongst other things, is an absolutely classic man-falls-in-love-with-sculpture story, but when you go to Knidos, you find the archaeology there has been driven and framed by our much better knowledge of what Hadrian's reconstruction of the Aphrodite of Knidos and her temple was like at Tivoli. So actually it's in a kind of loop.

FH Totally, it's a hall of mirrors. So Hadrian's fantasy-copy of Aphrodite's temple is driving twenty-first-century archaeology of what is supposed to be the original.

MB Yes. How do I know that what I've found on Knidos is the temple that originally contained the statue of Aphrodite? I know because I am looking at (and using as the checklist for what it has got to be like) Hadrian's own fantastical interpretation…

FH I can see why you don't want any more self-consciousness or self-reflexiveness within the actual methodology – there's enough in the subject-matter! And this brings us to the whole question of the copy, which is at large in all the types the unit has looked at. It's there in the fragment, because the fragment's copied. It's there in the ruin, because the ruin is endlessly copied through interpretation. It's there in the collection that installs the canon, because the collection itself often consists of copies…

MB And what you see, centrally, *is* Rome. I think what is interesting about all these things is that the context, within

Antiquity itself, in which those big ideas began to take shape was Rome's relationship with Greece. The paradox that is built into any study of the classical world is that twosome, which is not just the twosome that is represented by most modern popular culture – which is that the Greeks are airy-fairy and the Romans are building bridges and conquering the world. It is the sense that we have inherited from the Romans *their reconstruction of Greece.* So it's kind of a wonderful Derridean un-centred business, because we see everything through Rome, and although there were some Romans who were saying the Greeks were a nasty load of smelly, perfume-sodden effete wimps, as a culture, Rome was both casting itself as an inferior heir of Greece and at the same time not just reconstructing but constructing the canon. I was thinking, if you go to the museum of classical archaeology here, you can see all these plaster casts: 500 of them, they're just amazing. You look at all this stuff and it says – because in this case we're inheritors of the nineteenth-century arrangement – 'fifth century BC', etc., and then underneath it actually admits: 'Roman copy of…' There's the sense that Rome has delivered to us its vision of 'Greekness'. It would be very nice to take all our plaster casts and move them around a bit to demonstrate that there's almost nothing from Greece at all, apart from some architectural sculpture, some archaic *kouroi* – the rest of it is all a Roman copy…

FH So is it right to say that Rome invented the culture of the copy?

MB That's what I think. That's what I would say.

FH And it is exactly that culture of copy that has kept Rome alive.

MB That's right. It has kept Rome alive, and also to some extent devalued it – well, since Romanticism at least, because they are telling us that what they are doing is copying, we then see them as a secondary culture in value terms as well as in chronological terms.

FH But so effectively propagated that they are guaranteed immortality, so the value doesn't really matter.

MB Yes, but the price they pay is that they are 'copyists'. And recent scholarship on Roman art, for example, while it claims to stand against the notion of seeing the Romans as mere copyists, is actually embedded in that, because it wants to say (as I did) that these statues are 'versions'. Because if you say it's a version it becomes a constructive reinvention!

FH OK, so this is what you mean by the distinction between the 'version' and the 'copy'. If they are versions then they are somehow working on their artifice, they are arch artifice-makers.

MB Yes, that's right. So while accepting that Rome gave us the culture of the copy, you give them back a sense of independent cultural drive by saying it's a 'version'. And actually, maybe what we ought to be saying is: 'It's a bloody copy!'

FH But the Romans didn't have any problem with copying.

MB Nope. And you know classical scholars are the victims, as literary scholars, just as much as scholars of art (I'm not sure about architects). Do we think Horace is *better* than his Greek models because what he's doing is using Greek models and re-presenting them? Or somehow would it be better if we had more Alcaeus left? And I remember, being the terribly naive undergraduate that I was, listening to a lecture by a guy who'd made his name in Roman rather than Greek literature. I remember him saying, and it kind of stuck: what was it that made us think that Pope's translation of classical literature was somehow less original than Sylvia Plath's autobiographical account of her encounter with the milkman? …

FH It's a chip on your shoulder – a 'copy complex'. But without the copy you would be out of business.

MB That's right, and so we should actually celebrate it. And the way we've found of celebrating it is to rename it as a 'version'.

FH [laughs] OK, we won't use the 'c' word anymore.

MB Well actually I think we ought to reclaim the copy. 'Great, this is a copy! Yippee!' What's so bad about being good at copying?

FH [laughing] I'd like to come to another copy, or another much-copied subject: the Villa of the Papyri...

MB That's another nice one like Tivoli, because you can't visit it...

FH ...Because it's under 20 metres of lava. I thought we could use the Villa of the Papyri to discuss the relations between the artefact in the dig and the artefact in the collection.

MB Yes! Of which Papyri is absolutely the most brilliant example – almost the *reductio ad absurdum* of the dig and the collection, simultaneously. A dig that was somehow the *mise-en-abyme* of digging – nobody could ever get into it, so it was actually tunnelled.

FH Yes, the drawing of those tunnels would have been the drawing to have, but it doesn't exist, or only partially exists, it seems...

MB No, but you can sort of reconstruct it ...

FH ...There's presumably a whole load of bits that only the Camorra or whatever know about, as with the tunnel system under Naples and Palermo.

MB And it is phenomenally dangerous too. This is where archaeology meets potholing. This is not like Pompeii, it's not like just brushing aside the layers and there's the town – this is going down into the bowels of the bloody earth.

FH Have you been into the tunnels?

MB Oh no, but you can go to the recent excavation on the edge of the Villa of the Papyri and look at the cross section of the lava where it has been partly removed. Just the sheer depth of it is scary!

p 102
Letizia Bagheria
*The Secretary of the
Christian Democrat
Party in Palermo,
March 9, 1979*

p 103
Karl Kjelstrup-Johnson
*Subterranean System
for Naples Waste
and Archaeological
Extraction*

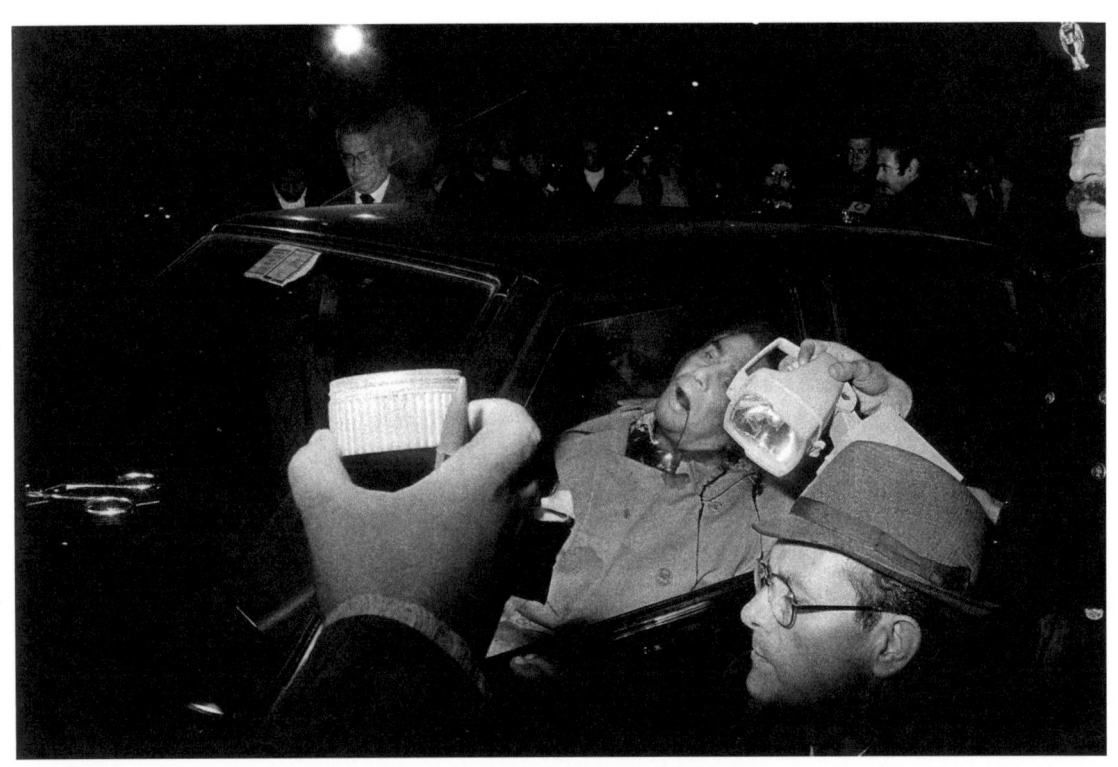

5   10   20   40

FH That makes me wonder whether one of the 'super-types' we should have pulled up – along with the copy, the ruin, the fragment, the triumph, and so on – is the whole question of the 'underground', as a key vehicle through which Antiquity has been rethought…

MB Yup. Underground would have been good. And you now get an interesting sort of twentieth-century spin on that, which is 'underwater'. I think the twentieth-century fantasy of excavation, in terms of what National Geographic *want*, has been not just the underground, but the diver.

FH Atlantis?

MB Yeah or Alexandria. You know, you go under the sea, and there is another world.

FH It's all very Jules Verne.

MB Yes it is. I was always struck by the huge popularity of the exhibition of the underwater finds at Alexandria, by the way that sense of adventure has been turned into the 'underwater'.

FH If you remember, with Jenny's proposal, she was proposing to take the artefacts removed from the Villa of the Papyri – these amazing figures with enamel eyes, which are now in the museum in Naples – and to reinstall them above the villa in an open-air museum. The point was to invert the normal relations – if one normally thinks of the vector of the dig feeding the museum, and the museum recontextualising the artefact – and instead to have the artefact recontextualising the contemporary urban landscape of Ercolano, the kind of hopelessness of Ercolano now. This was in a sense a particularly romantic project from a particularly romantic student, but I remember it throwing up all kinds of questions about the puritanical desire to put the artefact back in the proper place, which of course was not her agenda at all. And I wanted to revisit the question of what is behind that desire, and why must it fail (because it must fail, one cannot simply put things back and think it's all OK)? On top of this, if you do go along with that agenda or Jenny's

p 105
Jenny Elisa Schafer
Enamel Eyes

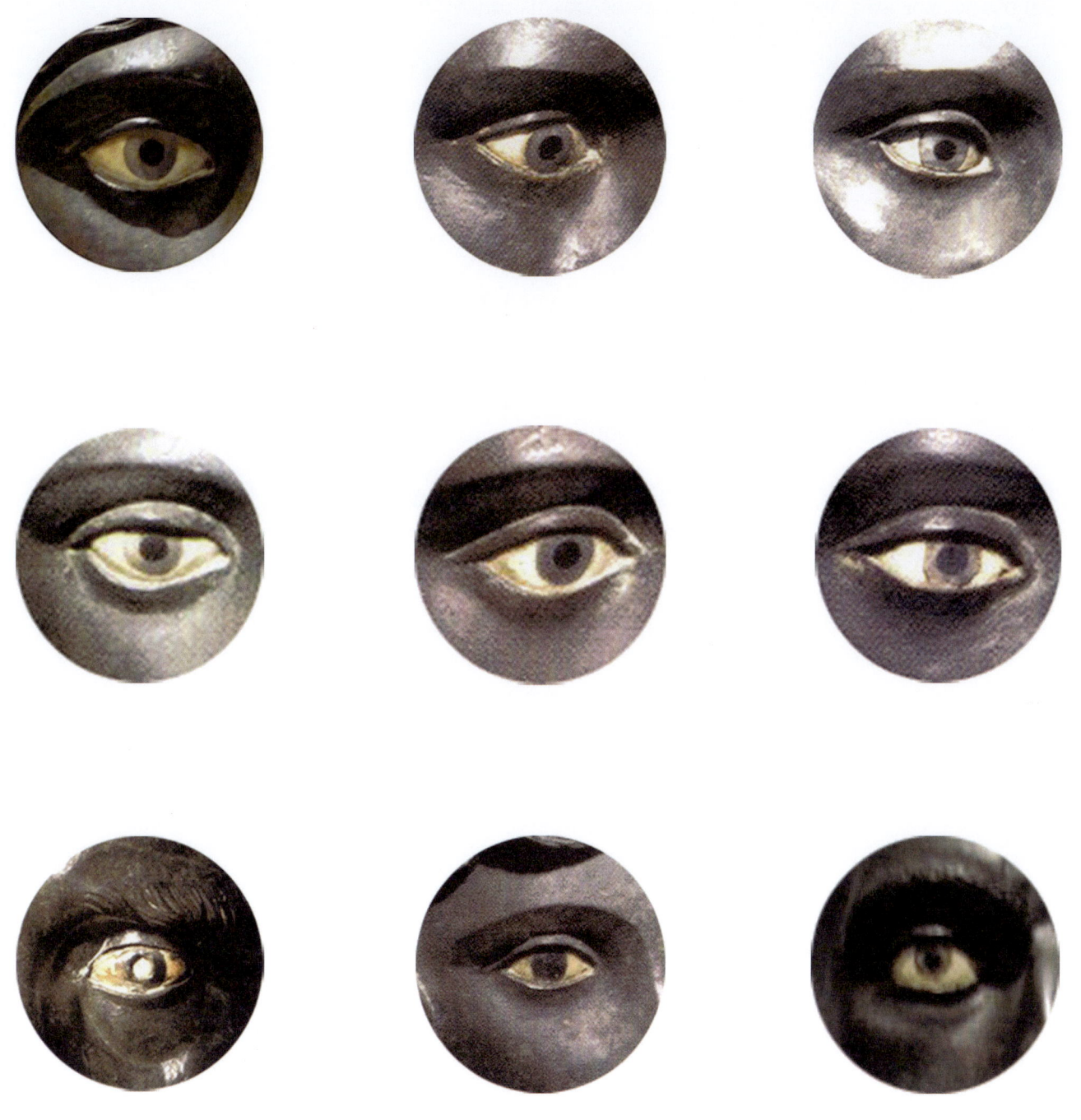

agenda, what becomes of the object when it is put back into the hole in the ground, which is in a sense no longer a hole in the ground: it has become a dig, something placed in the crosshairs of scholarship and all these other things…

MB Yes, I think that is more interesting than I realised when I was with you, because I have done more work since then on the history of the excavations in Pompeii and Herculaneum, and what you see is that from about 1890 onwards the idea of 'putting back' was one extremely strong strand in Italian archaeology, with interesting consequences. There was an enormous push to remove stuff from the Naples museum and put it back on the site of Pompeii. Up until that point everything found in Pompeii was removed first of all to the early museum at Portici, and then on to what's now the National Museum in Naples. So 120 years ago they are thinking about bringing stuff back and they partly do that by changing the nature of the museum – by thinking about what a museum is, how it can be an open-air site – and they are thinking about breaking down precisely the barriers that we want to repair. But I've only been able to find one sole object that actually goes from the museum back to the site, and it's the *cave canem* – 'beware of the dog' – mosaic. The absolutely most famous fridge-magnet icon of Pompeii is the one object that was removed from the museum and put back. But that initiative at the site of Pompeii went with the whole sense of reconstruction. There was an attempt to keep the site a living site, and to say that you don't want these houses dismembered, and bits of them put in the museum – you want to keep them as real houses. The mid-nineteenth-century practice had been to take any painting they found and put it in the museum and turn it from Roman wall decoration into gallery art, but they put a stop to that, and pretty much everything stayed on the site. Now, for one or two things that was fine – and thanks to the use of Vaseline, the petroleum jelly, the Villa of the Mysteries was fine – but the irony is that most of the paintings then faded. More than 50 per cent of the stuff they kept on the site has now been utterly destroyed. It was either ripped off, or when it wasn't ripped off it faded, or got water damage. So you can see Pompeii over the last 120 years has been an interesting series of test cases for the impossibility of either the site or the museum ever to satisfy, really, whereas Herculaneum is a kind of different case, because what Maiuri did, in the years immediately before and after the Second World War, was…

FH Yes, the 'dead city' is probably another type we should have looked at…

MB Up to the mid-eighteenth century Herculaneum was more important than Pompeii. It was more exotic. But after that, Pompeii took over, and it became very loaded, so you could always play more during the twentieth century with what you did at Herculaneum. And what Maiuri did was to start, quite explicitly, to build a museum city. If you go round Herculaneum now looking for his bits of museology you can see that he's got repro cabinets and things. The irony – as Andrew Wallace-Hadrill has discovered, just by looking at exactly what Maiuri did – is that the whole thing is a fiction. And it was a fiction driven in part by a desire to narrativise, and to say: 'So, who was in this room?' 'Who died here?' So all sorts of stuff has been put together to say, you know: 'Here is a bed with a bracelet and some weaving'. And [conspiratorial whisper] none of it was actually found together. But it becomes Maiuri's vision of a living–dying city. You could never quite have got away with that at Pompeii. So I think Pompeii, more than I realised, is a really important example of the ambivalence of ruin versus not-ruin, site versus museum, excavation versus gallery, with constant unexpected paradoxes. So the house in Pompeii that we now worry about most of all, that suddenly collapsed two years ago, becoming a kind of thorn in the side of Berlusconi, the so-called 'House of the Gladiators', is also a house that was bombed by the British in 1944. And so you get all sorts of different versions of preservation, destruction, display, non-display, ruination, conscious ruination, unintentional or intentional ruination.

FH And it seems that these can be triggered by the return of the artefact or the reinstallation of an artefact, for fictitious reasons, that was never there.

MB Yes, because it always makes a difference.

FH It changes the significance.

    MB Yes. And whereas for much of the latter half of the twentieth century there was a rather unthought out archaeological position that somehow it was better to be on the site, I think two things have conspired to problematise that, even for the most kind of dyed-in-the-wool 'how it really was' sort of archaeologist. One is some sense of the museum as an interesting institution in itself, and the other is the fact that if you take an intelligent party of ordinary visitors around Pompeii, they go around the site and they look at these drab, dirty, faded walls – and they go to the museum and they say…

FH 'Aren't the colours lovely'?

    MB Aren't the colours lovely! Yes. Now actually, of course, the joke is that the colours aren't quite what they were. It's a wonderful object lesson about the impossibility of fixing the past. You know you see something and think: 'Well, that looks great' and then of course you discover how much of it has been repainted. And yet on the other hand do we want the past as ruined?

FH So what would be the most radical way to re-engineer the relations between the museum and the dig, or what would be the way that would rattle the cage the most?

    MB Oh, I know what would rattle the cage in Pompeii. It would be to leave the excavation in an 'as excavated' state. Because one thing that's very interesting about comparing modern reactions to Pompeii with early nineteenth-century reactions, is that Pompeii, for most tourists, now works every time. No matter what the artifice, no matter how much you want to lament whether the Italians are maintaining it or not, it looks like a city. You're going to the 'City of the Dead'. By contrast, a hell of a lot of tourists in the early nineteenth century were very disappointed with what they saw. It was a big razzamatazz and then they went there and… So why the difference now? It's totally obvious: it's because it has been rebuilt. The reason Pompeii satisfies us is that it's recon. If you look at the pictures of the houses as they were excavated, it's just a mess – they've been fucking destroyed by a volcano, haven't they? But somehow the idea that you might in Pompeii *not* put a roof back on, or not rebuild the wall, or not remove that bit of the upper floor…

FH So being absolutely puritanical, in terms of not engaging with the artifice, and actually aiming at that unmediated contact, would reduce the figure of the ruin so much that the figure would no longer be there – it would an incoherent pile of rubble.

MB Yes, and it would force you to recognise, and I think to celebrate, the artifice that every ruin is. I would take a little corner of the ancient city and I'd say: 'Let's just have it as it came out of the ground.' And then as you walked round this city you'd understand that what you were seeing is our reappropriation of it, because that's all you ever can see. If a Roman building is standing, that is because somebody has rebuilt it. And I'm happy, I'm fine with that. I'm just not fine with that artifice somehow not being recognised. So I think I would say: 'Look, come and see it for what it is.'

p 41, 110
Theo Wyatt Petrides

FH In relation to the artifice of restoration I want to show you drawings of Theo's project. We went to the Valley of the Temples and, if you've got your back to the sea, the Temple of Hera is the one furthest to the right on the escarpment. And on the slope that falls away from it are a whole load of boulders and fragments of this temple that have yet to be dragged back up the hill – actually mostly boulders from the fortifications along the escarpment. And Theo started to propose a kind of 'Sisyphean' choreography of using the potential energy of one boulder to drag another boulder up. *[Mary starts to giggle.]* So to raise this one here, this one over here would have to be lowered, like a kind of 'snakes and ladders' of the eternal reconstruction of this temple. So this drawing plots out the 150-year choreography of that project, in a sense as a comment on the relations between the fragment and the whole, and the relationship between restoration – the desire for restoration – and the futility of restoration.

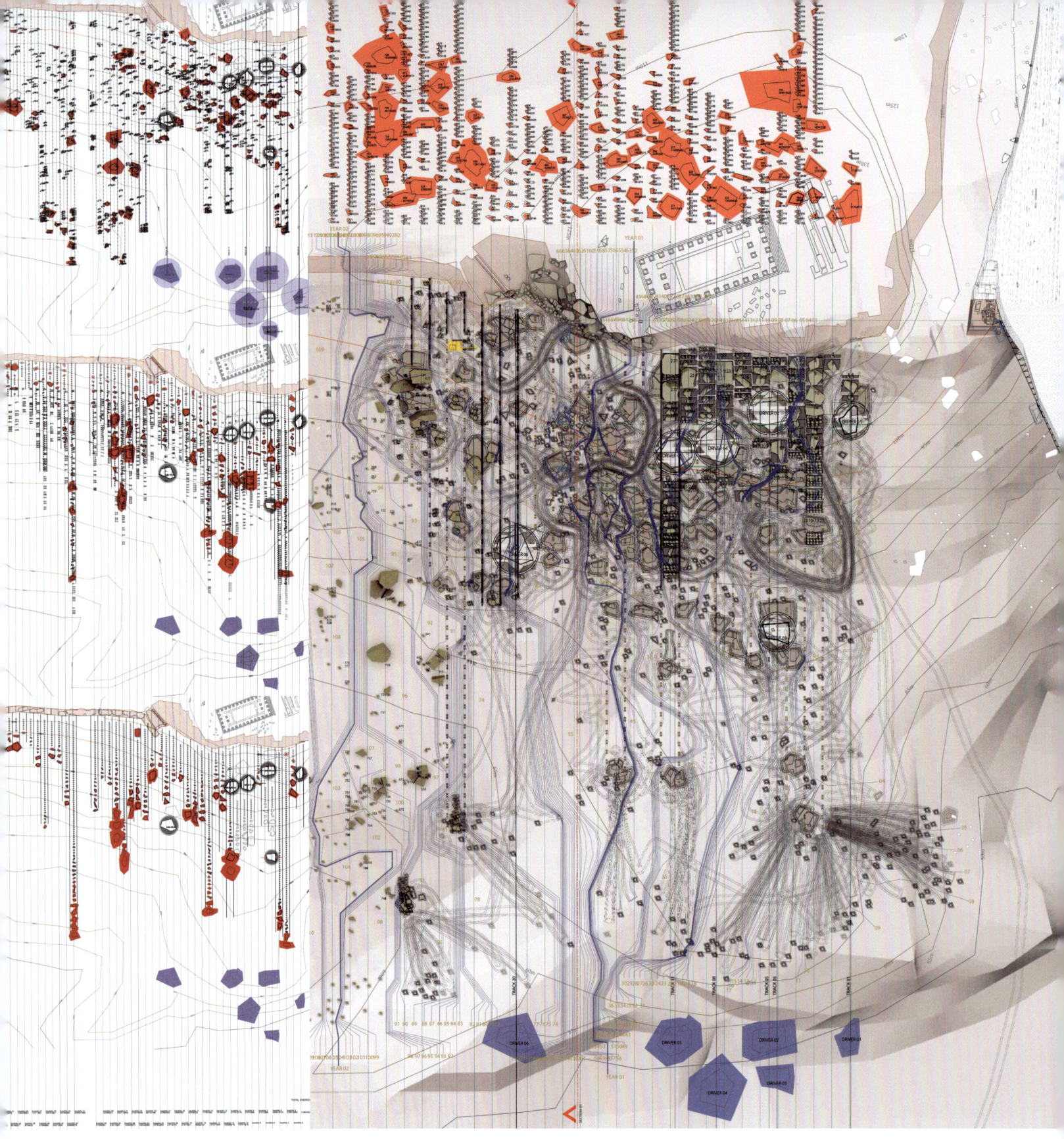

MB Yeah, as now represented most of all by the Acropolis restoration project. Which is both an achievement on *the* most extraordinary scale, and completely bonkers. And if you look at the architectural stuff that has been done, particularly on the Parthenon but also on the Propylaea, what's interesting is that they're using diagrams – and their diagrams look like Theo's project, but for real! You know, instead of saying, 'this is about modelling a version of the paradox of restoration', as Theo is doing, what they have done is they have gone around and tagged every stone on the bloody Acropolis and they have then worked out its trajectory from its original position to where it is now, and then how to replace it. So it's just like this *[Theo's drawing]*, but for real!

FH That's hilarious! And it's not tongue in cheek? It's totally serious?

MB So far as I know, it's not tongue in cheek. I might have missed the irony…

FH *[Laughing].* No subtlety there.

MB I might have missed the subtlety, but I don't think so. And it's had millions and millions and millions of euros… Of course the irony about the Parthenon project is that it has taken longer to put these blasted bits of marble back (or not put them back) than it ever took to build the bloody thing.

FH So it *is* becoming a kind of futile endless Sisyphean task. And paying for it certainly will be.

MB Yes. And it also, in that case, raises the question of what our historical engagement with it is. Because you then say, well OK, so what date Parthenon are we putting back? There was a mosque in it at one time. But we don't have the mosque – oh no, no, no, we don't have the mosque. And I think the Christian church that was in the Parthenon is going to be represented by a sort of 'trace'. So you'll go from the fifth century in this mad recon project, with all these new bits of marble inserted, as exact copies, with enormous skill and enormous razzamatazz about

'How can we find a bit of marble as big as they did in the fifth century?' or 'You know, they really, really were giants then!', and all this kind of stuff. And then you'll go through and you'll have a trace of the church – but no trace of the mosque. And so what's interesting about Theo's project here is that, intentionally or unintentionally, he's commenting on that particular form of reconstruction.

FH And ultimately what's behind that? What's driving that kind of eternal, endless futile labour of reconstruction? What's driving it in general and what drives it for you?

MB In general, it's another version, isn't it, of the power of the fragment and the problem of the ruin. The ruin in some ways is perhaps even more interesting than the fragment here, because the question is: in what state do we want it? What sort of ruin do we want?

FH Yes, so I guess the ruin is a subset of the fragment.

MB Yes. And the ruin is an interesting subset, because unlike Fuseli's foot it's completely unstable. The other thing that amazes people (when you point out something that is obvious to any architect) is that the only way forward for a ruin is to become more ruined – *unless* you decide to undertake a massive intervention. And so the pleasure of ruins in that old sense is one that requires an enormous amount of work. And then of course you have to say, OK, why was it that we wanted the Colosseum without its hermit and without its flowers? Why do we want to see those basements – they're horrible! The Colosseum now is quite an extraordinary building, because it's great on the outside – wow! – and you go inside and they've had to put a bloody gallery in there because there's nothing to look at.

FH [laughing] It's the same all the way around…

MB Yes. And you can't go on most of it because it's a bit too dangerous, so what do you do? You've had to pay a lot of money, you've had to queue for two hours, you've got to do something, and so you have galleries with temporary exhibitions and a gift shop. So the issue is that the material ruin is the most artificial of all forms of survival from Antiquity – unless it's on its downward spiral. Because the ruin can never be the same next year as it is now, unless there is *total* intervention. And then of course that brings you face to face with everybody else's previous interventions. On the Acropolis, something like the Temple of Athena Nike is actually a reconstruction work-in-progress of quite extraordinary dimensions, because nothing of it survived at all. Since the blocks were discovered in the Turkish bastion wall there have been three attempts to take it to pieces and put it back together again as a 'fixed ruin'. And it has been the victim of a kind of teleological progress. You know: 'Their reconstruction was that. My reconstruction is always going to be better, so we're going to take it to bits again, and put it all back together.' I think in many ways what drove the Parthenon 'restoration' (it's always put that way) is the practicality of it. I mean, you had to take out Nikolas Balanos' iron clamps, otherwise the whole thing was going to fall down. That was always the practical driver for getting money from the UN. But what it's about is a constant attempt to recapture a particular version of semi-truth better than the previous version of semi-truth.

FH Right, so this is very much driven by thinking about progress.

MB A rather narrow conception of progress, because otherwise we wouldn't have ended up with a Colosseum like the one we've got. I mean, it would be so much nicer if it were a botanical garden with a hermit!

FH Absolutely, with all of these extraordinary endemic flora and so on. So I hadn't realised – and it's very interesting – that the kind of thinking around the ruin is tied in with a whole kind of thinking about technology, and the teleological project of technology.

MB Yes, that's right. And I think that came out for me very clearly when I went round the Parthenon quite recently with one of the architects who is working on it. The big thing for him was whether they could get the quarries to *hew* a marble lintel as *big* as the one they had in the fifth century. So there are two senses of progress going on here. One is: can we restore it better than the guys in the nineteenth century? And the other is: can we match ancient technology? So there's a rivalrousness and sometimes, too, the sense of how it would appear on a television programme. *[Silly boffin voice]*: 'Do you know what was amazing? … No kind of mechanism today could ever…' We might laugh at that, but actually it goes right to the core of our relationship with Antiquity. And that was really my other encounter as a five-year-old in the British Museum. One was getting the bread out, and the other was seeing the Elgin Marbles, and actually doing just that manoeuvre. My dad was an architect who worked on historic buildings, so somehow I'd got the impression that medieval buildings were kind of worse than ours. I'd internalised a sense of progress.

FH Not just from your architect father, Mary!

MB Right, we'd gone round all these shacks, you know, and then we went to see the Elgin Marbles… And I thought 'God! Nobody told me they could be good at things!' And then you come across all those tropes, like, 'It wasn't until Michelangelo that…' I was doing it myself, in a different form, in this series of television programmes [*Meet the Romans*]. We're looking at Rome from the point of view of the ordinary citizen, but we're also looking at Rome as a metropolis – and what do I find myself saying? 'It wasn't until 1800 that London was as big as Rome!' You know. And of course I say that, because it has an impact with people. People think: 'God!' And yet it's another version of precisely that trope.

FH Listening to you talking about the faked stability of the ruin, or the massive effort required to keep the ruin stable, while at the same time the ruin is standing for the thing that has resisted the sands of time…

MB Yes, it's always a kind of self-referential symbol, I think…

FH … It reminds me of Joel Sternfeld's *Campagna Romana* photographs of fragments of the ancient Roman aqueduct in Rome's suburbia.

p 116
Joel Sternfeld, *Lovers parking beneath a pyramidal tomb of the second century AD*

MB Oh, yes, I just went out there when we were filming *Meet the Romans*. That's right, it's precisely this kind of conjunction with the Mussolini apartment blocks, the railway line, the aqueduct and the seedier aspects – you know, the syringes – and the daytime blokes with their sons riding their bicycles. Yes, it's absolutely extraordinary.

FH Yes, I mean in terms of the relationship between the fragment and the context it's highly ambiguous, this coming together of suburbia and some kind of pastoral setting with the sordid underbelly, the works.

MB Yes, and a sort of reappropriation of the monuments. Looking at the very varied social life around these ruins, it reminded me of when I'd heard Tariq Ali talk about growing up in whatever Pakistani city he grew up in, and he was trying to describe how things like the statue of Queen Victoria 'fitted in'. The interviewer was trying to get him to say: 'We wanted to deface it'. Whereas he said, 'No, we used to meet under it.' It had become part of our environment in a completely different way.

FH OK, going back to the question of what the object becomes when you put it back in the dig, in a sense these hulking Sternfeld aqueducts are giant artefacts that never left their dig, but they've become a place where you shoot up, or where you have a picnic with your dad who you have a difficult relationship with, or where you burn a car, or whatever… There's a kind of different potency to them.

MB And there's a potency because you don't have to pay to get in.

FH Yeah, and because they're not defined, not fixed in their meaning, so they can become whatever you need them to be. Which is extraordinary. In terms of making something become what one needs it to be, perhaps you remember Gergely's digital forensics on the mad fisheye lens that Piranesi 'used' for this projection [*Veduta dell'Anfiteatro Flavio detto il Colosseo*, 1757]. From this, Gergely came to the speculative conclusion that actually the only way to do it is to think of the Colosseum

p 117
Giovanni
Battista Piranesi

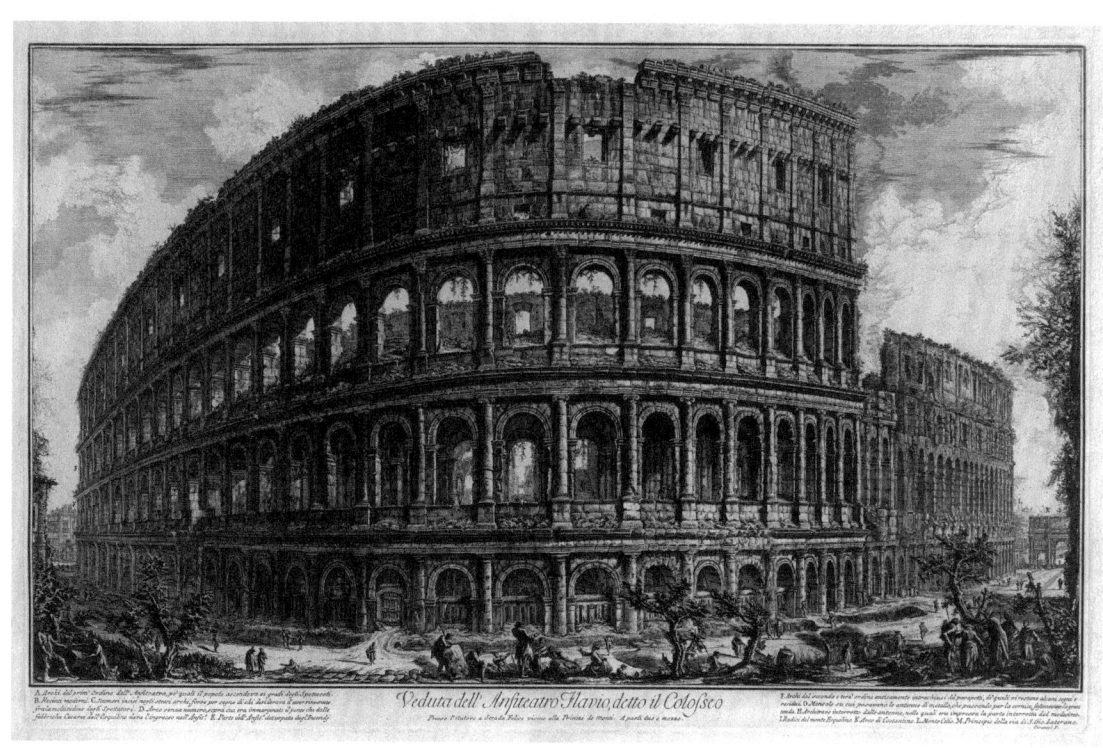

A. *Archi del primo Ordine dell' Anfiteatro, pe' quali il popolo ascendeva ai gradi degli Spettacoli.* B. *Archivo moderno.* C. *Numeri incisi negli stessi archi, forse per copia di essi che servivano l'avvenimento fra la moltitudine degli Spettatori.* D. *Area senza numero, come sia una comparsata il passo che dalla fabbrica Cavern dell'Esquilino dava l'ingresso nell'Anfit.* E. *Porte dell'Anfit.* disterpate degli Barroli.*

Veduta dell' Anfiteatro Flavio, detto il Colosseo
Presso l'Autore a Strada Felice, vicino alla Trinita de' monti. A paoli due e mezzo.

E. *Archi del secondo e terz' ordine anticamente intrecchiavi del parapetti, de' quali restavano alcuni segni e residui.* G. *Muro de'che in cui componesi le colonne di metallo, che passavano per la cornice, sostenevano i gran volti.* H. *Archi ove inservono dalle antenne, nelle quali era impresso la porta intercetta del medesimo.* L. *Radici del monte Esquilino.* K. *Arco di Costantino.* L. *Meta Sed.* M. *Principio della via di S. Gio. Laterano.*
Piranesi F.

117

not as a loop but as a line that's cranked with a kind of funny armpit condition on the inner face here where stone has to overlap stone. Through this he was asking (a bit like Angelo was with Turner): what was Piranesi up to? What did he need the Colosseum to be? Again, what was he using Antiquity as a context to invent? What was his agenda? To what extent might it have been a commentary on the line and the circle, the kind of politicising of geometry in Roman urban space? Or was Antiquity simply the alibi? Was it about something else altogether?

p 119
Gergely Kovács

MB With a monument like the Colosseum I think there's also a kind of rivalrousness between Piranesi and the past. The artist is saying: 'Look, what does everybody know about the Colosseum? It's a bloody oval, right? And how am I going to draw it? So it's no longer an oval. Just because *I can*.' And what's interesting is that he can do that, and it can still be the Colosseum. In a way that *that* [Gergely's drawing of the straightened Colosseum] isn't. I mean that has become Mussolini, that's EUR. It's another version of how far we want to make the past our own. I mean one way you can do that is by saying 'I'm now going to reconstruct the House of the Vettii and I'm going to put a roof on it, and who cares if it isn't really like this and the garden isn't like that?' The Piranesi is a slightly cleverer version, I think, that says: 'This is what I can do for you, I can make the Colosseum anew.'

FH And so your understanding is that Piranesi is making it his own in some way?

MB That's what I think. I mean it's a really self-confident gesture, isn't it?

FH It's an extraordinary thing to do. It's a kind of spatial pyrotechnics.

MB Yes, well it's a V-sign to the Colosseum as well as being a tribute to it. You know it's a bit like Salvador Dali and the Venus de Milo.

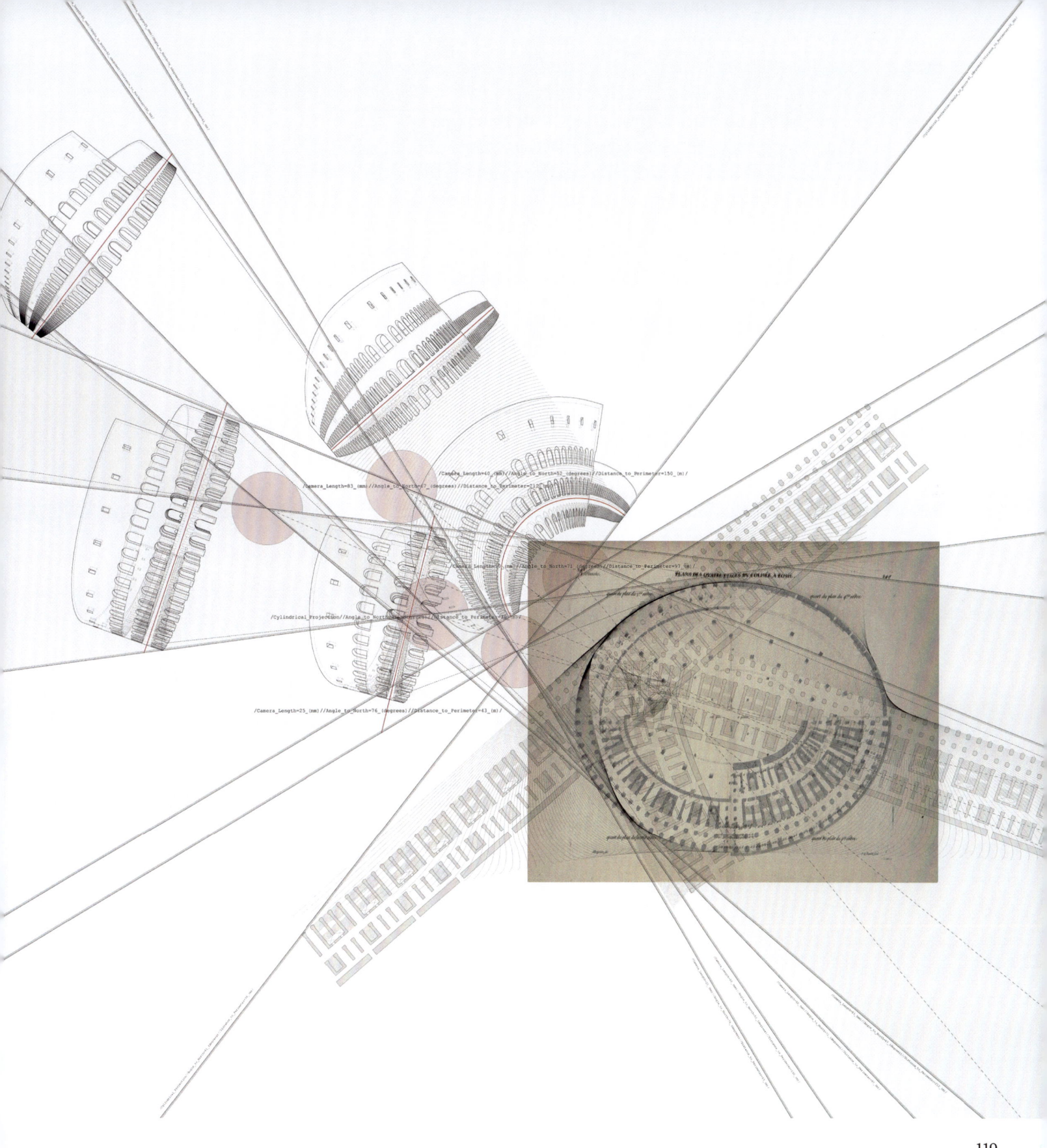

/Camera_Length=40_(mm)//Angle_to_North=52_(degrees)//Distance_to_Perimeter=150_(m)/

/Camera_Length=83_(mm)//Angle_to_North=7_(degrees)//Distance_to_Perimeter=112_(m)/

/Camera_Length=0_(mm)//Angle_to_North=71_(degrees)//Distance_to_Perimeter=97_(m)/

/Cylindrical_Projection//Angle_to_North=78_(degrees)//Distance_to_Perimeter=75_(m)/

/Camera_Length=25_(mm)//Angle_to_North=76_(degrees)//Distance_to_Perimeter=43_(m)/

FH But so much better.

MB Well yes, so much better, agreed... One thing that's interesting, though: I didn't rate the Dali that highly until I was in the Louvre and happened to spend time with the Venus de Milo – I had some students with me – and I suddenly saw that he'd observed it quite well, that actually from one angle she has this gigantically long neck. And in turning her into a giraffe Dali had actually said, I can see. It was an exploration of the flaws.

FH So of all the *Vedute di Roma*, which are all, in a sense, very servile to their subject...

MB Yes, this one is interesting, because it's not.

FH Why this one? Why the Colosseum?

MB Who knows? But I think one way of explaining it is that ever since Bede or whoever first said 'While the Colosseum stands, Rome will stand', this has been the iconic monument of Rome. And it's the most loaded one, the most difficult, the most myth-ridden, whereas who could give a toss about the Forum – it's the bloody *campo vaccino*. The Colosseum is the monument, more than any other, that was actively recuperated into the life of the city *as a ruin*. This is where the Pope comes every Good Friday – we've even got a cross here!

FH I am wondering then, why the Colosseum is out there on its own spatially, along with the *carceri*, when everything else Piranesi did is quite sensible (well, except for *Campo Marzio* – but even that is quite sensible, it's a jigsaw). Why the Colosseum and the *carceri*?

MB Well there's a link between the two. I mean, what *is* this? [pointing to Piranesi's Colosseum]

FH The prison? It's also the machine.

MB Yes, it's the prison, the machine and it's also, in terms of the ruins of Rome, the most aggressively in-your-face *challenge*, isn't it? We can see this from the different way it's used in modern cartoons: the difference, I suppose, is that in the nineteenth century the cult of the gladiator changes the Colosseum in a significant way. I think if you'd asked Piranesi about gladiators, he wouldn't have had a clue, wouldn't have made the connection. For him the Colosseum is about martyrdom.

FH I'm reading Hilary Mantel's *A Place of Greater Safety*, an amazing account of the French Revolution. And Rome is all over it, and the machine is all over it – the machine of the guillotine, the printing press for Camille Desmoulin's pamphlets. (Not to mention everyone throwing away their powdered wigs and getting a bad Caecilius haircut the moment the revolution happens).*

MB Yes, this is industrial slaughter.

FH So maybe this [Piranesi's Colosseum] is also about that horror?

MB Yes, and I think it relates to the prisons. It cannot be a coincidence that this is the closest *real* ancient monument to the prisons. It is odd because our students look at bits of Piranesi's *vedute* quite a lot, but they leave this one to one side – it doesn't do.

FH Why? Because of the evident distortion?

MB Yes, I think that's it. And I think they think – because most of them are not particularly interested in this bit of it – that perhaps he couldn't do it, perhaps it defeated him. So who defeated whom? Is this Piranesi saying 'up yours' at the Colosseum? Or *[conspiratorial whisper]* has the Colosseum defeated Piranesi?

*Anyone who studied Latin at school in England will be deeply familiar with Caecilius's hairdo, which, like Bede's Colosseum, stands eternal. Caecilius is still the key protagonist of the blissfully unchanged illustrations of the *Cambridge Latin Course* books that generations of schoolchildren have doodled or snoozed on.

FH I wonder if the students are saying: 'Ugh! The artifice is too in-your-face. That's so self-conscious, I can't stomach it.'

MB It could be that. Though our approach to Antiquity is always mediated, we nevertheless like to be given an alibi for forgetting the mediation. Turner allows it. But when somebody does that, you can't forget it.

FH But you see, what Turner is doing is even wilder, but it's concealed. Unless you go in and do what Angelo did, you simply don't know. It's much more stealthy, but also way more radical, because in a sense the Colosseum in Piranesi's treatment is still intact – it has become a cranked line (according to Gergeley's forensic analysis), whereas here [in Turner's *Dido building Carthage*] we have a complete fragmentation of space.

———————————————————— p 124–125
Gergely Kovács

MB A disaggregation. Yes, that's right.

FH I want to end with your practice as an Antique scholar, which is so amazing. In a sense you have to negotiate in your work so much that is didactic, that is puritanical, that has a kind of pompous agenda. I mean, I remember you going through the standard analysis of Aristophanes' response in Plato's *Symposium*: how one can understand the desire to unify and to make whole the classical world as being a collective erotic desire and that this is *the* Biggest Project and so on. But you seem to keep this at arm's length, and your own practice is much more about revelling in a playful set of relations with the past.

MB It's also much more muddled, don't you think? Or rather it's very hard to see structure within your quotidian practice… And of course what you do everyday seems muddled. And it would be something awful if it didn't – you'd be with Mussolini in that case!

FH Yes, this is true…[laughter]

MB So, there's an awful lot of improvisation about what one does. But I think what happens when you get older is that you have a greater fearlessness about revelling in the paradoxes.

You don't see the inconsistencies and the paradoxes as part of the problem any longer. You think: *that's* what it's about. And the more you read about the people in the past – and I don't mean the ancients, I mean any old nineteenth-century figure like Jane Harrison – the more you can see that, in their own slightly rebarbative jargon, *that's what they're doing too.*
You know it's impossible to study the ancient world, and the only way to make it make sense to anybody is by a series of compromises, which sometimes means forgetting the artifice – or at least pretending to forget the artifice.

FH And presumably at other times remembering the artifice, and adding to the artifice?

MB Yes, that's right. And you find that with students, they want both – they want to play with the fantasy of unmediated access while at the same time saying 'Somehow, if I knew Latin better, I would be closer.' But there's no way. If you know Latin better, you'll see different things in the texts you're reading, but you'll be no fucking closer to the Romans than you are now. But of course that's the Aristophanic lure we offer them: 'If you know your Greek properly, know your subjunctives and your optatives, my dear, that project of wholeness will be so much easier.'

FH What a carrot!

MB It's a terrible carrot, isn't it? Of course it works every time. There is an interesting analogy here, because one thing you're doing is saying: 'Look, the better you know the Latin or Greek language, the closer you get. You get really up close.' *[Breathy whisper]* Which is both true and untrue. But they also become very interested in the idea of the mechanisms by which they learn the language. Particularly if they've done Latin at school, they've been brought up to think that Latin grammar is a kind of inheritance that we have from the Romans – that the Romans would have sat down and said: mensa, mensa, mensam, mensae, mensae, mensa. And you say: 'Well, in the form in which you've got it, sunshine, some nineteenth-century guy sitting not very far from here invented this system.' Kennedy didn't do it entirely by himself, of course – there is actually a tradition stretching

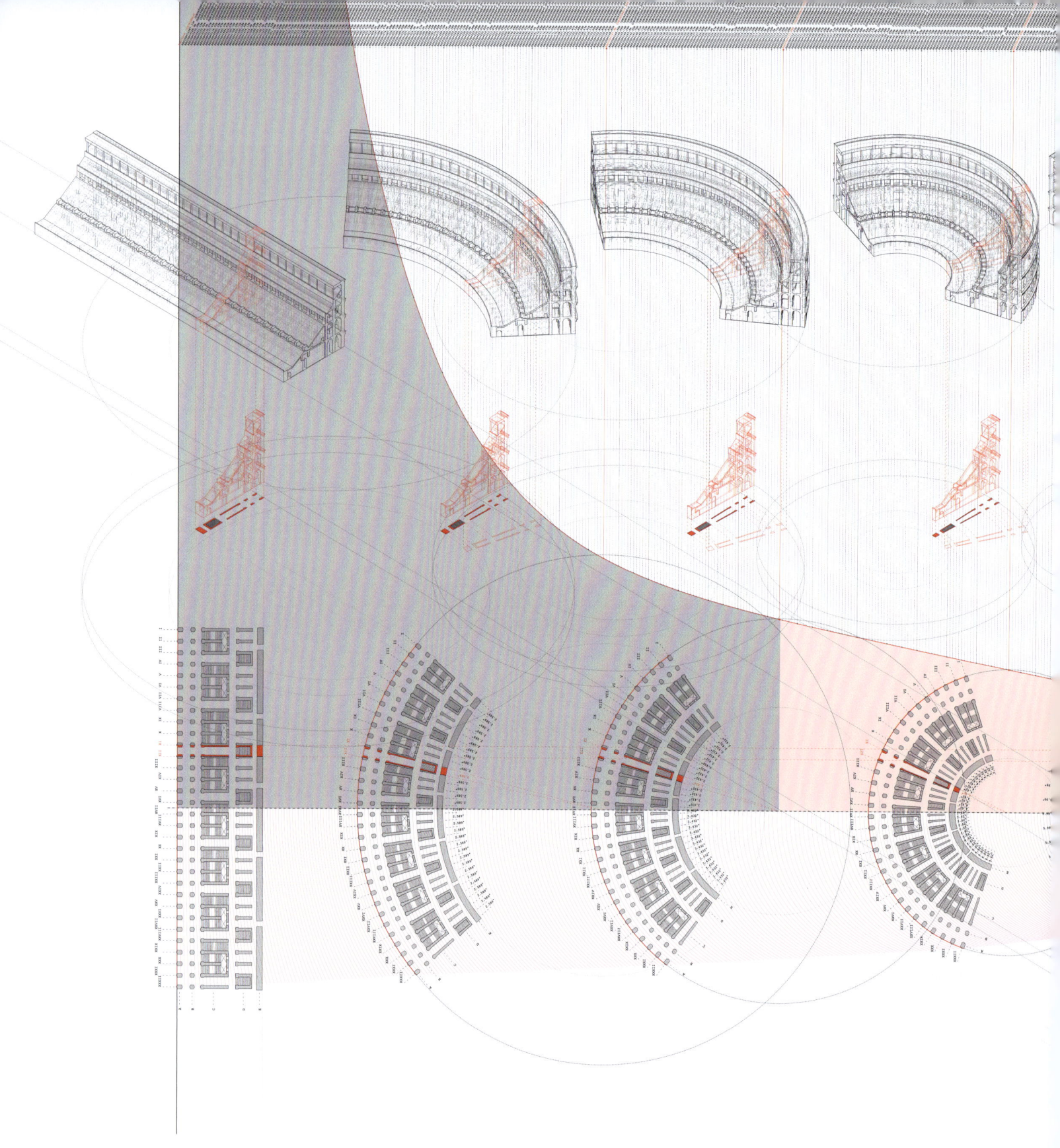

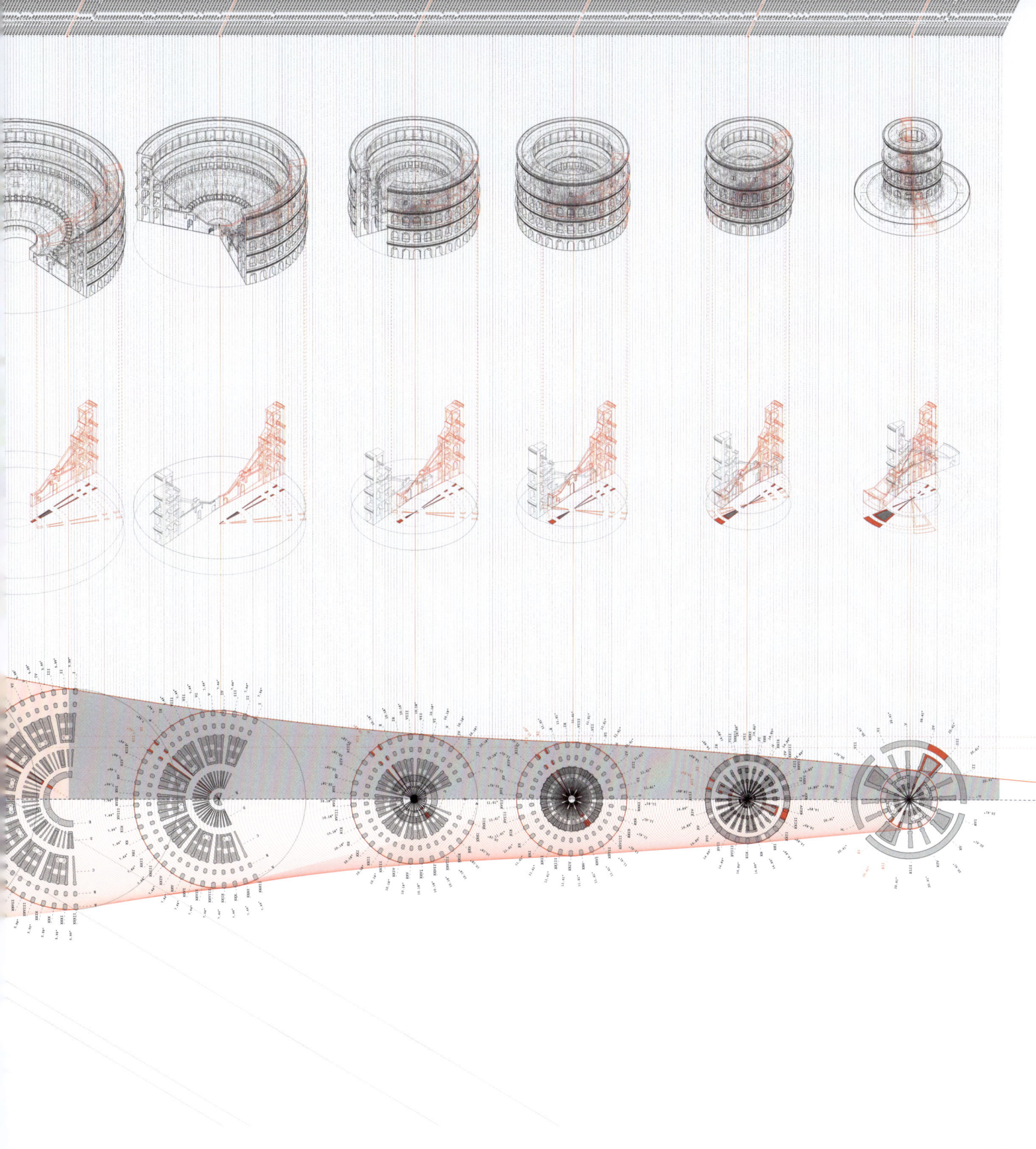

back to the middle ages – but when you read his Latin primer you are reading the artifice of language. It is always an eye-opener to tell students that the reason why there are exceptions to rules in Latin or Greek is because the structure was part of the artifice. What happened was that somebody said, 'How can I describe this from now?', and then sat down and tried to work it out. And of course he couldn't: there are some times where the bloody verb takes the genitive and then you have to explain that – 'Ah, it takes the genitive in those cases where there is perhaps an *element of doubt*.' And you say: 'No, no, it doesn't!' And of course you can't describe it – Kennedy has a totally failed version of artifice to start with. He has a public school Latin primer and he's using German grammars and the whole tradition of Latin grammar going back to the medieval school, but he's making it anew for nineteenth-century Britain. His first version is called *The Public School Latin Primer* and it's completely hopeless, it's the artifice of grammar that nobody uses, it doesn't ring, doesn't sing. And the story goes – this is also a nice bit of artificial mythology – that his daughters then take over, and they reconstruct the artifice, and they get it right with *The Revised Latin Primer*, that is, revised by the young Kennedy daughters. So the message, from a peculiarly linguistic analogy, is that there is of course an artifice between us and the ancient world, but sometimes it doesn't work for us.

FH And what made it not work?

MB Just too fucking dense. *[Laughs]*

FH Too dense? Too difficult? Or didn't sound right?

MB It's very interesting to know, isn't it? I mean it's easy to see productive and successful forms of artifice in our engagement with the past. But it would be interesting to think about or to see where you or your students think the artifice fails. You need also to think about what kind of vehicles of artifice have *not* worked? And that's always much harder to spot.

FH Yes, and to define why these ones work, and why other projections of the Colosseum or of Carthage couldn't have worked?

MB Yes, that's right.

FH That's a really interesting question.

MB We sometimes can see for ourselves what doesn't work, for example in movies. But this is quite hard. I suspect you need to think about what doesn't work.

FH We do. A good and difficult point. Also, one would expect certain artifices to work at certain times, and at others not to speak to us at all. So it's always about our relation to the present.

MB Yes. Modern studies of Alma Tadema have been quite interesting because somehow we …

FH Oh my problem with Alma Tadema is they're such gruesome paintings, I can't look at them…[laughing]. Do you like them? You must have developed a way of liking them.

MB I think his project's interesting.

FH OK, I will squint at the paintings and see the project.

MB I think the stuff that is about the relationship of the ancient viewer to the ancient art object is extremely interesting, and his insertion of himself into those paintings as the ancient consumer is extremely smart.

FH I want to ask you a last question. I remember your commentary on the Iraq war 'triumph', with Bush on the aircraft carrier, declaring victory ten years before it didn't happen.

MB [Laughs] What did the banner say? … 'Mission Accomplished!' That's it.

FH And in a sense, having read the Hilary Mantel recently, I am really beginning to understand more clearly how Rome is always at work, always there. And the question is perhaps a silly question, but where, in your mind, is Rome now? What is Rome up to right now?

MB [Laughs] You *know* perfectly well that that will only be apparent to us after the event. We couldn't be good cultural practitioners if we simultaneously *knew*. There has to be a delay – though it might even be only ten seconds later that you see what is happening…

FH I think that your Bush commentary was probably about a month later, so it can be pretty soon.

MB Yes, so you can see that. Now, in due course, I would want to reflect on how the present travails of Europe – and its money and its sense of whether it's a state, or a continent, or an odd amalgam of different countries – is being debated in relation to Antiquity…

FH That's certainly going to require hindsight, especially with Athens in the very centre of it.

MB Yes, and the thought that the self-proclaimed proud birthplace of democracy has become a sort of non-voting subsidiary of Germany, which of course is what the modern state of Greece started as. You know, little King Otto, where did he come from? Bavaria! This goes back to 1830 and the major powers of Europe deciding that they would recreate 'Greece'. Where the hell are they going to get the king from? Eventually they find little King Otto, because he's too young to say 'no', and his dad is dead keen on Classics. And then what do they do? They recreate the state. The recreation of Greece as a model of fifth-century culture and democracy (the democracy bit was slightly iffy in 1830) is a product of German classicism.

FH And a German project?

MB A German project. Who were all the little advisers when they started to excavate the Acropolis? They were Germans! So there is a certain sense in which we can't avoid thinking about this in terms of the *recently* recreated classical past in Greece, which is what has generated claims to primacy. This is where our problems about Rome and Greece stem from – our productive problems about their relationship, and about Rome as the culture of the copy, Rome constructing Greece as a copy. It would of course have been entirely different in the early eighteenth century.

FH What would it have been then?

MB Well, we certainly wouldn't have known a damn thing about Greece! There was still a sense of the culture of the copy, but it would have been much more indistinct, I think. I mean imagine having Rome's version of Greece without having seen the Parthenon! So it will be interesting to see what happens. It's not that I think that the history of Europe is in some way inextricably tied up with the inheritance of the classical world, because that's cheap relevance talk, but that our *way* of thinking about Europe and how it means something to itself is still enmeshed with how we think about ancient Greece and Rome. And I would be very surprised if that wasn't changing at the moment.

FH Yes, I remember there was a point a couple of months ago when Sarkozy said in despair to Cameron: 'You know, we are not just a trading zone, there has to be a loyalty, a project beyond that.' And Cameron responded: 'Well actually I thought we *were* just a trading zone.'

MB [*Laughs*] Yes! So, I think that if it is true to say that you can't have Western European culture without at least half an eye on how you construct that in relation to the ancient world, then there must be a shift going on right now. Though I don't quite know what it is.

FH And you don't quite know when you're going to know either, because this might take a while?

MB No. It might be next week, or it might not be for ten years!

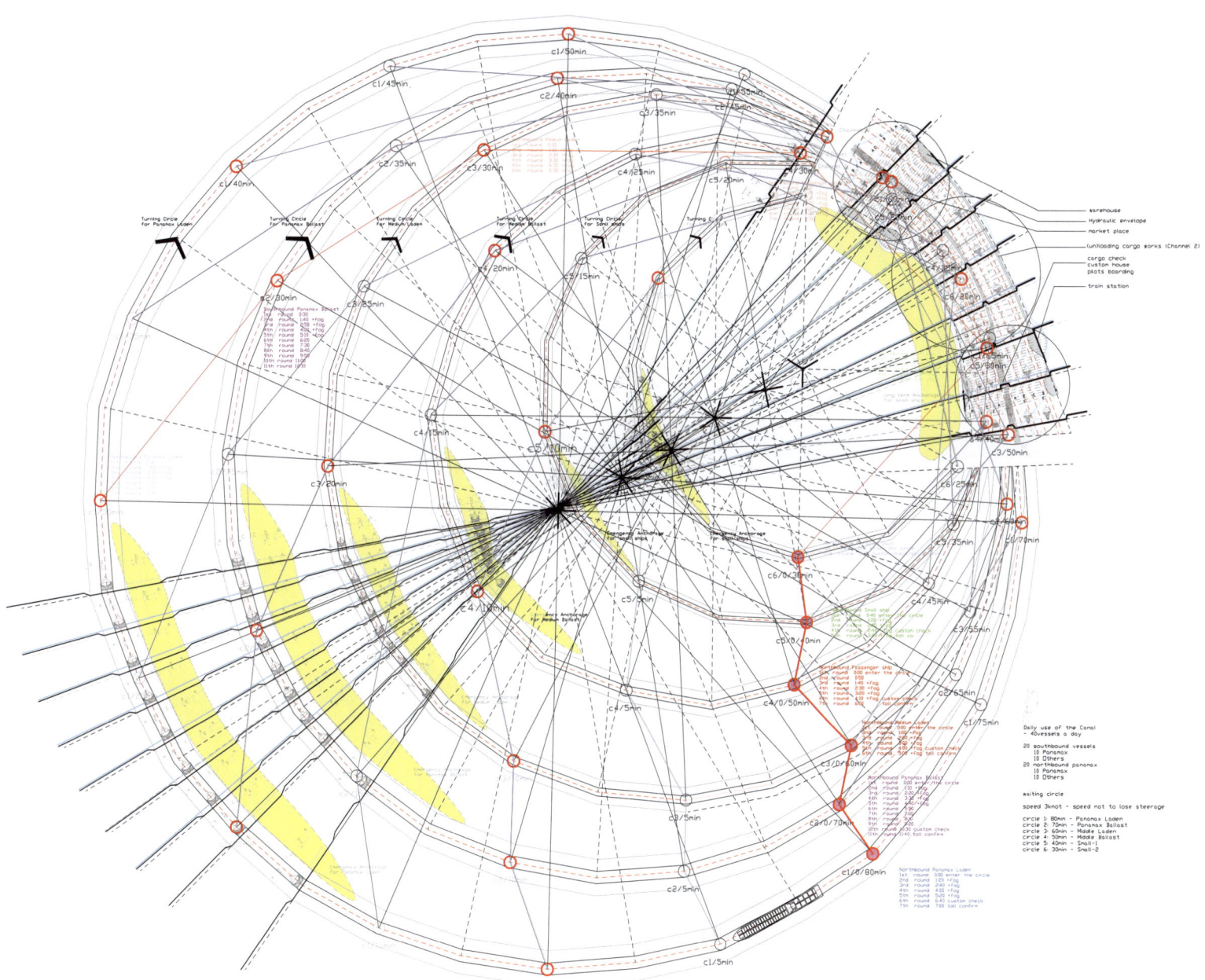

131

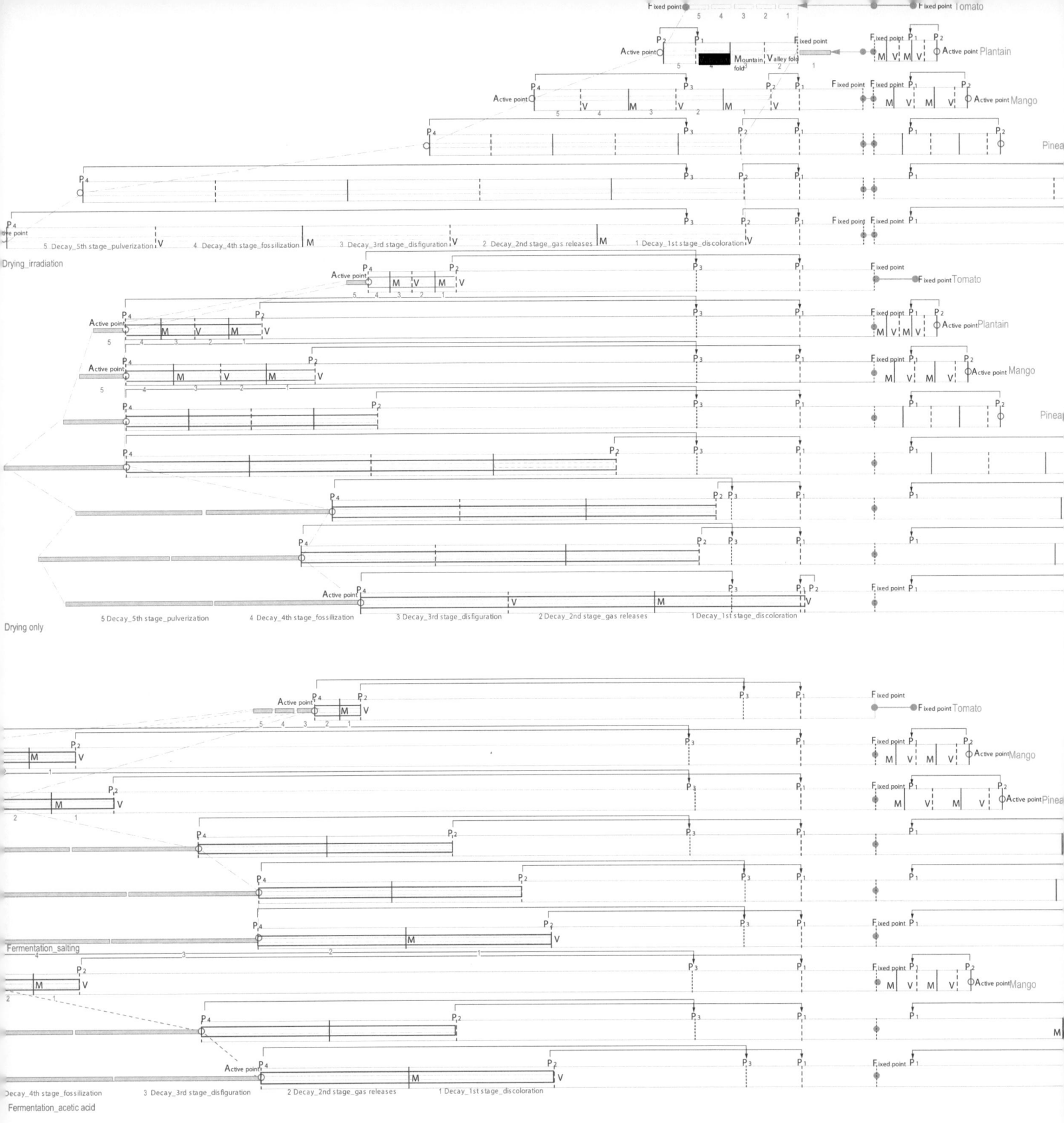

Fixed point 5 4 3 2 1 Fixed point Tomato

Fixed point
Active point P₄ P₁ Mountain Valley fold fold M V M V Active point Plantain
Mountain Valley fold 5 4 2 1 M V M V

Active point P₄ P₃ P₂ P₁ Fixed point Fixed point P₄ Active point Mango
V M V M V 5 4 3 2 1 M V M V

P₄ P₃ P₂ P₁ Pinea

P₄ P₃ P₂ P₁

P₄ P₃ P₂ Fixed point Fixed point P₁
the point
5 Decay_5th stage_pulverization V 4 Decay_4th stage_fossilization M 3 Decay_3rd stage_disfiguration V 2 Decay_2nd stage_gas releases M 1 Decay_1st stage_discoloration V

Drying_irradiation

Active point P₄ P₂ P₃ P₁ Fixed point Fixed point Tomato
M V M V 5 4 3 2 1

Active point P₄ P₂ P₃ P₁ Fixed point P₄ Active point Plantain
M V M V 5 4 3 2 1 M V M V

Active point P₄ P₂ P₃ P₁ Fixed point P₄ Active point Mango
M V M V 5 4 3 2 1 M V M V

P₄ P₂ P₃ P₁ Pinea

P₄ P₂ P₃ P₁

P₄ P₂ P₃ P₁

P₄ P₂ P₃ P₁

Active point P₄ P₃ P₁ P₂ Fixed point P₁
5 Decay_5th stage_pulverization V 4 Decay_4th stage_fossilization 3 Decay_3rd stage_disfiguration 2 Decay_2nd stage_gas releases M 1 Decay_1st stage_discoloration V

Drying only

Active point P₄ P₂ P₃ P₁ Fixed point
M V 5 4 3 2 1

M V P₂ P₃ P₁ Fixed point P₄ P₂ Active point Mango
1 M V M V

P₂ P₃ P₁ Fixed point P₄ Active point Pinea
M V 2 1 M V M V

P₄ P₂ P₃ P₁

P₄ P₂ P₃ P₁

P₄ P₂ P₃ P₁ Fixed point P₁
M V

M V P₂ P₃ P₁ Fixed point P₄ P₂ Active point Mango
Fermentation_salting 2 1 M V M V
4 3 2 1

M V P₄ P₂ P₃ P₁ P₁
2 1 M

Active point P₄ P₂ P₃ P₁ Fixed point P₁
Decay_4th stage_fossilization 3 Decay_3rd stage_disfiguration 2 Decay_2nd stage_gas releases M 1 Decay_1st stage_discoloration V

Fermentation_acetic acid

132

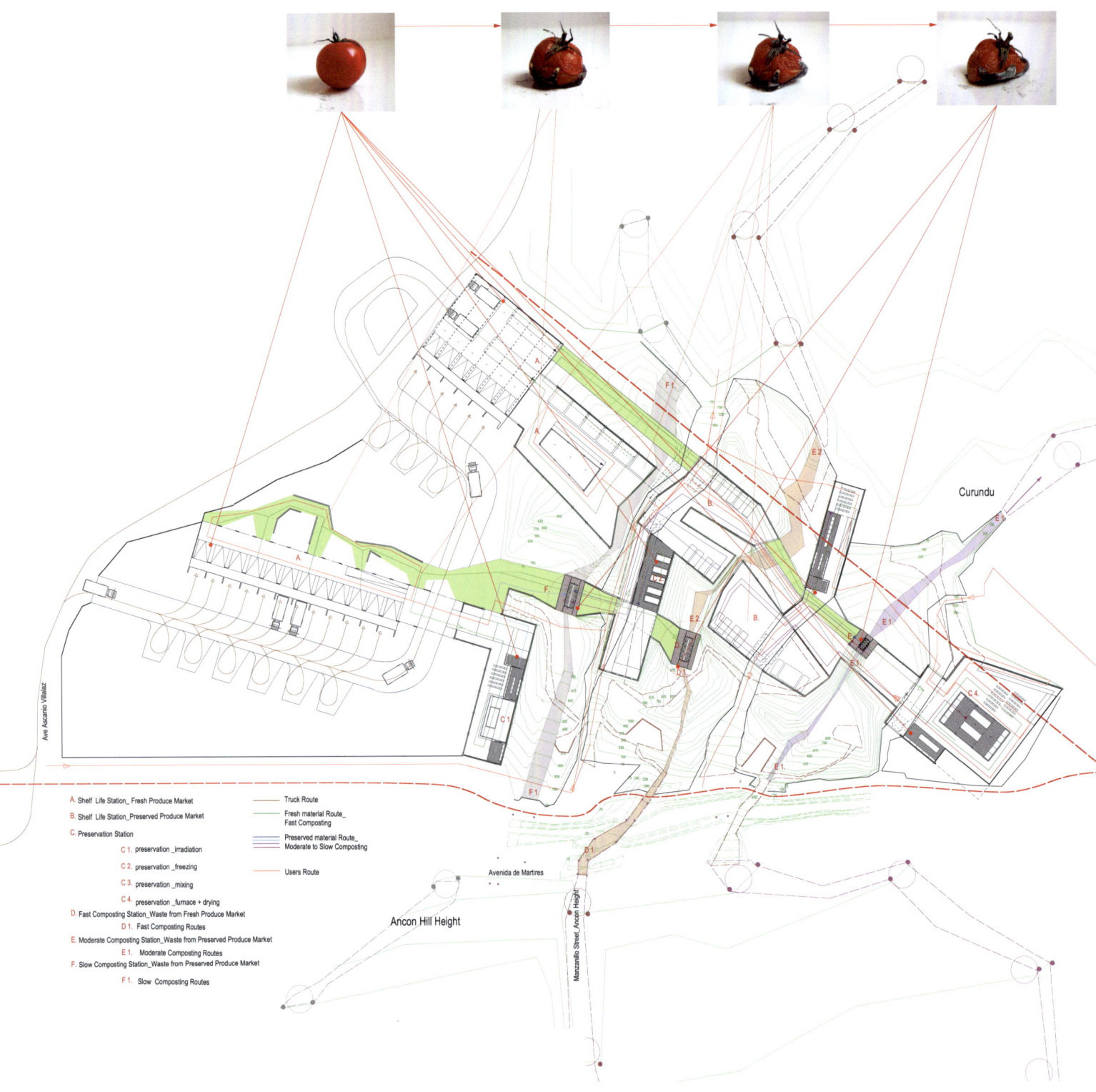

A. Shelf Life Station_ Fresh Produce Market
B. Shelf Life Station_Preserved Produce Market
C. Preservation Station
       C 1. preservation _irradiation
       C 2. preservation _freezing
       C 3. preservation _mixing
       C 4. preservation _furnace + drying
D. Fast Composting Station_Waste from Fresh Produce Market
       D 1. Fast Composting Routes
E. Moderate Composting Station_Waste from Preserved Produce Market
       E 1. Moderate Composting Routes
F. Slow Composting Station_Waste from Preserved Produce Market
       F 1. Slow Composting Routes

——— Truck Route

——— Fresh material Route_
     Fast Composting

——— Preserved material Route_
     Moderate to Slow Composting

——— Users Route

Ave Ascanio Villalaz

Curundu

Avenida de Martires

Ancon Hill Height

Manzanillo Street, Ancon Height

134

By the Time it Takes to Count

Unlike calculation, counting is tied to the material: the crumb, the circular counter, the leaping sheep even – all bind integer to object. Counting not only has a material footprint but, like all labours, it takes time. The materialisation of the temporal – an architecture that accrues, and the clock that writes it – is central to much of the unit's work. Periodicity, duration and interval are accordingly key elements of our repertoire's syntax. Sayaka Namba's space for getting

p 17–18
Sayaka Namba

lost, *A Qanat Park for Palermo* [*Get Lost: A Qanat Park for Palermo*, p 17–18], addresses the loss of both spatial and temporal orientation: being physically lost does strange things to time. Jean Wang's clock in *Shelf-Life: The Preservation and Decomposition of a Political Border* p 133, 134 is matter-specific and thus multiple: time accelerates with the rapid decay of the tomato in the Panama tropics and slows with the reluctant decay of citrus. Time inflected by the 'material subjectivity' of decaying organic matter thus compacts and stretches space in her hypercontextual regime. By contrast,

Gergely Kovács' time is the time that denies subjectivity: the endless, repetitive, looped patience of the algorithm. Around and around his human computer goes, as inversion is mapped upon inversion, *ad absurdum* and *ad infinitum*, creating a spatial and temporal prison of sorts. The poignant circuits of the

p 175
Gergely Kovács

algorithm's prison yard in *Paths in a Field of Inversion* [*Studies in Inversion: Paths in a Field of Inversion*, p 175] or *Inversion of a Generic Grid* [*Studies in Inversion: Inversion of a Generic Grid*, p 137] remind us, amongst other things, that the looped temporal line of this repetition *is* the invisible dominant space of now, the space *behind* all the extraordinary spatiality we can now make in the computer.

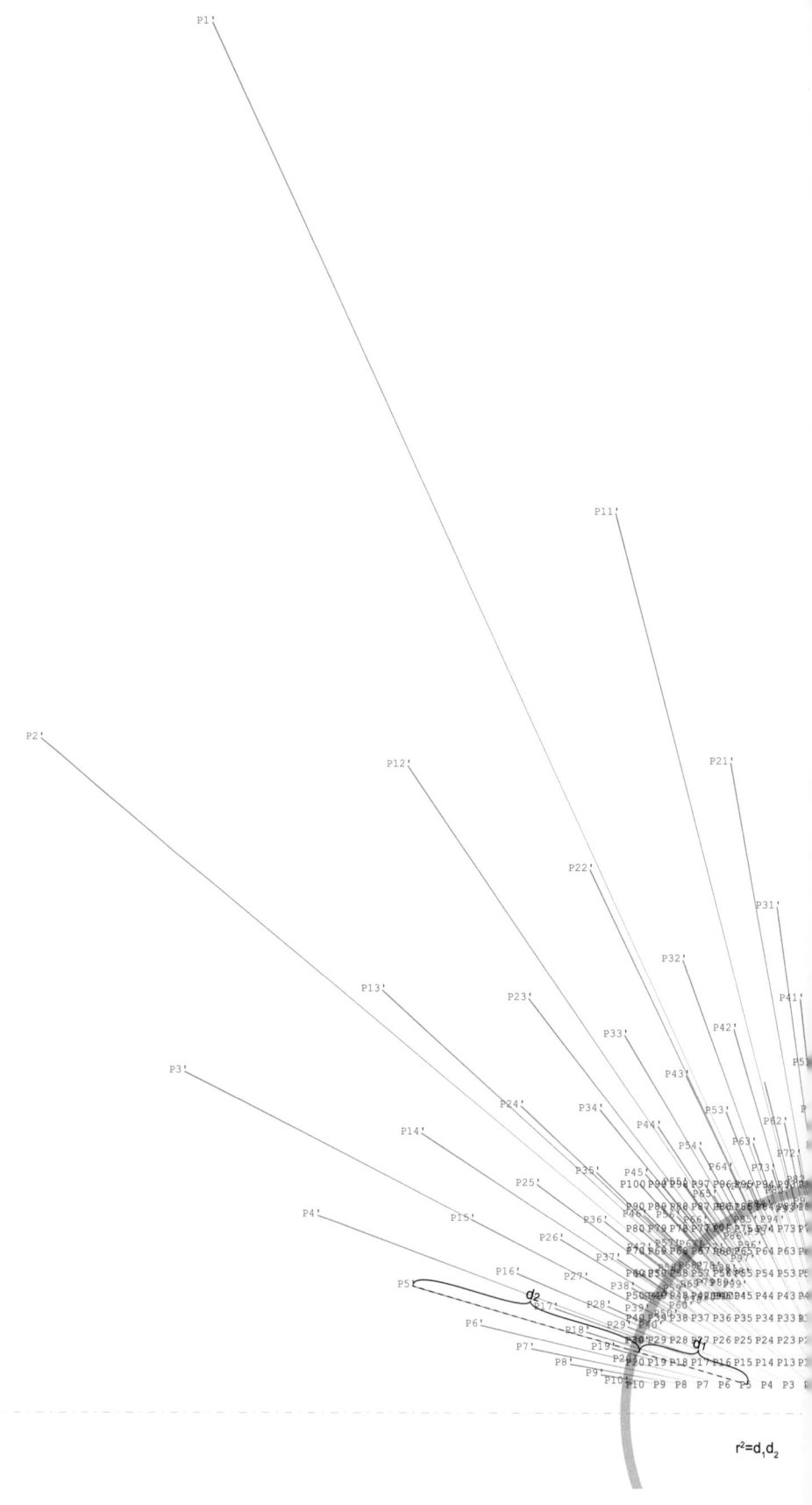

$r^2 = d_1 d_2$

136

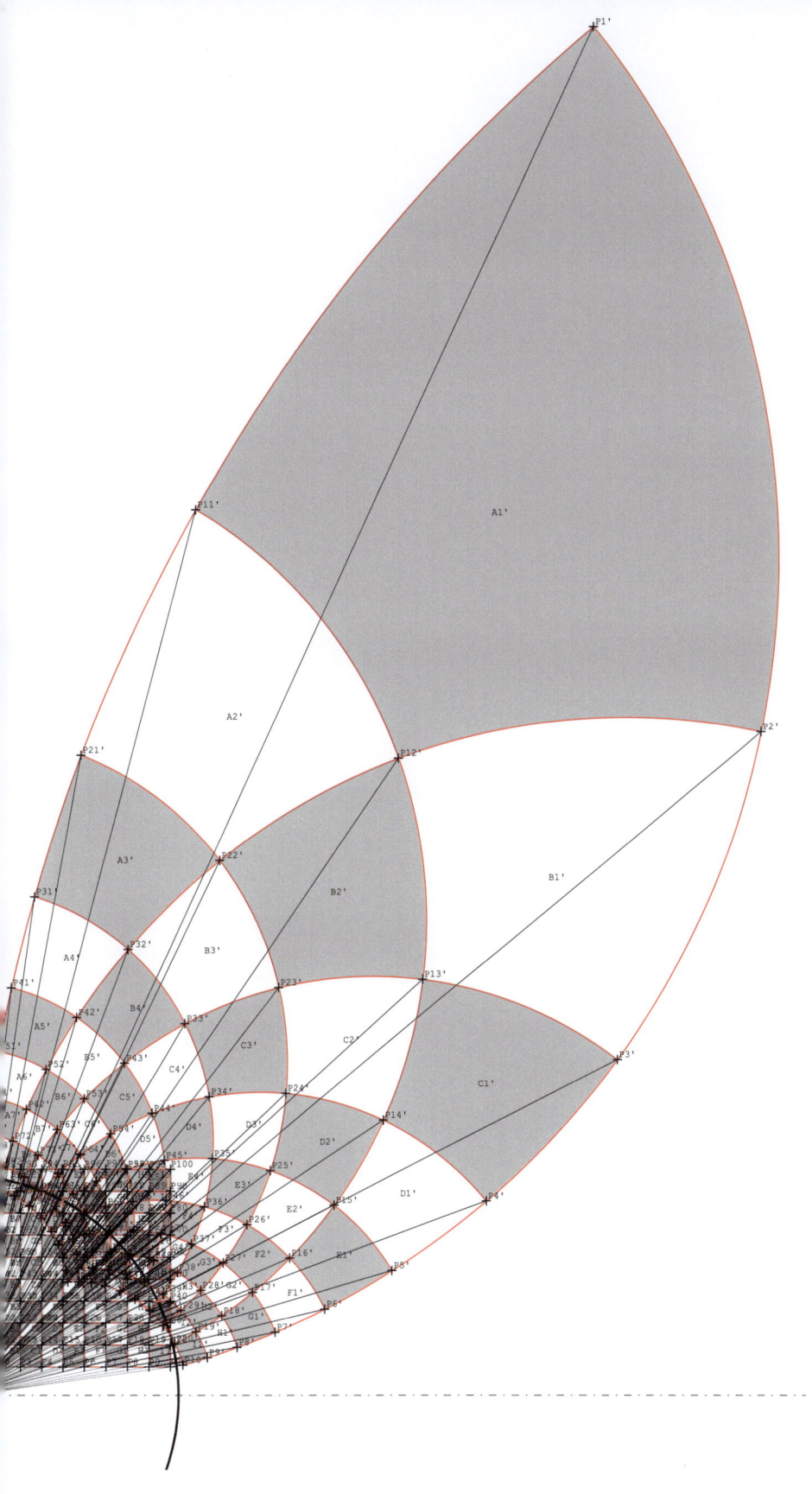

137

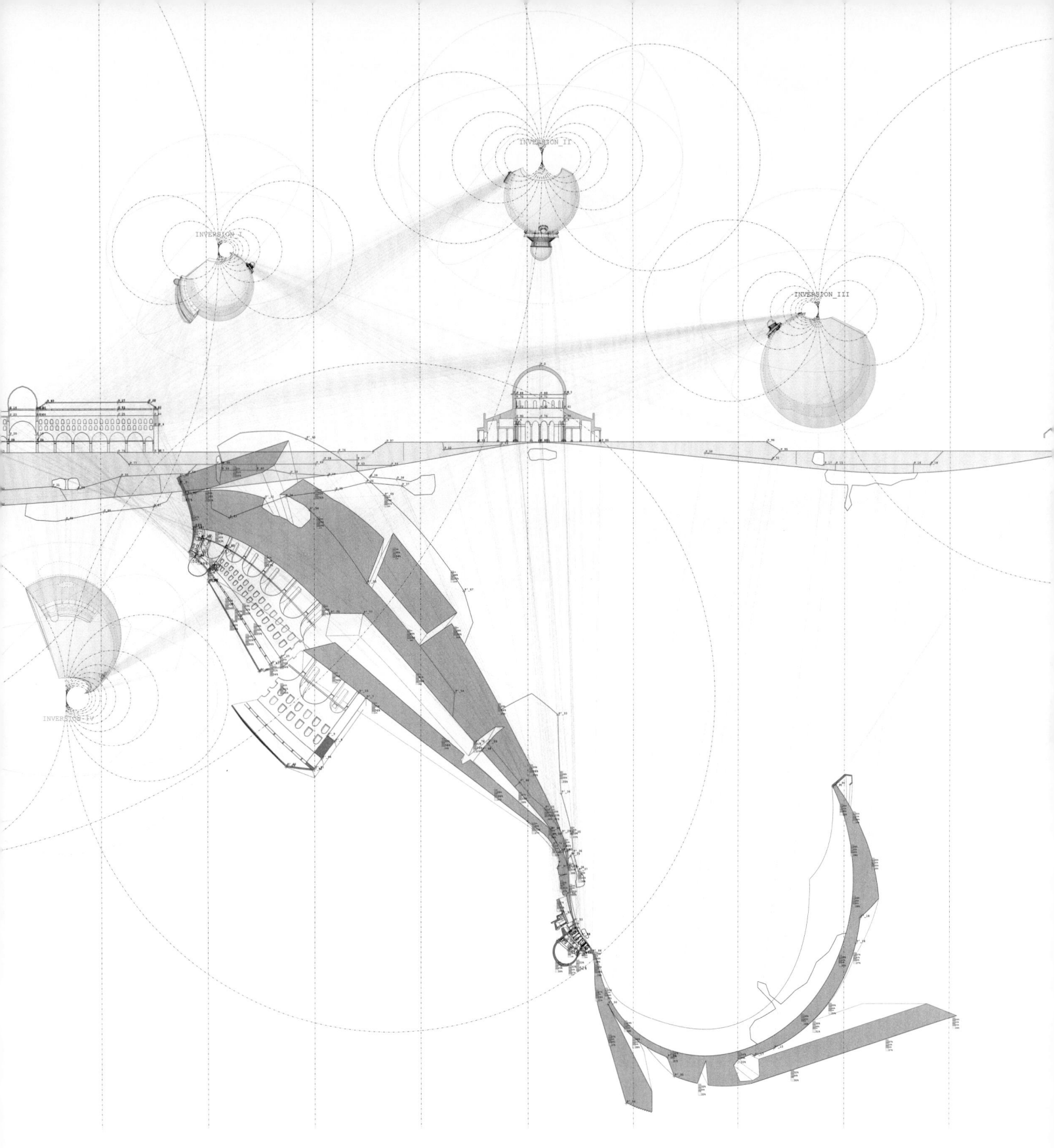

INVERSION_I

INVERSION_II

INVERSION_III

INVERSION_IV

139

And the Word Became Technology

— David Edgerton

Until the mid-twentieth century technology barely existed. For it was not until then that this late-eighteenth-century coining became a master concept in modernity. In its original sense, it was simply an *ology*, a 'study of' the technical arts (*techne*); it would appear in such phrases as 'the Manchester College of Technology' and hardly anywhere else. Only in the fairly recent past did technology come to denote not just a branch of knowledge but the things produced by that knowledge. While many languages retain a distinction between, say, *technique* and *technologie*, or *técnica* and *tecnología*, this is losing its grip, and the Anglo-American technology is the future in the bones of modernity everywhere. *Technology* now means something either broad or narrow, depending on the argument, but above all it means a digital novelty.

In the nineteenth century the future emerged as a key category for social commentary – only the future was not with *technology*, but with science, inventions, machines, instruments, apparatus, devices: with novelties. There was no question that contemporaries saw the nineteenth century as a time of spectacular advance. By the end of the century the early 1800s were described by some, referring to Britain, as the period of the 'industrial revolution'. In the 1950s, in Britain at least, scientific intellectuals thought this industrial revolution had been superseded by a 'scientific revolution', one associated with nuclear power and electronics and automation. Later – it is not clear exactly when – changes in the late nineteenth century were labelled a 'second industrial revolution' and the idea of a 'scientific revolution' was firmly fixed on the *seventeenth* century. Past and future changed together.

The first and second industrial revolutions had, in these schemes of history, quite different characters. The first was the result of a 'wave of gadgets' – particularly for the making of textiles, but also in agriculture and in mining. The dominant machine in most narratives was the steam engine, which converted coal into a new source of inanimate power of unprecedented scale. The idea of the second industrial revolution focused on two sectors. The first was industrial chemistry, and in particular synthetic organic chemistry, mainly concerned with

p 143
Angelo Sanghoon Han
*Lord Byron's
Front-Crawl Down
the Grand Canal
as a Representation
and Transportation
Machine*

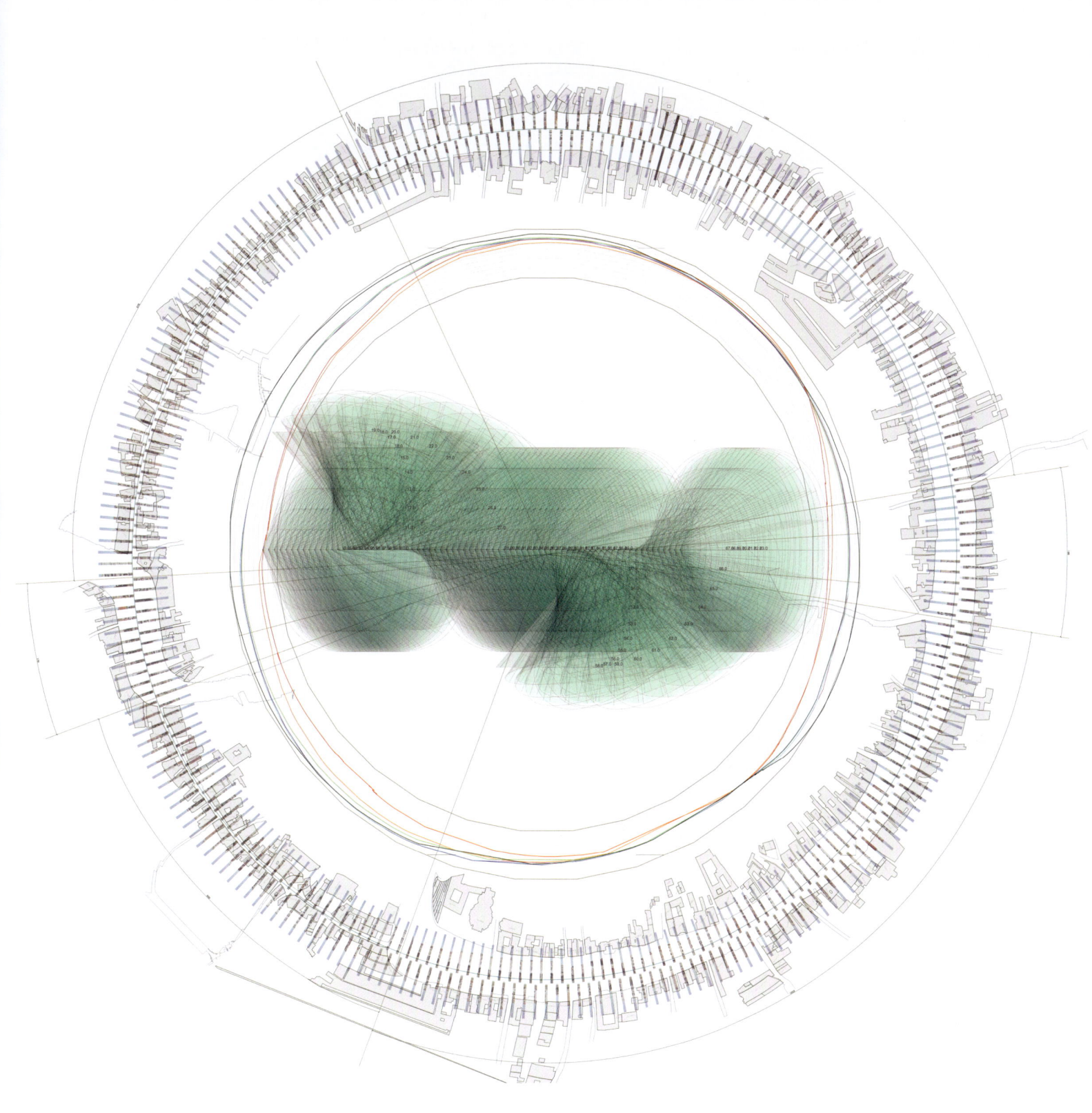

143

the making of new dyestuffs and also synthetic versions of natural ones like indigo and alizarine. The second was electricity, a startling invisible force that produced lighting, traction and many mysterious chemical and other effects. The first industrial revolution was broadly speaking the work of mechanics, artisans, the ingenious inventor; the second the work of scientists, working in laboratories, in great firms like General Electric or BASF or Bayer. It is striking that most of the 'industrial revolution' gadgets are known by earthy English names – the spinning jenny, flying shuttle, water-frame, self-acting mule, steam engine, railway – while later ones tended to be given new names derived from ancient languages – hence photograph, kinematograph, oscillograph; telegraph and telephone; any number of scopes, say stereoscope, praxinoscope, kinetoscope; and automobile, taxi, aeroplane. Whole new classes of living things and chemical compounds were given names derived from Latin and Greek, as were some new elements (Helium, Argon, Xenon…) New sciences were embellished with names conjured out of the past – biology, technology – as were new medical specialisms, say psychiatry.

These are compelling, standard stories, which are granted authority in both positive and negative accounts of modernity. Fortified by the knowledge that these stories have very particular histories, we need to challenge their hegemony. One might have thought that this was done long ago, not least by 'post-modernism' – which surely pushed aside all grand narratives and took off into a new eclecticism. Yet po-mo thought was itself the latest variant of such modern narratives: was not post-modernity intimately tied to post-industrialism, to a technical revolution which was dwarfing the industrial revolution, and the second industrial revolution too? The po-mo grand narrative too often required a crass version of Enlightenment, an industrial society as described by its ideologues.

For historians the picture of the past was always more variegated, and indeed some directly challenged such accounts. Raphael Samuel, in a devastating paper of 1977 ('Miners, Quarrymen and Saltworkers'), showed the nineteenth century was as much about expanding old gadgets as it was about inventing new ones; that the appearance of coal-based power did not reduce human effort, but instead often created new kinds of intense human work – say, de-clinkering boilers. Novelty was not all, nor was it what is was said to be. We may enter similar reservations about the late nineteenth century. *This* was the great age of coal, or steam engines, of textiles. It was indeed a moment of extraordinary creativity, but it was not concentrated in two sectors or in universities or giant firms. Rather it was very general – this was the great age of invention right across the board

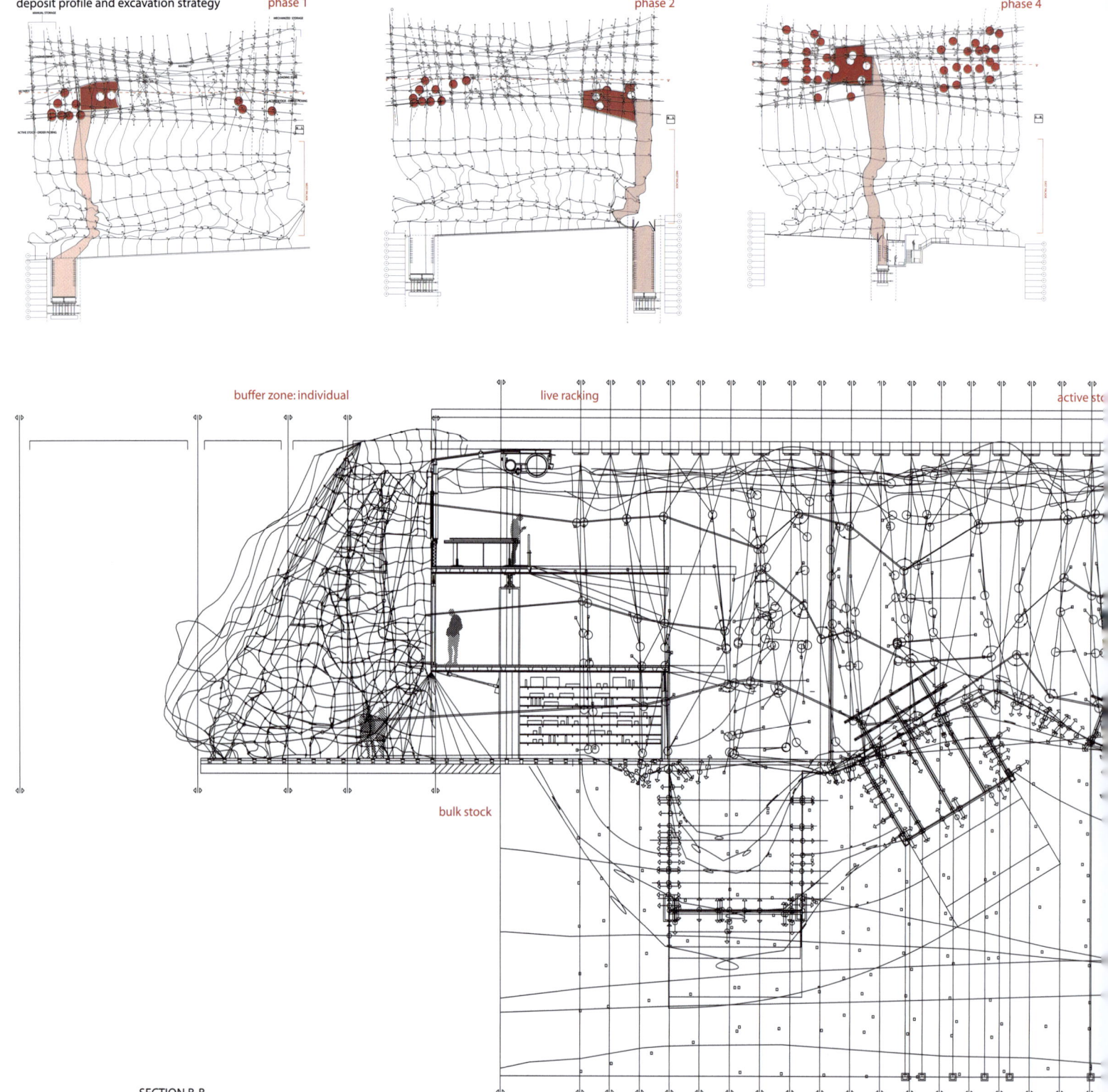

deposit profile and excavation strategy   phase 1   phase 2   phase 4

buffer zone: individual   live racking   active sto

bulk stock

SECTION B-B

p 146–147
Jenny Elisa Schafer
*Zoetropic Space
and the Construction
of Suspicion*

p 140
Geo R Lawrence Co,
Union Stock Yards,
Chicago Union

– in steam, in textiles, in mechanical engineering, in everything. Modern wonders came in all sorts of shapes and sizes, in all sorts of materials. Great wheels, optical tricks, unheard of power, giant guns, tea services for all, capstan lathes – on and on went the list. The wonder is that anyone could believe one could show all this – but they did, for this was the great age of international expositions, stretching to the new world with the World's Fairs in Chicago (1893) and St Louis (1904).

Organisers of the latter pointed out that one could reach St Louis, Missouri from Paris, France in *days*, by train and steam-ship and train again. These were years of unprecedented globalisation (unmatched until very recently) – of new imperialism, of mass migration, especially to the Americas, of new routinised means of communication. The great triple expansion reciprocating steam engine made long-distance transport fast and predictable and relatively cheap. The greatest ever ships powered by such engines were the *Titanic* and her two sisters, but more typically these engines drove ships which carried cargos, central among them food. Indeed St Louis and Chicago were all about food. They processed it and they made equipment for agriculture. Chicago was the home not only of massive slaughterhouses around the Union Stockyards, but also of the International Harvester company (and both feature in Upton Sinclair's *The Jungle*, that great muck-raking call for socialism, one of the great new doctrines of the era). Sigfried Giedion made much of course of the stately dispatching of beasts by hand in La Villette in modern Haussmannian Paris versus the frantic attempts at mechanising the killing of hogs in the Midwest. Yet these attempts at mechanisation failed – the mass killing of hogs and cattle lingered well into the twentieth century (the work of the sledgehammer or pollaxe and the knife), just as the great ships, and the great trains, remained steam-powered well past the middle of the twentieth century. The late nineteenth century was the great age of the horse, in the countryside and in the city. In the great wheatfields of the North American plains, the new agricultural machines were horse-powered, producing the most labour-efficient farming the world had ever seen. The white settler territories – horse-powered and land-rich – became as wealthy as any industrial centre of the world around 1900. The urban horse population peaked somewhat earlier, around 1900, stimulated by the need in rich cities to transport more and more goods and people; before the motor car, bus and lorry, it was the horse that complemented long-distance transport by train and ship.

But if there was a seamless fast connection between Paris and St Louis, or between Buenos Aires and Naples, the web of communication was deeply fractured. Until about 1900 the emigrant from Basilicata in southern Italy

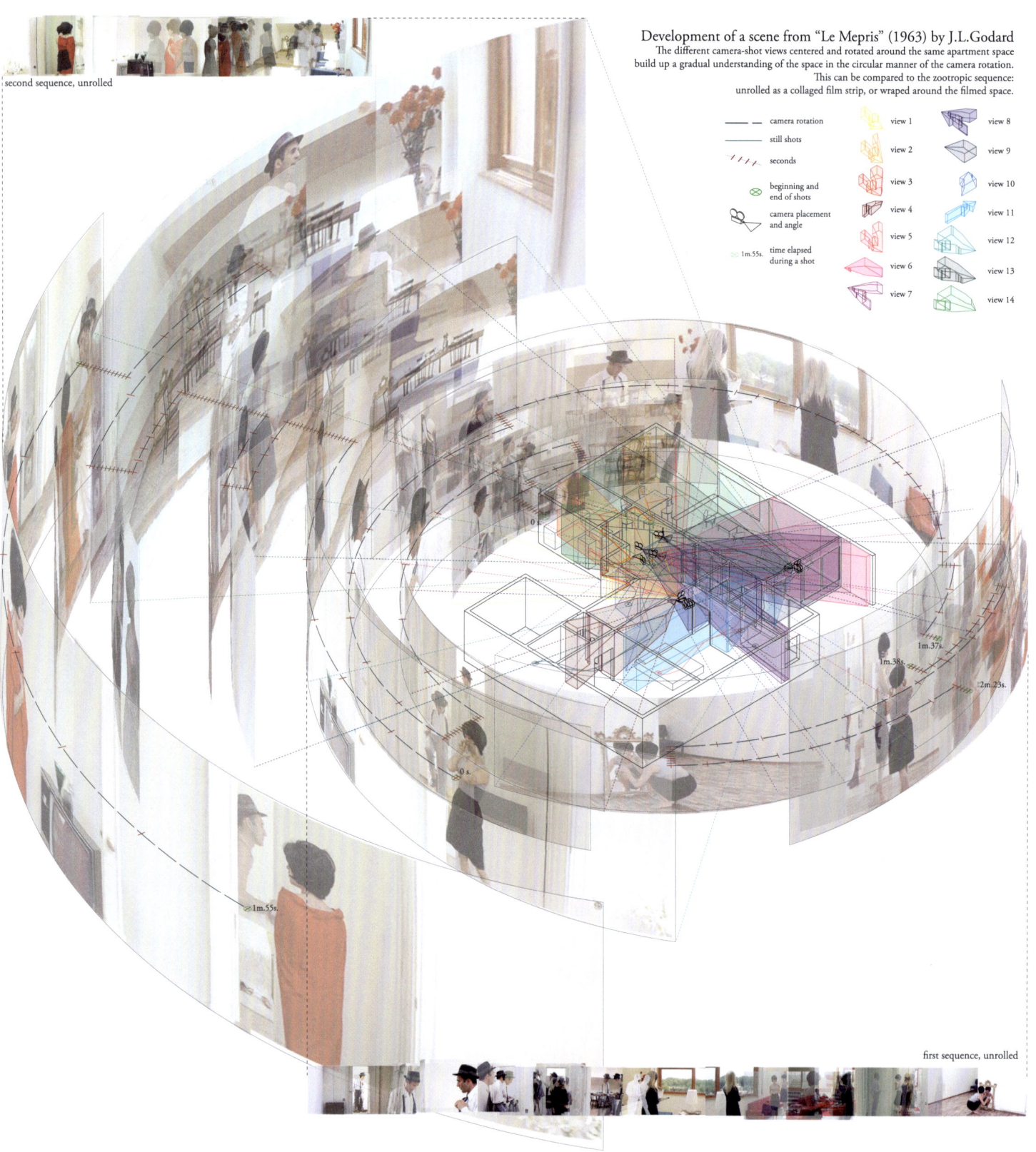

second sequence, unrolled

Development of a scene from "Le Mepris" (1963) by J.L.Godard
The different camera-shot views centered and rotated around the same apartment space
build up a gradual understanding of the space in the circular manner of the camera rotation.
This can be compared to the zootropic sequence:
unrolled as a collaged film strip, or wraped around the filmed space.

camera rotation	view 1		view 8
still shots	view 2		view 9
seconds	view 3		view 10
beginning and end of shots	view 4		view 11
camera placement and angle	view 5		view 12
1m.55s. time elapsed during a shot	view 6		view 13
	view 7		view 14

0 s.

1m.37s.

1m.38s.

2m.23s.

0 s.

1m.55s.

first sequence, unrolled

146

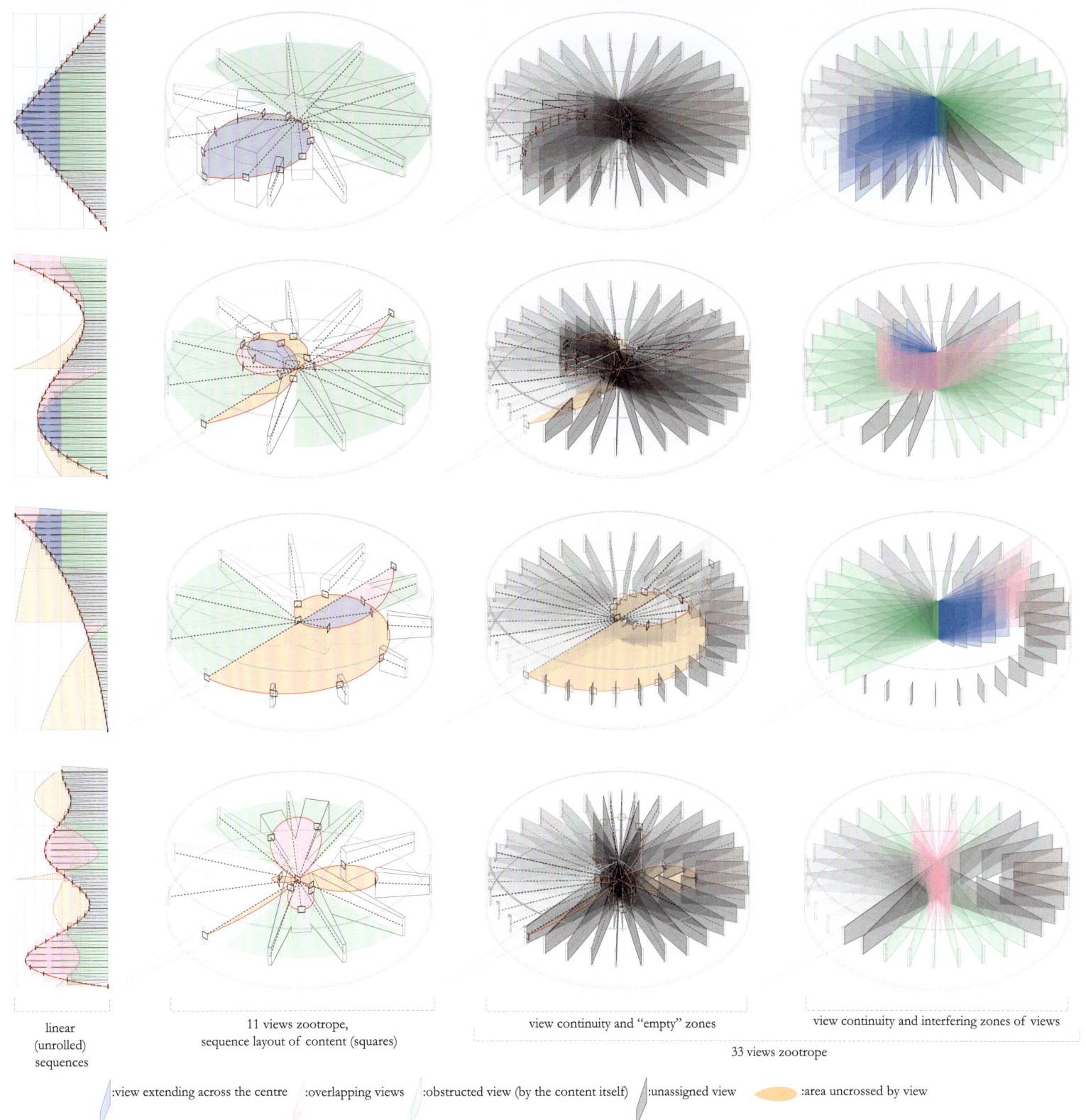

linear (unrolled) sequences

11 views zootrope, sequence layout of content (squares)

view continuity and "empty" zones

view continuity and interfering zones of views

33 views zootrope

:view extending across the centre   :overlapping views   :obstructed view (by the content itself)   :unassigned view   :area uncrossed by view

would have to trudge to Naples on foot, or be conveyed by animal power, a journey that might well take longer than the sea-crossing to Buenos Aires or Ellis Island. Fast transcontinental ships docked only in some places; only so many tunnels and bridges crossed great rivers and great mountains carrying railways. Only with improved land-communications could modern nations be built, and these were years when this was done. Hence the seeming paradox that this great era of globalisation was also the era of Magyarisation, Russification, Ottomanisation, of pan-Germanism; the time in which *paysans* were made into *citoyens*, and so on. Modern machines – cheap books for education, postal systems sustained by trains, national markets by national infrastructures, and national conscript armies – were indispensable to modern nationalism. For Ernest Gellner nationalism was precisely a response to the new global industrial civilisation – the only tolerable way of engaging with these forces was to do so in one's own language. But many would never speak, and especially write, the languages of the new nationalisms. Our emigrant from Basilicata never spoke Italian, but instead used Lucanian dialect and later English; she probably couldn't write, but her children could – in English only.

In our accounts of machines and inventions we are apt to focus on serious matters, on production, on communication and transport. The ludic gets short shrift – wrongly so, for the ludic is much more important, even for machines discussed in serious registers, than we have allowed. The vibrator was a remarkably early electrical innovation which featured in the Sears catalogue alongside entirely respectable gizmos; photography, still and moving, had an important hidden pornographic side from the start; the early telephone was a means of entertainment, the motor car too. What were the great exhibitions, for all the uplifting talk about them, but giant spectacles? And through them, and especially the US fairs, came modern gigantic variants of older ludic machines: the Ferris wheel, the roller-coaster, the whole ensemble of the lunar park. This is also the great age of the theatre, and of the opera house – from Buenos Aires to Hanoi, from New York to Wellington, all acquired new opera houses between the 1880s and 1914.

The world of machines, of modern factories, of ships, of mines, was not the subject of much literature. There might be what was called muck-raking about capitalists, and there were plenty of machines in the illustrated magazines, and in the cinema as it emerged, but in fiction little or nothing. In any case, as Raphael Samuel insisted, the descriptions of machines in the technical and trade press were descriptions of novelties, not of what was in use. There were hardly any *flâneurs* of the machine shops, the engine

p 148
Eadweard Muybridge
*Animal Locomotion,
Female Spanking
a Child*

149

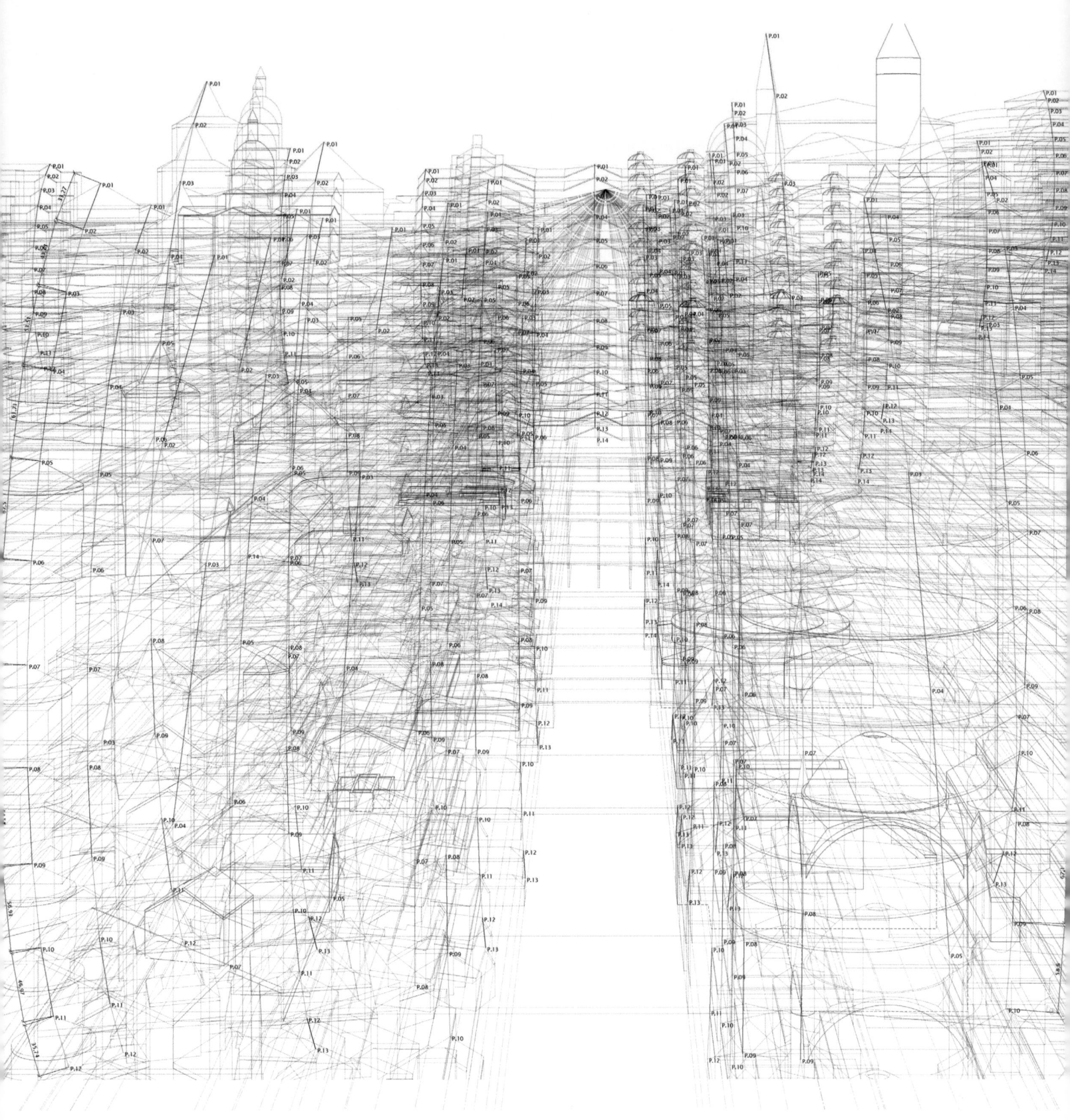

151

rooms or the mines. Yet there was one immensely important branch of literature that propelled certain authors to international stardom of a rare kind – the 'science fictions' of Verne and Wells. The point about these is of course obvious but hugely important – they are set in the future. Futurism and reflection on the machine were now intimately tied together. To say that they are prescient is to buy into the schemes of modernity they themselves represent; that we think them prescient is in fact testimony to the poverty of our thinking about machines, to how much it still owes to the peddlers of techno-fantasies of over 100 years ago, not least in its continued futurism. We still have visions of global villages, of great wars, of giant guns and atomic bombs, of submarines and time machines, of worlds of order, worlds where technicians ruled. But culture isn't everything, and indeed it is a great mistake, especially for materialists, to assume that culture reflected the material at all directly.

It is perhaps no accident that some of the best work on the material has been done by authors who take it for granted that the material is made, architects and urbanists among them. Perhaps the most influential general treatment of the topic ever has been Lewis Mumford's *Technics and Civilization* of 1934 (note the term technics, and his use of *neo-technic*) and a richer (to my mind) 'contribution to anonymous history', Sigfried Giedion's *Mechanization takes Command* of 1948. Yet the history of the material is hard to get at, even for architects. Most histories of architecture are contextualised chronologies of designs for particular types of building; they are not histories of what was built, or how things were built. They are at best histories of some (though certainly not all) futures in the making, which is what might be said of most science and technology studies, and the history of science and technology.

The history of the material is hard to get at; we have been over-impressed by the conclusions of scribblers and boosters. We might note this problem was present in the greatest ever materialist history, Marx's *Capital*. What Marx is describing is hardly the average means and modes of production of mid-century British capitalism, but rather what he took to be the novel – the origins of the future. And he got this from bourgeois boosterism, from the works of the chemist Andrew Ure and the mathematician Charles Babbage, a man then better known for his mathematics, his political economy, than for his calculating engines. Yet Marx quoted from the Roman poet Horace to tell his German readers that the British past and present was their future: *de te fabula narratur* – the tale is told of you.

p 154
Tom Burnford
Around the World in 80 Days or 3,188 Million Calories or £20,000

153

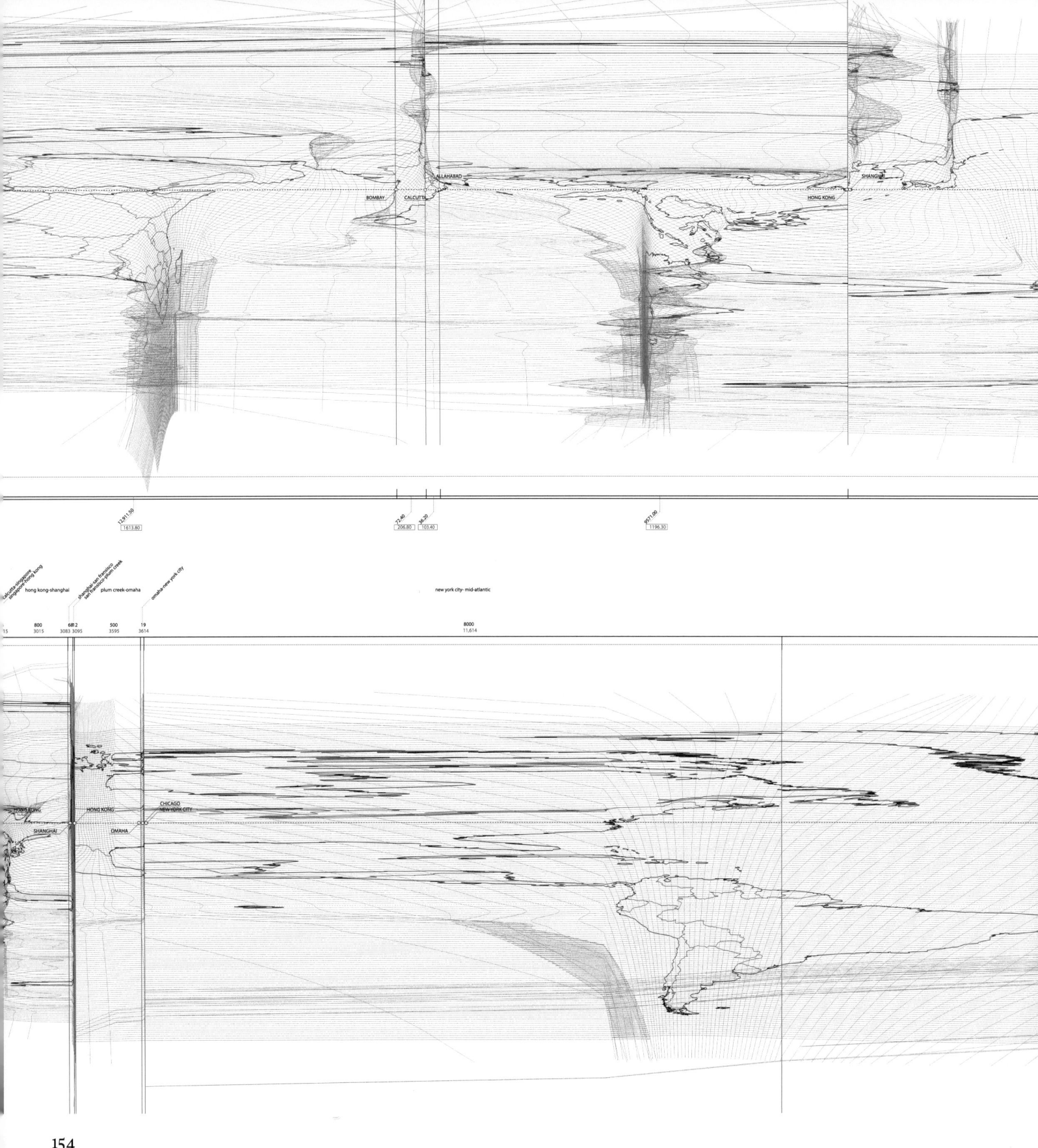

ALLAHABAD

BOMBAY   CALCUTTA

SHANGHAI

HONG KONG

13,911.50
1613.80

72.40   44.20
206.80   103.40

9571.00
1196.30

calcutta-singapore
singapore-hong kong

hong kong-shanghai

shanghai-san francisco
san francisco-plum creek
plum creek-omaha

omaha-new york city
new york city

new york city- mid-atlantic

15   800   68I2   500   19   8000
            3015   3083 3095   3595   3614   11,614

HONG KONG   HONG KONG   CHICAGO
                                      NEW YORK CITY

SHANGHAI   OMAHA

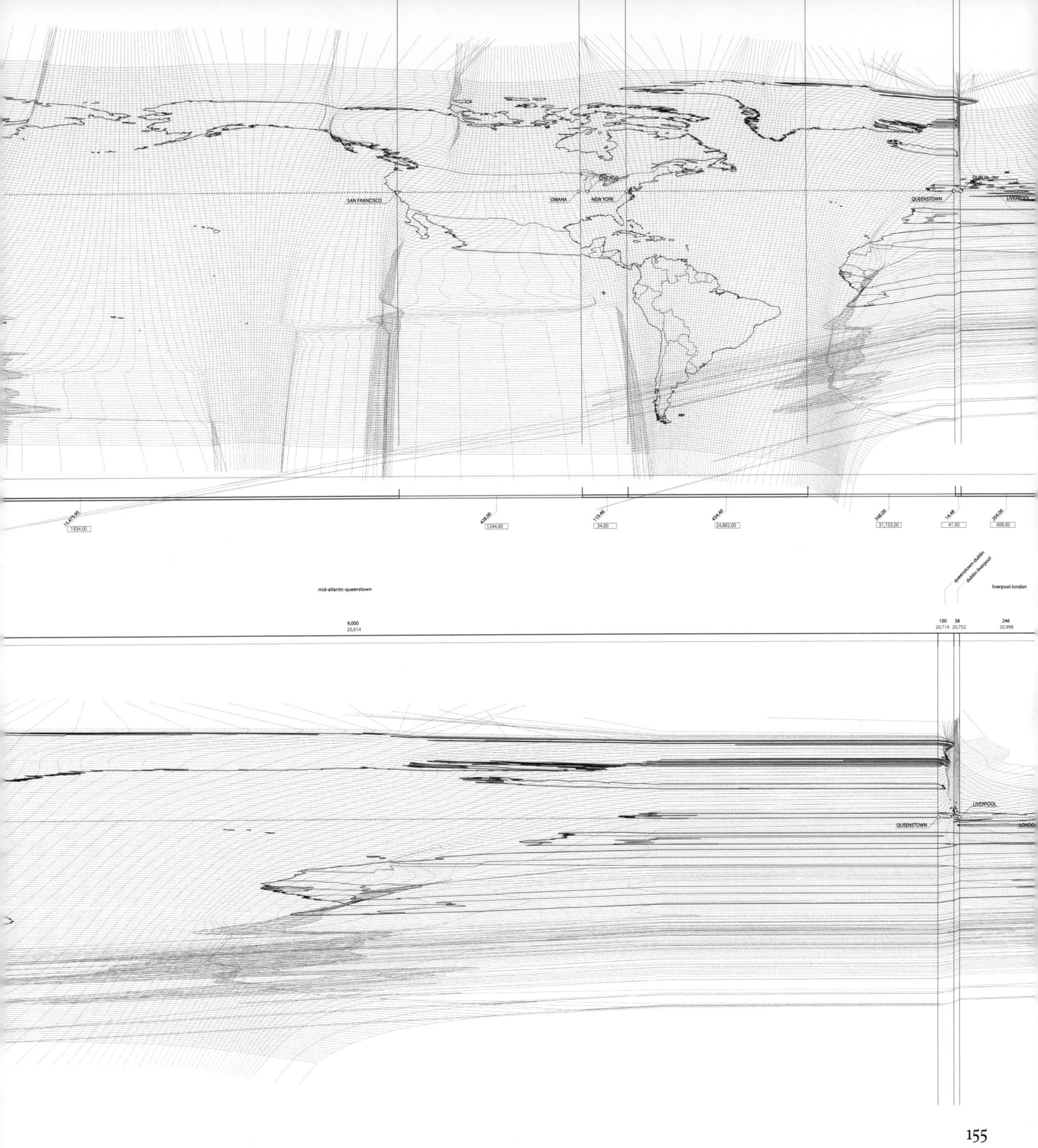

SAN FRANCISCO   OMAHA   NEW YORK   QUEENSTOWN   DUBLIN
                                                                                            LIVERPOOL
CHICAGO

15,475.95   428.00   119.40   434.40   348.00   14.48   204.00
1934.00   1244.00   34.00   24,882.00   31,103.00   41.00   408.00

                                                                          queenstown-dublin
                                                                          dublin-liverpool
mid-atlantic-queenstown
                                                                              liverpool-london

                                                                          100 38   246
9,000   20,714 20,752 20,998
20,614

                                                                    LIVERPOOL
                                      QUEENSTOWN   LONDO

155

Stepped Reckoner (1671 Leibniz)

Figuration and
its Discontents

It's fair to say that we didn't 'do' the final image. At a time when the figure, and in particular the rendered perspective, loomed large in the work of the AA, we insisted on the business of the line – on making every mark ourselves as a studio that strove to sweat out its drawings, to draw our thinking via the daily, incremental register of the notational. We were accused of never producing 'the money shot', of being 'a tease' – a strangely sexualised accusation that speaks volumes about the role of the figurative in architectural culture. But the figure is always a tricky creature. Its ability to shout the loudest – to disrupt the steady presence of the abstracted mark and take hold of the viewer – is always difficult to manage, as student and as teacher. The more the glossy render prevailed the more wary we became of its easy pleasures; as with the pinning of context to geographic location, we instinctively knew this was something to walk away from. But this is not to exclude the poetics of the figure (as if that were a possibility). We learned from the lessons of the ruin and the fragment, unpacked again here with Mary Beard – to walk the tightrope between having enough recognisable form (usually in outline) that the imagination could complete the missing whole, but not so much that the endeavour was pointlessly deterministic. Something Fusako Ishikara used to great advantage, especially in her drawings of Charles Babbage's Difference Engine [p 156 *Cascade of Numbers*]. Perhaps at the end of the day it was the determinism of figuration that we found problematic: the idea of 'this is how it definitely will look', not to mention the prioritising of visual form over performative form that this sets up.

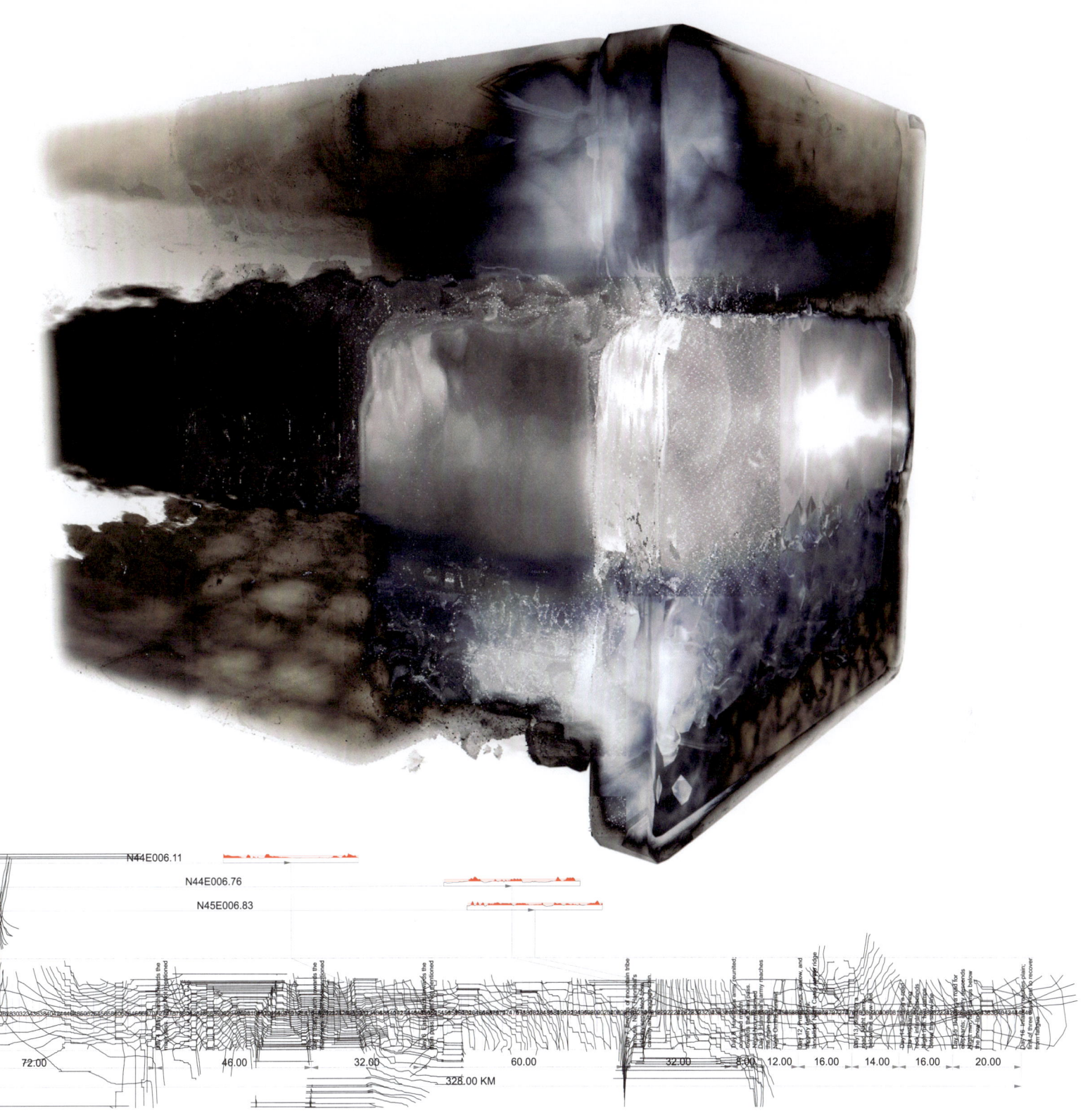

N44E006.11

N44E006.76

N45E006.83

72.00   46.00   32.00   60.00   32.00   8.00 12.00   16.00   14.00   16.00   20.00

328.00 KM

159

p 91
Karl Kjelstrup-
Johnson

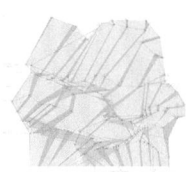

p 65
Marilia Spanou

We needed, without abandoning specificity to a morass of vagueness, a representational vehicle that espoused the indeterminate, as a counterpoint to the worst effects of parametricisation and what it stood for. Karl Kjelstrup-Johnson's intelligent struggle with the representation of indeterminacy led him, like Marilia Spanou, to the experiments of Op Art [p 91, p 65]. Curiously, however, when he applied the lessons from the indeterminacy of Hannibal's Alpine crossing to the archaeological underground of Naples and the virtual duplication of its data black holes into the inky dark of digital space, he unwittingly turned to figuration. His digital model of this hypercontext, *An Architecture of Indeterminacy* p 159, designed for counting known coordinates in a sea of unknowns, *looks like* a block of frozen ink; it can't help but conjure an impossible picture of unquantifiable stuff, of formlessness itself — the material architecture of the indeterminate. The figurative intervened and, to our bemused dismay, people suddenly got it.

Widari Bahrin in turn literally put the figure in a cage: her Kinotel in Hanoi houses the very particular iconography of Vietnam War films, detached from and distorted by the architecture of their containment. Like the chairs and floor tiles in Van Hoogstraten's peepbox p 161, the images in *Kinotel: Hanoi Peepbox Hotel* p 162 climb the walls and wrap round corners in their bid to escape. In a not altogether unrelated exercise, Gergely Kovács' forensics on the mysterious projective

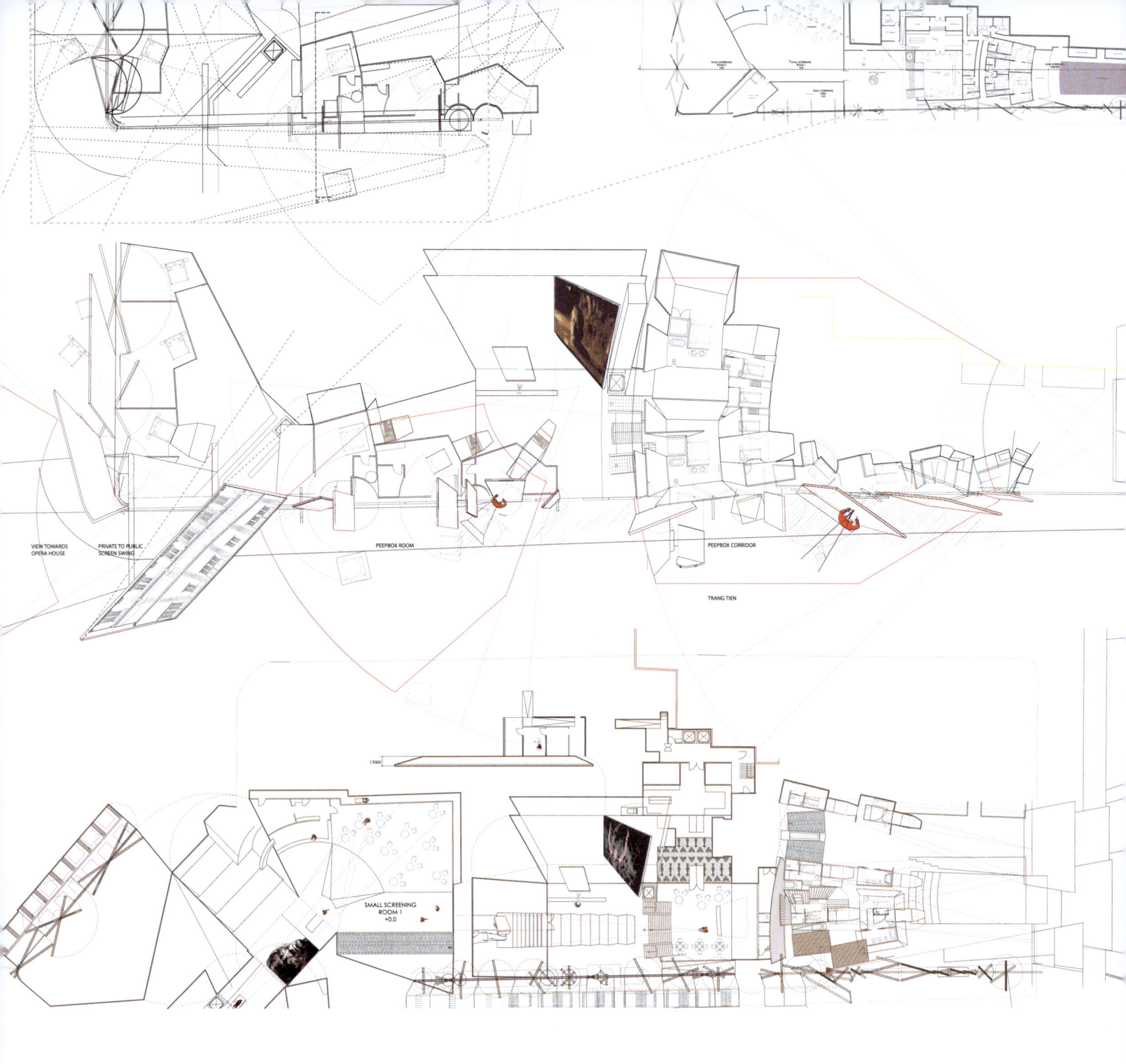

VIEW TOWARDS
OPERA HOUSE

PRIVATE TO PUBLIC
SCREEN SWING

PEEPBOX ROOM

PEEPBOX CORRIDOR

TRANG TIEN

SMALL SCREENING
ROOM 1
+0.0

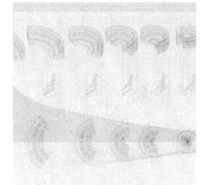

p 124
Gergely Kovács

geometry at work in Piranesi's Vedute di Roma series led him to turn the Colosseum inside out in *Lessons from Piranesi I* p 124. We read the shrinking of the radius via the illustrative capacity of the figure: arches, stepped seating, buttresses tell us what is going on here. The relations between abstraction and figuration, which Escher knew well, are rendered uneasy. Even more disquieting is his subsequent drawing, *The Topography of Neutrality: Inside is Outside* p 164. Here true inversion, in the algebraic sense, is registered by the melting outline of Jerusalem's Temple Mount. The undesired presence of Dali haunts. There is something deeply unsettling, and instructive to the architect, about the meeting of indexicality, the registering of a function plotted out on the page, and the figuration that we can't help but see in the stacked up answers. In the last year of the unit Hye-Ju Park tackled the illustrative capacity of figuration head on, via that arch genre, the comic strip, and the mnemonic ruse of crime

reconstruction, which is all about 'looking like' the event that has already happened in order to better know what did actually happen – a crafty loop from data to figure and then back to data that plots a symbiotic set of relations between the figuration and the indexical. Thus, *Case for the Prosecution: The People vs The City of Palermo* p 166, in its frame by frame reconstruction of two *omertà* murders, with its loving depiction of the 1970s steering wheel and the fatal pressing of the apartment doorbell, *is* an indexical drawing oh so thinly disguised as a picture.

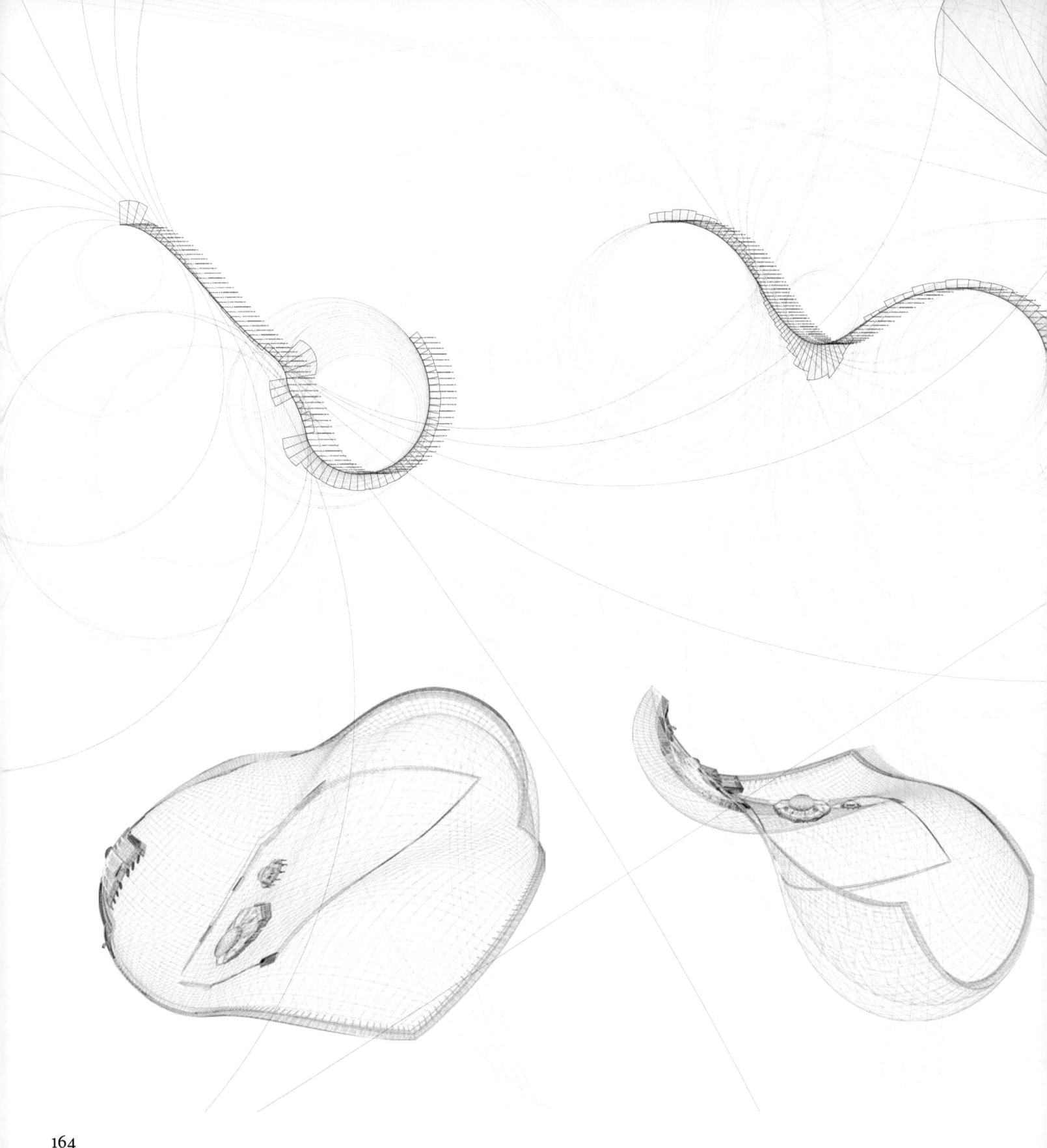

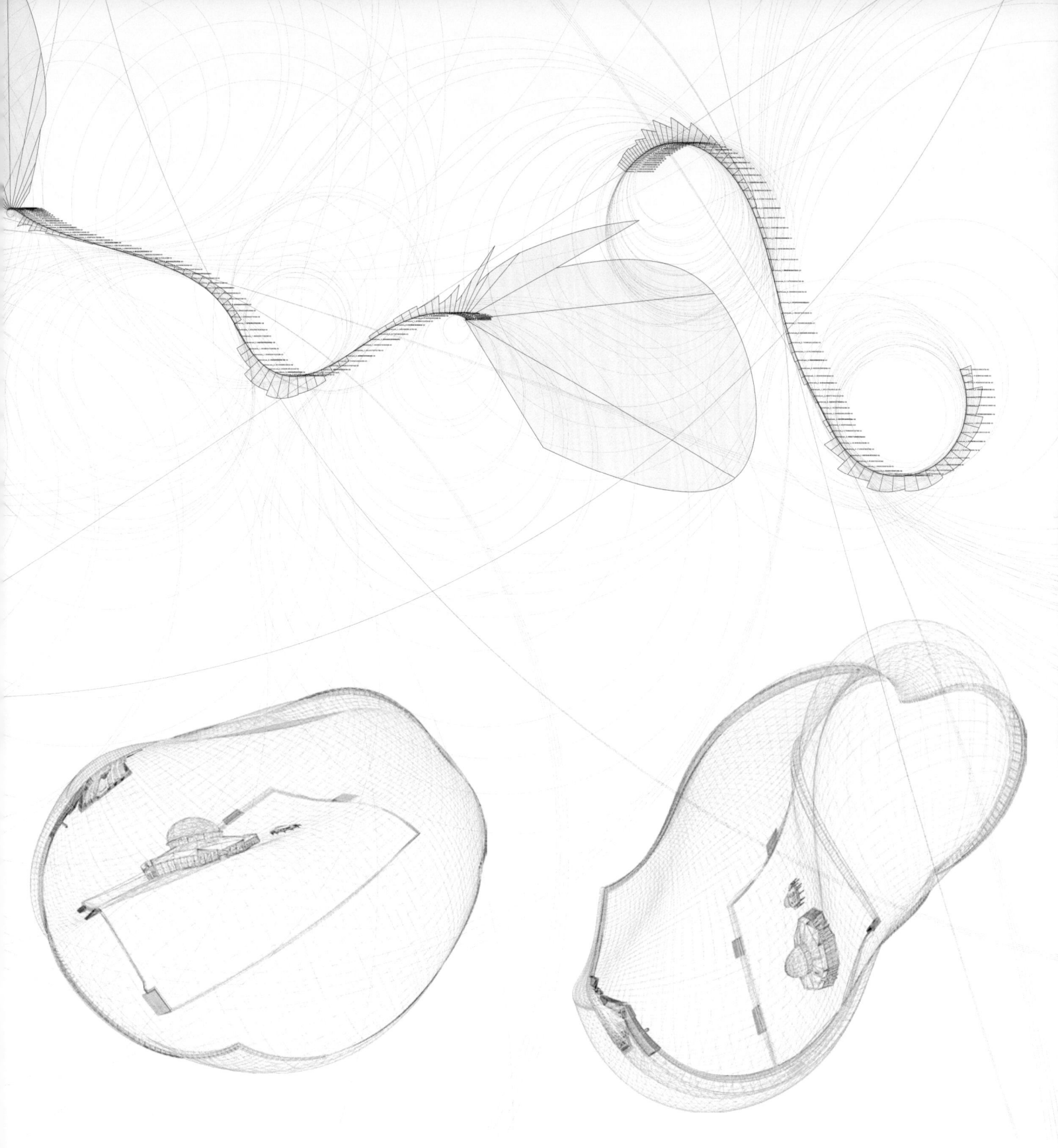

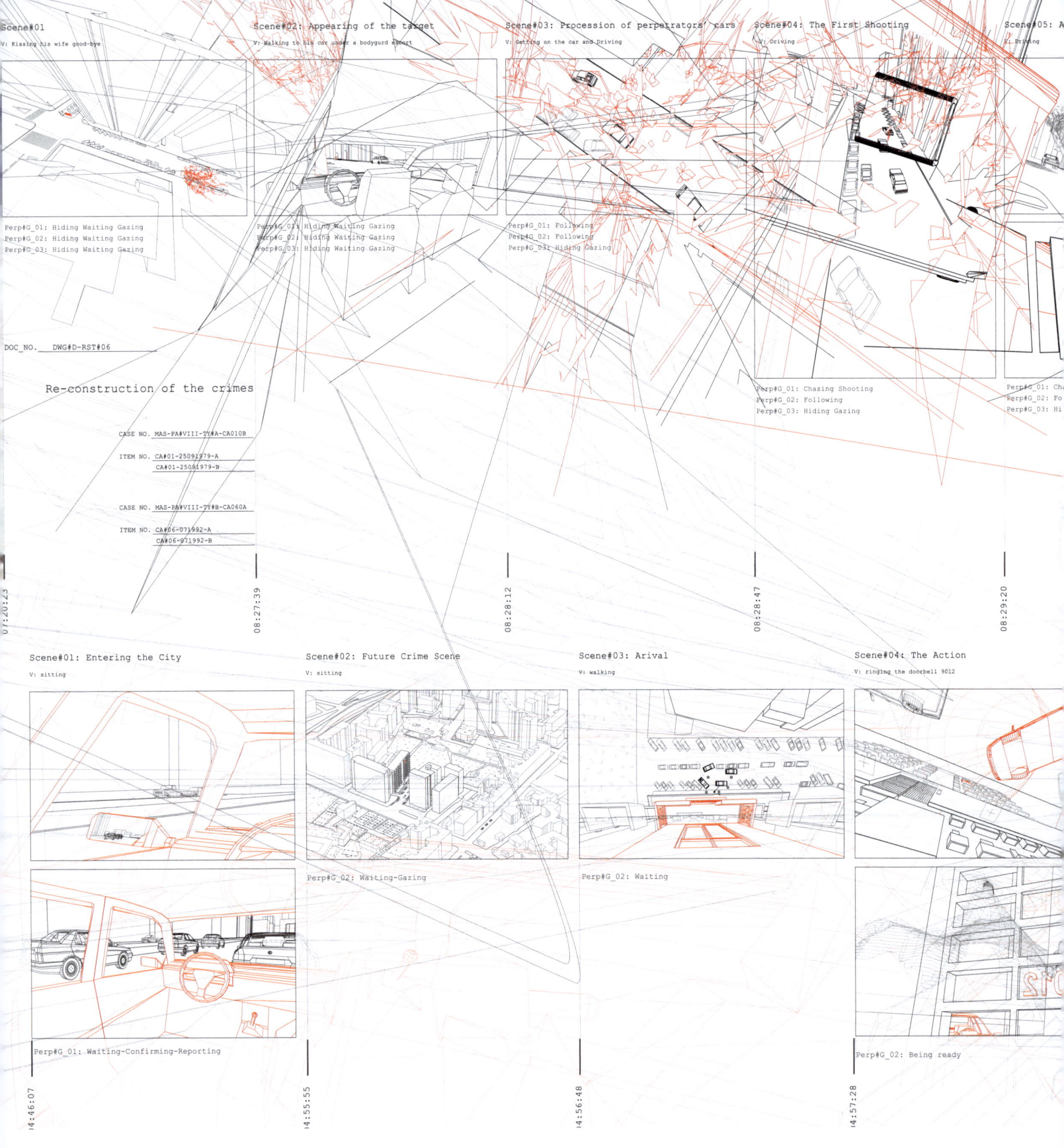

Scene#01
V: Kissing his wife good-bye

Scene#02: Appearing of the target
V: Walking to his car under a bodyguard escort

Scene#03: Procession of perpetrators' cars
V: Getting on the car and Driving

Scene#04: The First Shooting
V: Driving

Scene#05: A
V: Driving

Perp#G_01: Hiding Waiting Gazing
Perp#G_02: Hiding Waiting Gazing
Perp#G_03: Hiding Waiting Gazing

Perp#G_01: Hiding Waiting Gazing
Perp#G_02: Hiding Waiting Gazing
Perp#G_03: Hiding Waiting Gazing

Perp#G_01: Following
Perp#G_02: Following
Perp#G_03: Hiding Gazing

Perp#G_01: Chasing Shooting
Perp#G_02: Following
Perp#G_03: Hiding Gazing

Perp#G_01: Che
Perp#G_03: Fo
Perp#G_03: Hi

DOC_NO.   DWG#D-RST#06

Re-construction of the crimes

CASE NO. MAS-PA#VIII-TY#A-CA010B

ITEM NO. CA#01-25091979-A
          CA#01-25091979-B

CASE NO. MAS-PA#VIII-TY#B-CA060A

ITEM NO. CA#06-071992-A
          CA#06-071992-B

07:20:23

08:27:39

08:28:12

08:28:47

08:29:20

Scene#01: Entering the City
V: sitting

Scene#02: Future Crime Scene
V: sitting

Scene#03: Arival
V: walking

Scene#04: The Action
V: ringing the doorbell 9012

Perp#G_02: Waiting-Gazing

Perp#G_02: Waiting

Perp#G_01: Waiting-Confirming-Reporting

Perp#G_02: Being ready

14:46:07

14:55:55

14:56:48

14:57:28

166

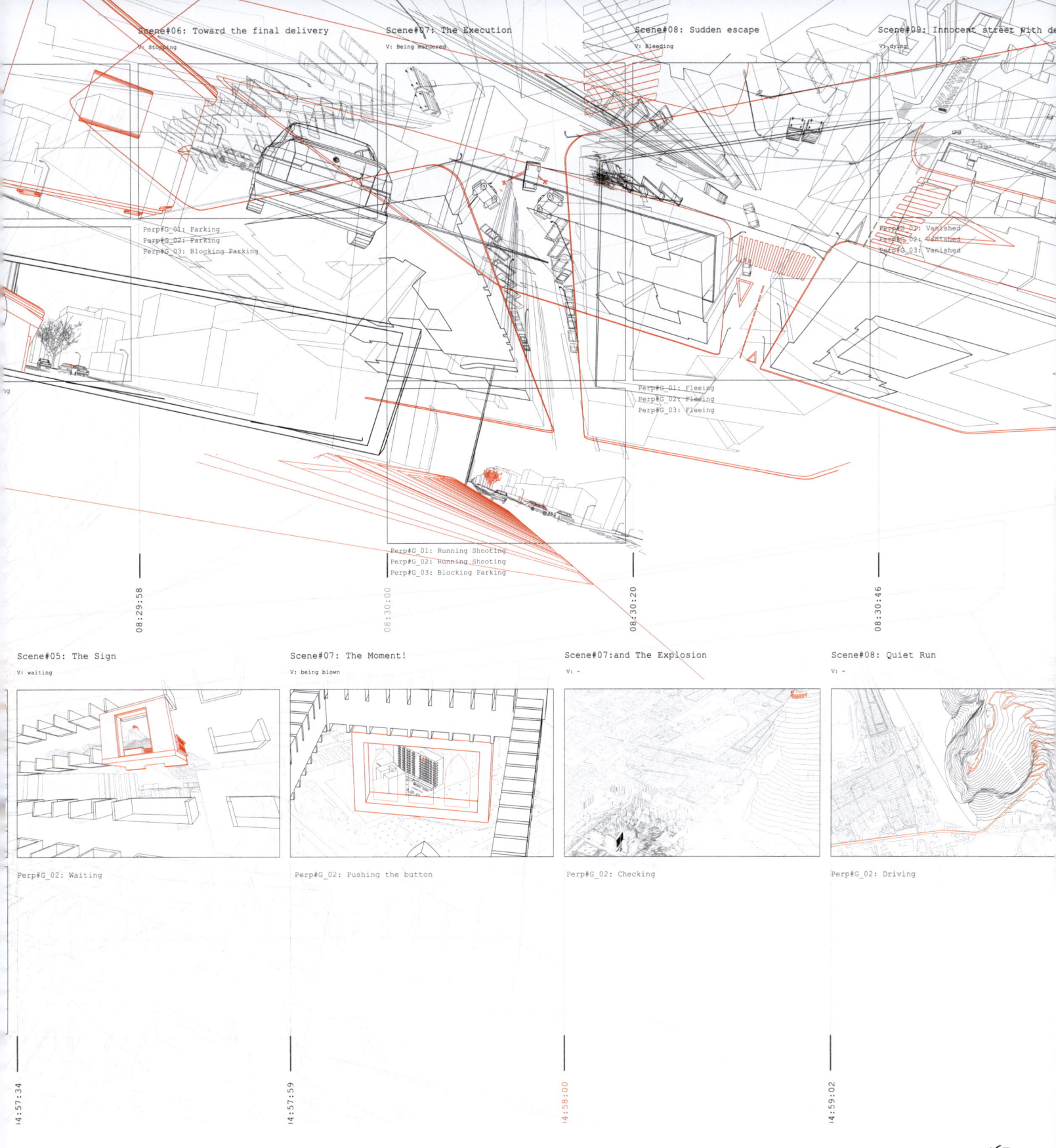

Scene#06: Toward the final delivery   Scene#07: The Execution   Scene#08: Sudden escape   Scene#09: Innocent street with de

V: stopping   V: Being murdered   V: Bleeding   V: dying

Perp#G_01: Parking   Perp#G_01: Vanished
Perp#G_02: Parking   Perp#G_02: Vanished
Perp#G_03: Blocking Parking   Perp#G_03: Vanished

                                                                    Perp#G_01: Fleeing
                                                                    Perp#G_02: Fleeing
                                                                    Perp#G_03: Fleeing

                                        Perp#G_01: Running Shooting
                                        Perp#G_02: Running Shooting
                                        Perp#G_03: Blocking Parking

08:29:58   08:30:00   08:30:20   08:30:46

Scene#05: The Sign   Scene#07: The Moment!   Scene#07:and The Explosion Scene#08: Quiet Run

V: waiting   V: being blown   V: -   V: -

Perp#G_02: Waiting   Perp#G_02: Pushing the button   Perp#G_02: Checking   Perp#G_02: Driving

14:57:34   14:57:59   14:58:00   14:59:02

167

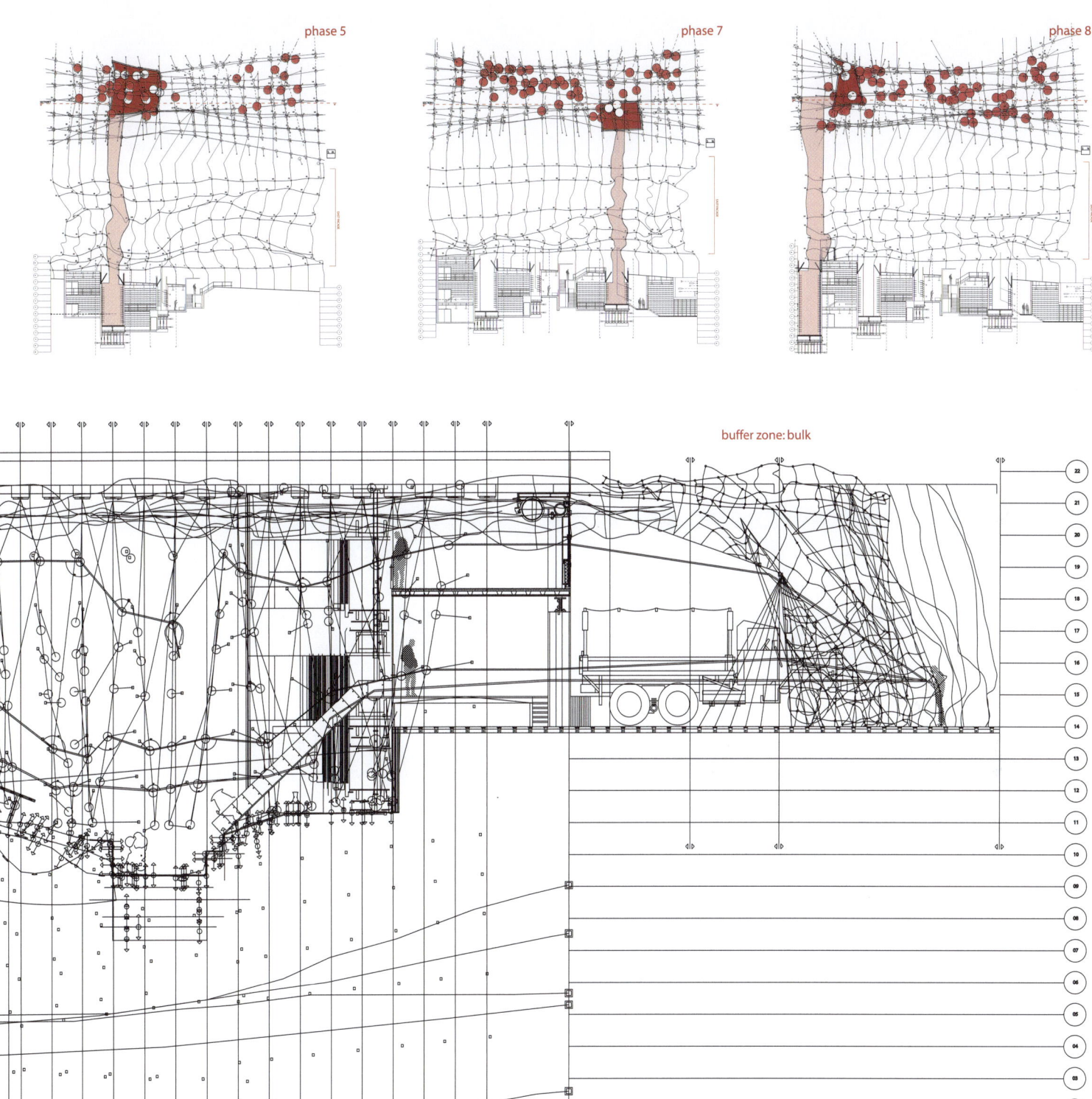

phase 5

phase 7

phase 8

buffer zone: bulk

22
21
20
19
18
17
16
15
14
13
12
11
10
09
08
07
06
05
04
03
01
0

169

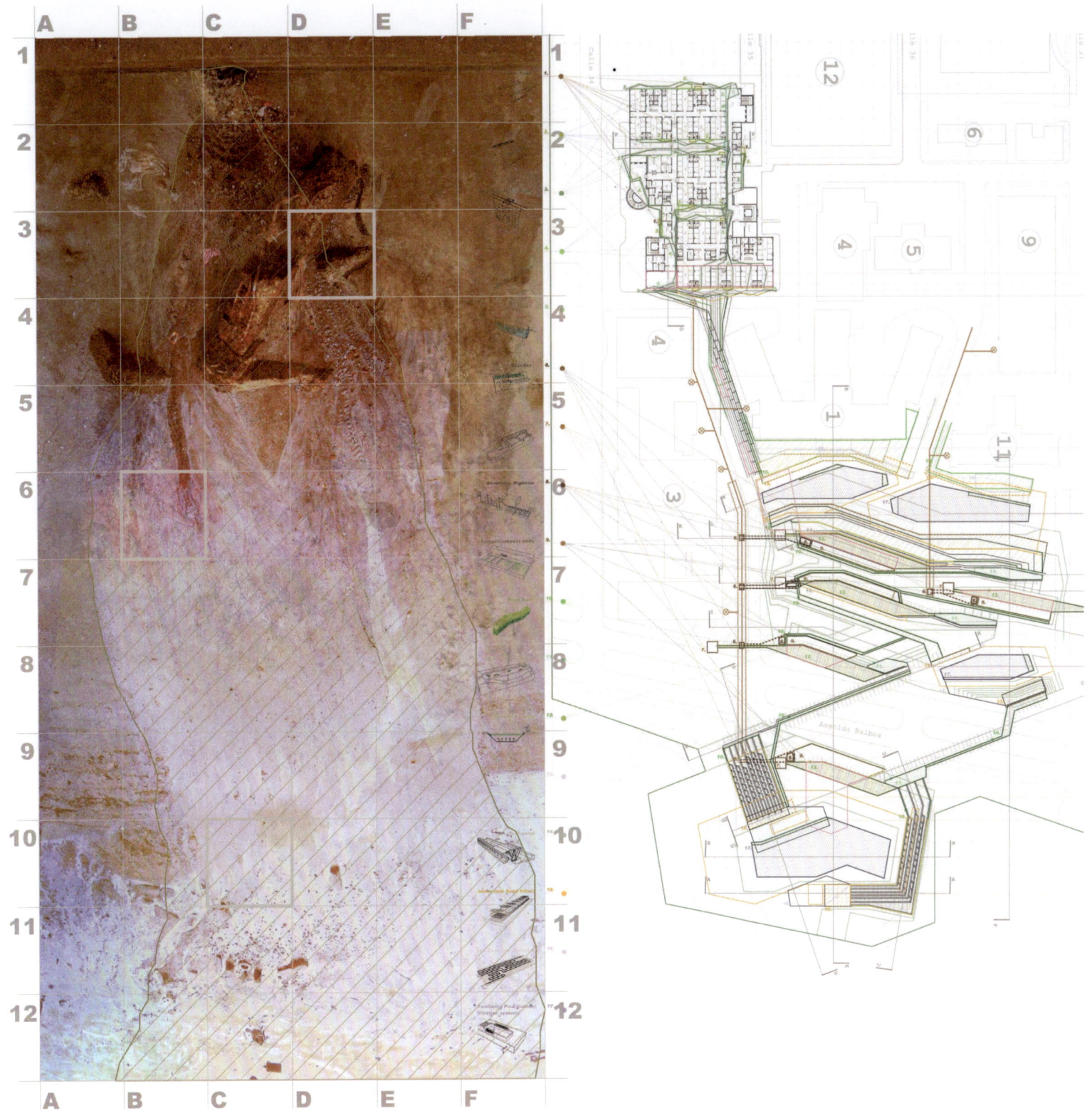

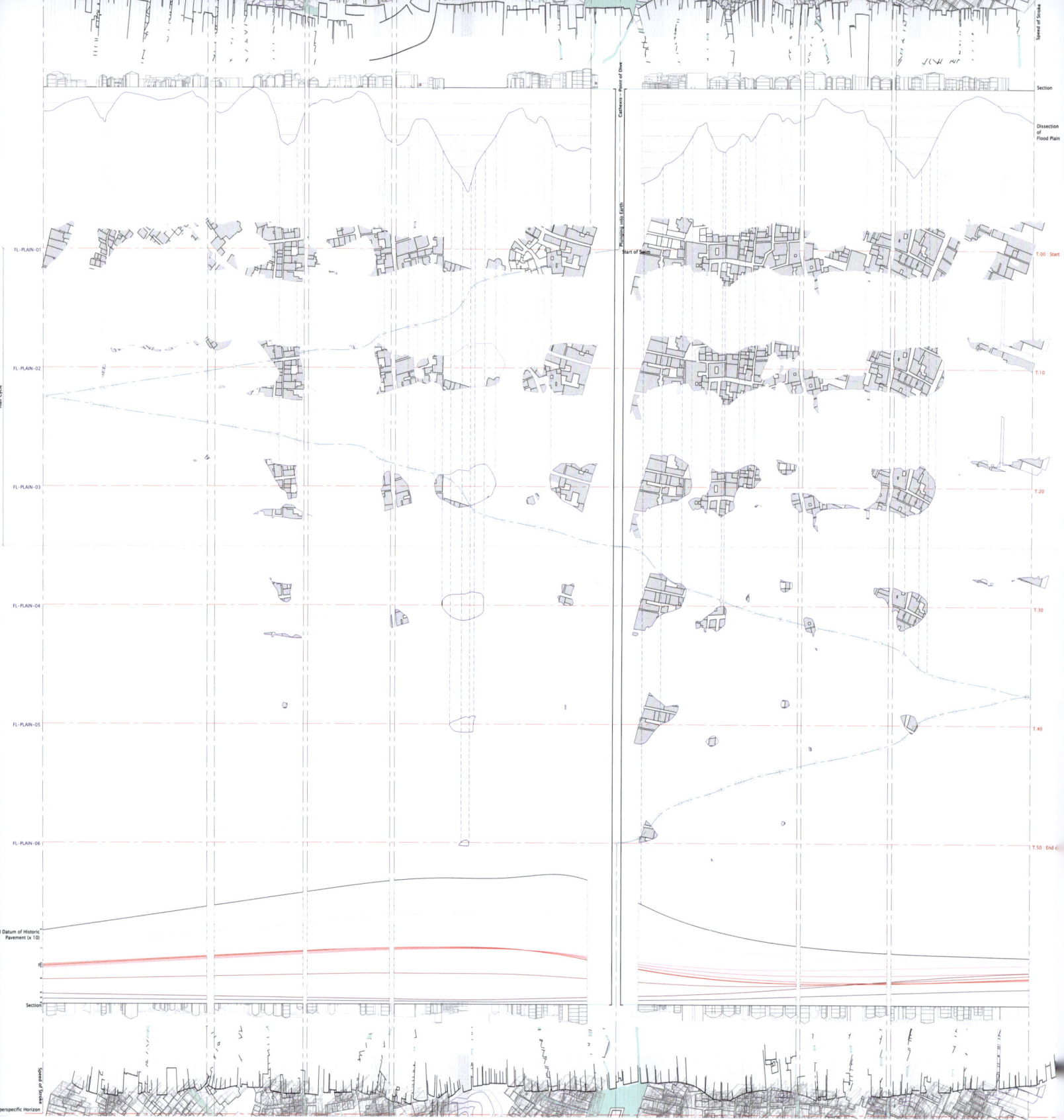

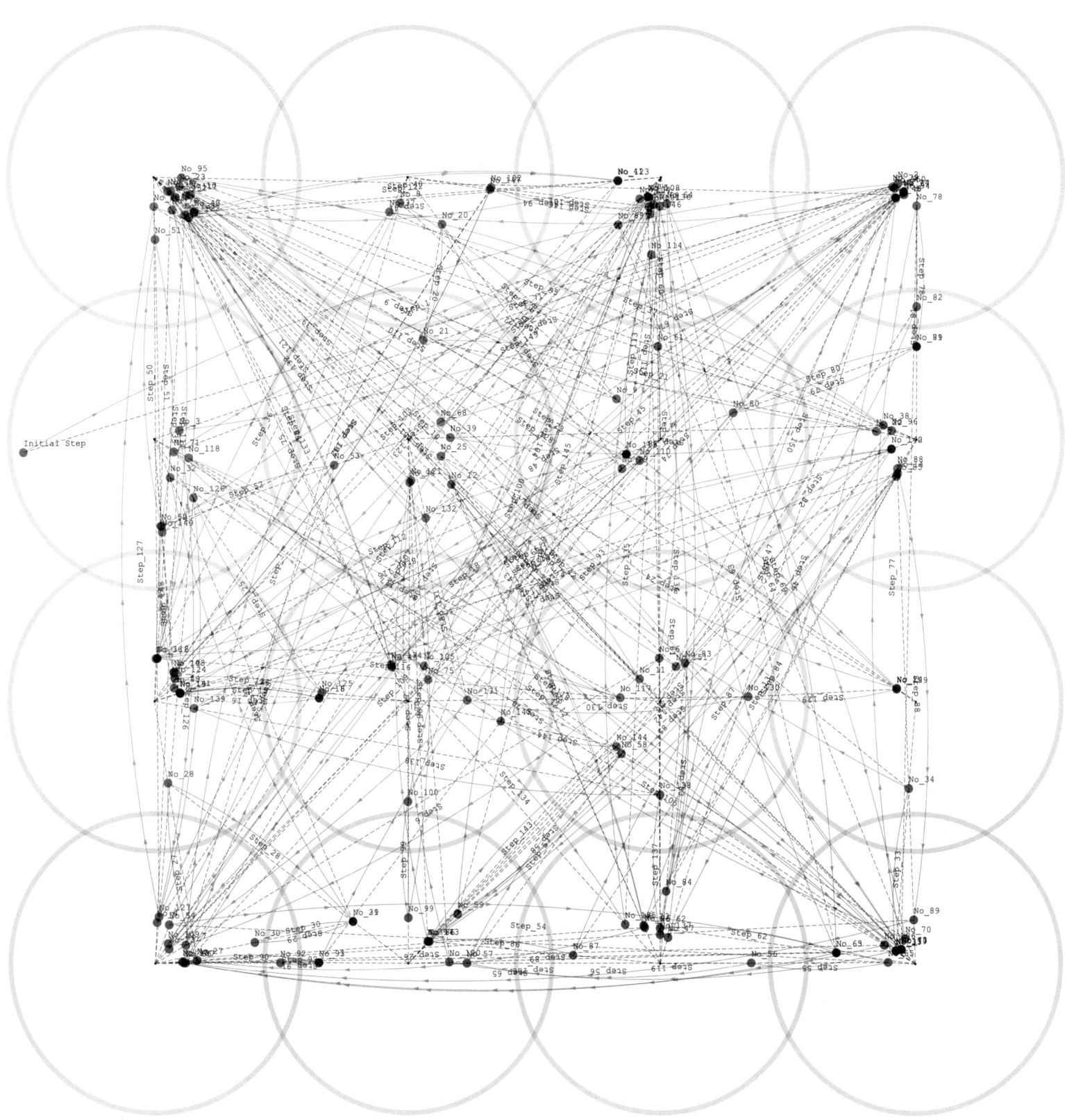

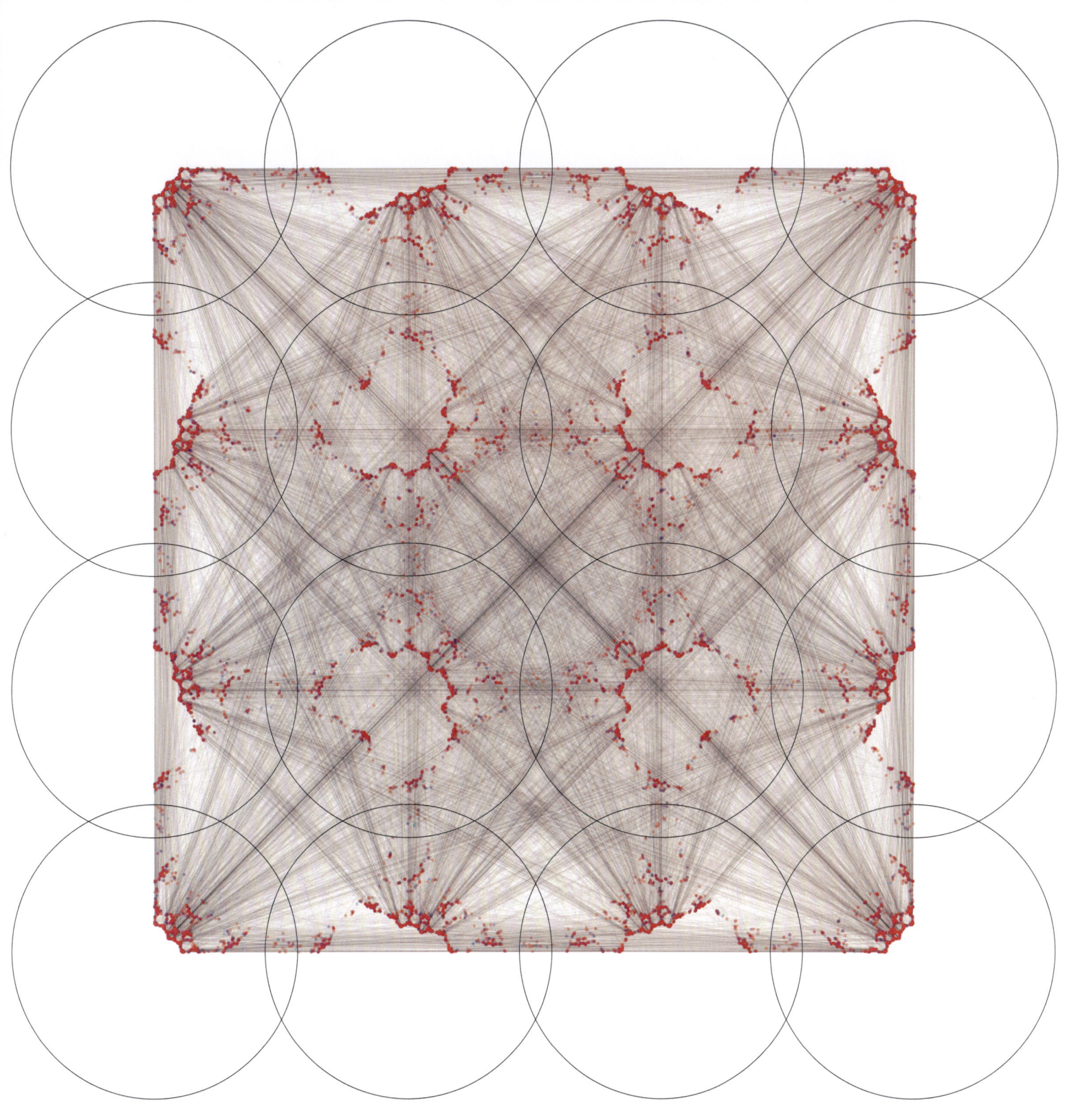

175

Projects

Noam Andrews, 2004–5

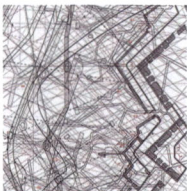

p 23
Murailles West: Ideal Battle
The Murailles West is a series of increasingly elaborate fortifications constructed in response to battles waged from the tenth to the eighteenth centuries. Unlike the Murailles East, which is reduced to an archaeological site, the Murailles West remains standing even today – a monument to the history of siegecraft and now a form without modern function. The drawing extracts backwards from the architectural form the idealised battle it was designed to defend against, as it might have been conducted with artillery technology of the time. It reveals zones of safety, strategies of attack (burrowing under the ground) and the modifications made to the landscape in order to pre-empt advantageous positioning. The development here of the sister structure, the Murailles East, deploys reverse-engineered strategies of economic, not military, defence.

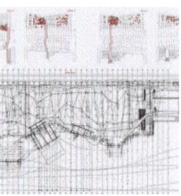

p 168
Murailles East: Hypertrophic Storage Facility; Phases in Excavation and Replacement Strategy
Section through a proposed market and storage facility situated on the grounds of a Renaissance fortress in the Spanish tax enclave of Ceuta, a border town on the edge of Morocco and the southernmost point in Europe. Goods produced in Ceuta are theoretically exempt from VAT in the European Union, but since the town does not have a functioning manufacturing sector it is unable to capitalise on this economic potential. In the Murailles East, 'Ceutan' archaeological debris is excavated and sold in order to make room for the storage of modern commodities. These goods, in turn, replace their ancient predecessors and are buried for a length of time deemed sufficient to give them 'originating product status' so that they may be exported to Europe in bulk, VAT free.

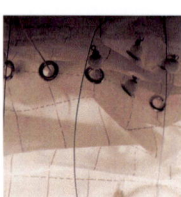

p 31
Murailles East
Facade Detail
The selling of Ceutan products is tied to commodity data from the Production Price Index (PPI), which dictates the most opportune time to sell. The data causes the flabby 'skin' that surrounds the building to expand and contract as goods are raised from the earth and replaced with others. The 'skin' has tensile properties that enable it to aid in the extraction and replacement of modern and antique matter, thus acting as a low-tech register of global economic trends. A structural 'skeleton', tied into the obese facade, rises and falls, aiding the digging up of archaeology and its replacement with cigarettes and alcohol.

p 67
Murailles East
Structure and Facade Detail
With a nod to the realities of life in Ceuta, where petty trafficking sustains residents on both sides of the border, the Murailles East market includes points of contact with the local communities. Here goods can be bought, sold and buried for profit. Strapped to the bodies of women who often double their weight in concealed commodities, goods are trafficked back and forth across the Moroccan border.

p 22
Diet-Induced Obese Body (DIOB)
Diet-induced obesity entails an asymmetry in food uptake, which results in the hypertrophy of cells and a consequent increase in bulk. The body becomes a container storing energy that cannot be easily accessed, and also expands in biologically predetermined areas. In an imaginative foray into an

essentially sedentary system the DIOB might also, in theory, develop the ability to absorb, through epidermal pores, decomposed morsels of food trapped in folds of skin. Produced prior to the development of the later architectural proposal, the DIOB served as a conceptual precedent for the aesthetics and spatial possibilities of storage systems.

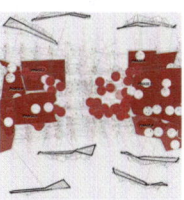

p 32
Murailles East: Nine Phases of Archaeological Excavation with Integrated Facade Operation
The storage facility continually digs into the ground, creating an archaeological upward drift. The holes created by the excavations are stabilised to provide permanent storage for commodities. The facade, structural and excavation systems are entirely integrated. The animation of facade folds with excavation renders the building both allegory and performance, enabling degrees of interpretability that speak both to economic incentives and to the 'a-functional' aesthetics of the obese body.

Widari Bahrin 2008

p 162
Kinotel: Hanoi Peepbox Hotel
The Vietnam War is one of the few wars that generated its own cinematic genre. As with the Wild West, the cinematic fiction it weaves is larger than the life it represents. Bahrin's proposed hotel for the Hanoi film festival draws on the techniques of obscuration deployed in Vietnam War films to deliver a peepshow-like engagement between tourist and the city. As images fold up walls and around corners, sundering the logic that ties surface to volume, the lessons of Van Hoogstraten's 1660 peepshow box are never far away.

Tom Burnford 2010

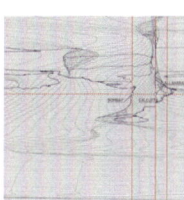

p 154
Around the World in 80 Days or 3,188 Million Calories or £20,000
One of the best-known demonstrations of the potential effects of Victorian advances in transport and communication technologies is to be found in Jules Verne's *Around the World in 80 Days*, written in 1873. In Verne's portrait of a closed system, time, fuel and information all work as a synchronous economy, transporting Phileas Fogg around the globe in a newly predictable mode of travel. In Burnford's analysis the journey

is represented as miles per pound and miles per calorie. His Sterling and calorific cartographies map key events in the itinerary that transform space/time relations: on day 76, for example, Phileas Fogg orders the skipper to maintain full speed, knowing that there isn't enough fuel onboard to complete the last leg, the Atlantic crossing; inevitably, the fuel runs out the next day. Fogg, in desperation, purchases the boat from the captain and sets about hacking up its woodwork, which is then fed into the ship's boiler. So closed is the architecture of Verne's economy that in order to complete the journey the crew are compelled to consume the vessel. The auto-cannibalised boat is stripped bare by the time it reaches England.

Sea Eun Cho, 2008

p 8
Fictive Infrastructure: Long Bien Bridge Water Puppet Theatre
As Hanoi rapidly expands, new Red River crossings are superseding the historic Long Bien Bridge, a central piece of the city's physical and psychic infrastructure. Once a symbol of Vietnamese ingenuity and defiance – it was famously rebuilt overnight each time it was bombed during the Vietnam War – it is now to be made redundant. Cho proposes to give the bridge new meaning by inscribing the Red River's indigenous form of water puppetry into the structure itself, transforming the rusting cast iron members into limbs that wave at the crossing viewers. Cho's choreography describes the set pieces of the

ancient tradition. Load-bearing structure dissolves at 15mph into the fictive space of puppet theatre.

Angelo Sanghoon Han 2009

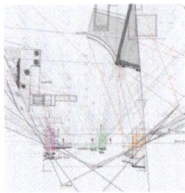

p 10
Perspectival Forensic Study, I, of JMW Turner's Homage to Claude Lorrain's Seaport with the Embarkation of the Queen of Sheba (1648), Dido Building Carthage (1851)
Han's analysis of Turner's tribute to Lorrain finds it is not as faithful as it at first appears. While the architectural fragments in Lorrain's Antique seaport are all located within the same vanishing point and sun angle, Turner's fragments not only have their own vanishing points but are also subject to different sun angles: the space has splintered into multiple spatial and temporal domains. Within the space of Antiquity Turner quietly suggests that the subject is either not stationary, or is itself multiplicitous, a crowd.

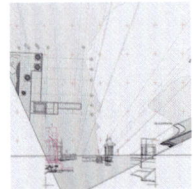

p 76–77
Perspectival Forensic Study, II
Han retraces Turner's actions step by step in this digital forensic analysis. Here he examines three questions: How might a single viewpoint set up to work with the perspective of one of the architectural fragments

distort the actual 3D forms of all the other architectural fragments? How would a default viewpoint – with a 60-degree view cone oriented perpendicular to the plane of the painting – distort all of the fragments? Lastly, what is the gap between these two viewpoints and the distorted geometries they each deliver?

Angelo Sanghoon Han 2010

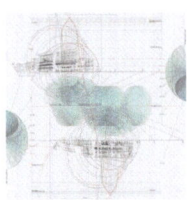

p 44
Lord Byron's Aquatic Venice: Horizon Zero
The swimmer's horizon is the zero-horizon. This conceptual swim – a reiteration of Lord Byron's legendary swim down the Grand Canal – proposes to straighten the canal, make its facades buoyant, enlarge ancient pavements and invert and resurrect the forest of pilings beneath Venice for the *flâneur* aquatic.

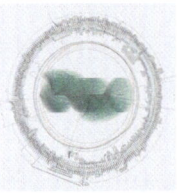

p 143
Lord Byron's Aquatic Venice: The Front-Crawl as a Representation and Transportation Machine
Drawing from the Ferris wheel and the panorama machine – which both blur the distinction between transportation and representation, and in taking you exactly nowhere also take you

somewhere else – Byron's legendary swim down the Grand Canal is redeployed in Venice. Stroke by stroke, the front crawl reconfigures the facades of the Grand Canal and the aquatic micro-horizons at the water's edge.

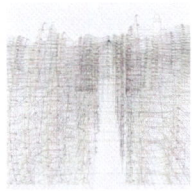

p 151
Machines That Do No Work: The Ferris Wheel
A technological artefact that does no work, gets you nowhere, yet endlessly redelivers the horizon: the visuality of flight as inscribed by the Ferris wheel.

p 172
Lord Byron's Aquatic Venice: Water Table
Detail

Fusako Ishikawa 2010

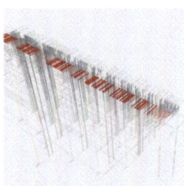

p 13
Writing Architecture in the Gap between the Countable and the Calculated
The process of mass-indexing, central to the nineteenth century, laid the foundations for the twentieth-

century's relations between the countable and the calculated – just in time for Wittgenstein's seminal crisis on the matter. Ishikawa's analysis of the friction incurred in Babbage's Difference Engine reveals that the amount of energy and time expended on a given calculation relates to the chosen route of the function through the space of the machine. That is, the commutative law does not stand when mechanised: 100 x 2 requires a lot more work than 2 x 100. Given that the mechanisation of calculation is simply the counting of cogs, the machines of Babbage, and of Leibniz before him, anticipate Wittgenstein's famous doubts concerning the reliability of calculation and its slippery relations to counting or surveying set out in *Foundations of Mathematics*

p 37
Counting the Glacier:
Vallot's Survey of the Mer de Glace
Joseph Vallot made the first systematic survey of the movement of the Mer de Glace in Chamonix. The method was as simple as it was beautiful. Once a year, from 1891 to 1899, he would align a set of painted and numbered stones across the glacier, always reinstalling the line of rocks in the same location. In this way he was able to measure the relative velocity of different parts of the glacier's surface over nine years.

p 39
Temporal Glacial Chronograph
In an attempt to write architecture backwards, Vallot's nineteenth-century technique has been adapted to develop a passive surveying system that harnesses the glacier's dwindling descent and steady retreat. Ishikawa here installs a self-surveying system in the Mer de Glace to create a fleeting architecture of voids that switch back and forth across the gap between the surveyed and the surveying. The system is a monument to twentieth-century cultural construction of weather as the warming ice counts itself away.

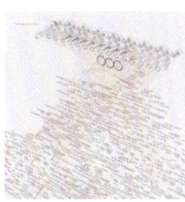

p 156
Cascade of Numbers
Cog analysis of Charles Babbage's 1820 Difference Engine with Ian Hacking in mind

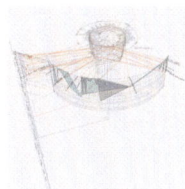

p 24
Jules Verne's
Palaeontological Calculator
In Verne's *Journey to the Centre of the Earth*, going down is literally going into the past, and space,

before carbon dating, is read through the combined lens of geology and palaeontology. In a central passage of the book, all geology disappears when the narrator crosses a dinosaur-filled subterranean ocean; in the absence of strata, Verne uses species identification to determine geological period and depth location. In the manner of Wittgenstein's question, 'Might I not use a table to measure a ruler?', Ishikawa reconstructs the subterranean ocean landscape backwards from the species data, inverting the established relation between geology and palaeontology, using dinosaur-time to draw rock-time.

Karl Kjelstrup-Johnson 2009

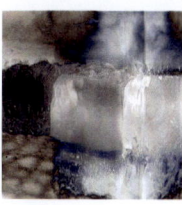

p 159
An Architecture of Indeterminacy
Kjelstrup-Johnson's proposed digital model of the indeterminate distribution of archaeological material in underground Naples explores the relations between geophysical and virtual data black holes. Here he employs a computer ray-tracing engine to bore through the subterranean blackness that belongs to both actual and virtual realms.

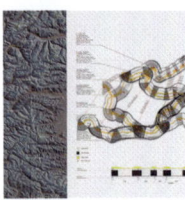

p 86, 87
**On the Road with Hannibal
and 37 Elephants**
We have no way of knowing the exact route by which Hannibal crossed the Alps with his entourage of 50,000 men and 37 elephants. In response, Kjelstrup-Johnson lays out the spatial and temporal discrepancies between seven historical accounts of the same event in order to erect the framework for an eighth narrative: one that is defined not by territory crossed in days and nights but by levels of determinacy and indeterminacy.

p 91
**Cartography of Relative
Indeterminacy:**
Hannibal's Alpine Passage
Using the 'marching day' in Livy's account of the passage as a space–time unit, Kjelstrup-Johnson maps a landscape of relative indeterminacy/determinacy for the Alpine topography. Each square is one marching day, with size indicating the difficulty of the terrain crossed: a big square means easy conditions, a small one more difficult routes. Embedded in this model is a semi-indeterminate event-network in which known instances – such as setting frozen rocks on fire, losing yet another elephant or skirmishes with hostile tribes – mediate with each other in order to establish the most likely 'optimised' route.

p 103
**Hypercontextual Waste
Infrastructure: A Subterranean,
Temporal Geographic Information
System for Managing Naples' Waste
and Archaeological Extraction**
A subterranean superstructure uses a 3D temporal geographic information system to carve out a space for aerobic waste processing and archaeological extraction in Naples. Navigating through the indeterminacy of toxic soil, Camorra activity and a matrix of cavities in the volcanic tufa, a responsive tunnelling system simultaneously constructs a virtual public database of subterranean Naples and a set of physical public spaces.

Gergely Kovács 2009

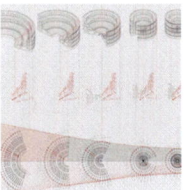

p 124
Lessons from Piranesi I
Kovács' digital forensics into the construction of Piranesi's famous fish-eye perspective of the Colosseum suggests that the artist notionally unrolled the structure into a linear element and then projected it back upon a curved picture plane. The line is thus found embedded in the circle. Here the process is extrapolated to its logical conclusion: as the Colosseum's radius tightens, it is turned inside out. The result is a highly political inversion of an ancient engine of power.

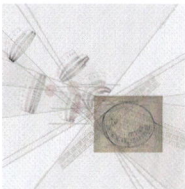

p 119
Lessons from Piranesi II
In investigating the uncanny distortions of Piranesi's representation of the Colosseum, Kovács unravels its hidden architecture: the 3D digital reconstruction of Piranesi's etching shows everything but the all too familiar elliptical edifice – depending on the projection method used, its geometry opens up; walls start overlapping other walls; or the building becomes perfectly linear where the area inside (the delimited arena) equals the area outside – the Roman Empire.

p 137
**Studies in Inversion: Inversion
of a Generic Grid**
Inversive geometry constitutes an alternate space (a mapping of Euclidean space through the algebraic transformation of inversion) that allows for the resolution of mathematical problems that cannot be solved in Euclidean space. The axis of inversion, unlike the axis of symmetry, is a circle of finite radius. It not only divides space but encloses it and sets up an outside and an inside. It flips the relation of these two domains by mapping the space inside the circle outside, and vice versa.

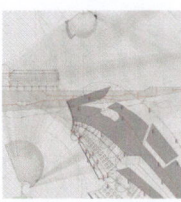

p 139
The Construction of Neutrality
An impossible complex of overlapping cultural and political territories, the Temple Mount in Jerusalem represents the ultimate site of conflict and a Holy Grail of constructed neutrality. Bill Clinton's proposed solution was a 1.5m subterranean neutral slab to separate Muslim surface from Jewish underground. As a critique of the impossible simplicity of this proposal, Kovács deploys LI Magnus's 1831 inversion formula –a space devised for solving otherwise unsolvable conundrums – to create an inverted reflection of the most contentious zones in the temple. The formula generates spatial liberties and convolutions which permit a joint occupation that would be impossible to achieve under normal spatial conditions and current political constraints.

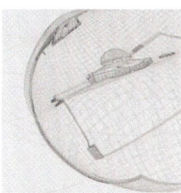

p 164
The Topography of Neutrality: Inside is Outside
Kovács' reconstruction of the Temple Mount in Jerusalem is scripted by the complexity of juxtaposing the three main religious calendars and the simplicity of the mathematical formula of inversion. Through the changes of its local surface curvature, the Temple Mount is able to negotiate the irreconcilable parameters of the shared occupation

of its domain. In the process, relations between inside and outside are dynamically altered: as they separate and connect, they become neither distinguishable nor reliable categories. Thus subject to inversion the Temple Mount, spatially at least, overcomes the limitations of a binary order in which one gains territory or access at the necessary expense of the other.

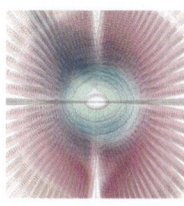

p 173
A Spatio-Temporal Plan:
The Society of the Colosseum
Within the confines of its walls, the Colosseum – a seminal engine of power – generated well-choreographed social orders: relative height, distance, angle, proximity and view were all carefully engineered. Kovács' temporal mapping of the Colosseum extricates a social hierarchy based on the time it took for various members of Roman society – from senators to slaves – to occupy their designated seats.

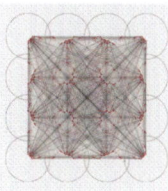

p 175
Studies in Inversion: Paths in a Field of Inversion
Kovács' study is a recording of 30,000 footprints at a point traversing a field of inversive circles. The architectural plan of this abstract mathematical space notates a regular grid of 16 circles, yet fails to register the intricate spatiality at

play. These footprints, like those in fresh snow, record the complexity of the space through the medium of the plan – a plan intact and untouched by the hands of the architect.

Ed McCann 2006

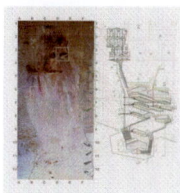

p 171
Scatological Beach
The imposition of the Canal Zone – until 1999 controlled by the US – forced Panama City to grow eastward along the coast, with little or no infrastructure. One of the smellier products of this haven of consumption is catalogued on the beach at low tide. In McCann's proposal the shit of the city – or more specifically its artful meeting with a proposed extension of the city's public hospital – generates public space from the private space that is its point of creation. As the hygienic and the pathogenic slide past each other, the body – central to the whole dialogue between consumption and waste – is placed at the axis of desire in the city.

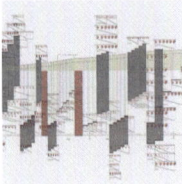

p 58
Forensic Analysis of a Vase that was Never Full: Van der Hamen's Still-Life with Flowers, 1627
Van der Hamen's still-life – typical of the seventeenth century – depicts a vase with flowers that would never bloom together in the same month. Murata explores the temporal artifice of this construction by plotting the flowering window of the various plants, how long they would last when cut, and the overlapping phases of their decay. In doing so she draws the architecture of complex adjacency behind the seventeenth-century still-life: the anticipation of flowers yet to come and the absence of flowers long since wilted.

p 66
Hanoi Still-Life: Cemetery Detail
A study of the temporal artifice of the still-life and its embedded rates of decay is brought to bear on the materialisation (or dematerialisation) of time in the Hanoi Cemetery. The high water-table of the Red River Delta has given rise to a double burial process (exhumation and reburial), in which the relative decay of adjacent bodies inscribes a complex temporal and material architecture. Within Murata's proposed choreography of substitution and deposition we find echoes of the structural grammar of the still-life.

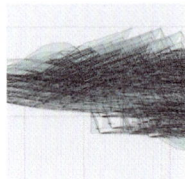

p 17–18, front fold
Get Lost: A Qanat Park for Palermo
Sectional detail through true and misnavigated paths
Jules Verne's *Journey to the Centre of the Earth* is, amongst other things, a portrait of the collapse of navigational paradigms and their attendant technologies. As the party explore deeper into the Earth's cavernous interior, their instruments and their magnetic and thermal orientation strategies fail: North appears everywhere, the centre of the Earth is mysteriously cooler. Hopelessly lost, and dying of thirst, they strike through a rockface in an attempt to reach an underground river. Only then do they realise that the water gushing through at their feet knows the way down. Namba's proposal to restore the eleventh-century Arab underground water channels (*qanats*) of Palermo as a space of public misnavigation engineers the collapse of orientation in order to explore the pleasures of getting lost and the expansion of psychic space this brings.

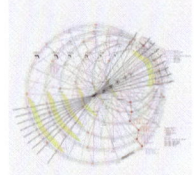

p 131
Sculpting in Time: A Futures Exchange on the Panama Canal
The miracle of the Panama Canal is that it cuts out around 20 days of shipping time, replacing it with 9 to 24 hours of transit through its various locks. This global trade valve provides incalculable benefits for international markets, but brings in limited revenue for Panama, since the canal zone was long controlled by the US (and only ceded to Panama in 1999). Oh proposes to aid its reassimilation into the local economy by establishing a trading floor to speculate on the value difference of the same commodities at opposite ends of the canal. His site is temporal, fiscal and climatic first; physical second. A nightly fog stops all traffic through the canal. Although it is difficult for a large ship to remain stationary and also dangerous to navigate in fog, it is possible to lock into a turning circle as a stable holding pattern. By moving the holding area for vessels away from the Atlantic and the Pacific ends and into the centrally located Gatun Lake, Oh establishes a futures exchange between the local market and the vessels held in tight turning circles. A proposed holding pattern maintaining three knots means even Panamax vessels (the largest container ships permitted in the canal) can safely stay in the designated one-way channel. While turning, trading decisions and transactions are made on the basis of both international and local speculation.

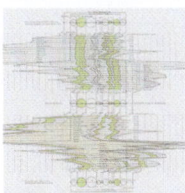

p 29
**Panama Canal Futures Exchange:
Sculpting in Time**
The waiting time in international
waters at either end of the canal is
relocated to the centre of the transit
through locks in Gatun Lake. Thus
in this drawing of time, transit and
space, the canal's middle swells with
waiting: the site of trading.

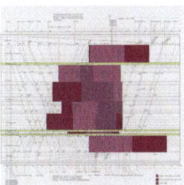

p 15
**Panama Canal Futures Exchange:
Fog and Lockage Time**
Study of the tolerance and deviation
of the transit time at particular
sections along the canal

Derin Ozken

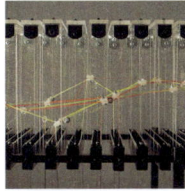

p 12
**Three Regimes, Fifty-One
Typological Transformations
and One Hundred and Twenty-
Seven Years: From Quatremère's
Anti-Model to Rossi's
Unprogrammed Type to Hanoi's
Hyperpromiscuous Type**
Throughout Hanoi's serial occupation
(by imperial China, colonial France,
the Soviet Union and latterly Doi Moi

capitalism) the loyalty of architectural
type to form has been stretched to
the limit – as hospital, for example,
mutated into an art museum. This
extreme typological promiscuity has
been the means of reconfiguring the
psychogeography of the city and
its institutions. As Hanoi's historic
relations between type, programme
and form verge on the arbitrary in
their convolutions, Ozken speculates
on the potential of counterfactual
history techniques to rewrite the city
via the architectural type.

p 21
Hanoi Hypercontext Analysis Model
End view

Hye-Ju Park 2010

p 166
**Case for the Prosecution:
The People vs the City of Palermo**
In Park's analysis of *omertà*
urbanism, the reconstruction of two
high-profile murders in Palermo
is presented as evidence: the People
contend that architecture itself
enabled, and acted as accessory
in, the murder of two anti-mafia
magistrates – Cesare Terranova
on 25 September 1979 and Paolo
Borsellino on 19 July 1992 – with the
motive of fuelling and funding its own
urban redevelopment.

Theo Wyatt Petrides 2009

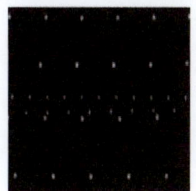

p 36
**Light Choreography for the
Twenty-First-Century Grand
Tourist's Alpine Passage**
Gotthard Base tunnel, interior still

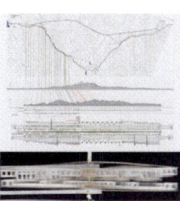

p 63
**Gotthard Base Tunnel:
Section and Choreographic Score**
The opening of the Gotthard Base
tunnel (due in 2016 and connecting
Germany and Italy under the Alps)
will further eclipse the Alpine
passage as a portal to the Grand
Tour. For contemporary Grand
Tourists – who will now take the
tunnel train – Petrides proposes
a light score that rewrites into the
dark the former drama of the ascent
and descent of Goethe's rocking
carriage and the sublime crossing
of Turner's *Devil's Bridge*.

Theo Wyatt Petrides 2010

p 41
**A Small Rock at the Top of the Hill =
A Big Rock at the Bottom of the Hill**
Hypercontext model
Survey of the negative potential
energy of the fallen rocks on
Agrigento's ancient ruined city wall.
Within the closed system of Petrides'
restoration choreography, the relative
potential energy of one fallen
rock is used to raise another rock,
so conserving mass and potential
energy. Each rock, in its journey
back up the slope, finds itself
following a complex snakes-and-
ladders itinerary.

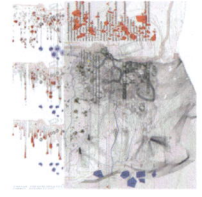

p 110
**The Sisyphean Engine
of Reconstruction or the
Perpetual Rebuilding of
the Agrigento's Ancient City
Wall by Man and Machine**
*'The gods had condemned
Sisyphus to ceaselessly rolling
a rock to the top of a mountain,
whence the stone would fall
back of its own weight. They
had thought with some reason
that there is no more dreadful
punishment than futile and
hopeless labour.'* – Albert Camus,
The Myth of Sisyphus
It is possible to calculate, with
varying degrees of indeterminacy,
the original position and orientation
of each stone that has fallen from

Agrigento's ancient city wall. Such
analysis would necessarily create
multiple potential 'true' arrangements
for restoration. In this allegory of
the Sisyphean futility of our attempts
to reconstruct the classical world,
Petrides proposes that the fallen
boulders of the ruined city wall
should be eternally rearranged in
the landscape by machine and man.

Jenny Elisa Schafer 2009

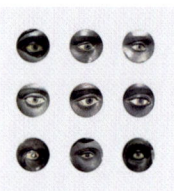

p 105
**Enamel Eyes:
Villa de Papyri Collage**
The figurines discovered in the
Villa de Papyri, Herculaneum, are
famous for their enamel eyes. Jenny
Schafer speculates on the role of the
intersecting gazes of these figures,
both in their current museum location
and in their potential return to their
original position in the Villa dig.

Jenny Elisa Schafer 2010

p 146–147
**Zoetropic Space and the
Construction of Suspicion**
In the rapid-fire development
of photography in the nineteenth
century several key devices were
superseded before their full spatial
and representational potential could
be explored. Schafer returns to one

such object, the zoetrope – which
captured successive phases of
motion – and brings its punctuated
visuality to bear on the space of
suspicion, most quintessentially
at play in Jean-Luc Godard's *Le
Mépris*. In her exhaustive analysis of
zoetropic visuality, a perceptual field
of suspicion is constructed through
the notional occupation of the
circular space inside the zoetrope.

Marilia Spanou 2009

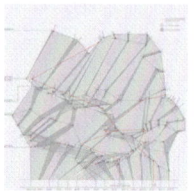

p 65
**Spatial and Temporal Conflict
in the Accounts of Hannibal's
Passage through the Alps**
Central to the artifice that
is Antiquity lies a process of
reconstruction always riddled with
indeterminacy. A seminal site for
this is the establishing of the exact
route of Hannibal's passage through
the Alps. Spanou's study explores
how the compound error of Livy's
account (using the marching-day as
a kind of space–time unit) produces
strange anomalies of its own, such
as a temporal landscape in which
odd hours of night are stranded in
the middle of the day. It is not only
geography but also the diurnal
structure that lies in ruins.

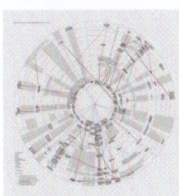

p 88
The Ruin of the Narrative
Within classical scholarship, archaeological and textual evidence are generally assigned equal value. And curiously for architects, the physical ruin and the ruin of a fragmentary text share many properties in relation to interpretation and indeterminacy. Spanou here examines the textual body of evidence concerning Hannibal's Alpine passage. Taking a wide array of accounts – Polybius, Livy, Whitaker, Cramer, Torr, Walbank, Lazeney, to Bradford in 1981 – she plots how interpretative licence and serial mistranslation (for example of the names of rivers such as the Durance) combine to unravel and make a ruin of the textual edifice.

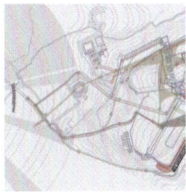

p 96
The Ruin of the Ruin: Analysis of Conflicting Interpretations of the Circulation Logic of Villa Adriana
As a seminal ruin, Hadrian's Villa in Tivoli has become a laboratory for classical scholarship and a template onto which we project our changing vision of the world of Antiquity. But this doesn't necessarily mean that we've made great progress: we still don't even know where its front entrance is. Spanou's analysis of conflicting theories regarding the circulation systems for servants, ice and guests is used to propose a revision of the archaeologist's Athens Charter. Within her Charter, the distinction between the textual and the physical ruin collapses; marginal and major spaces are valued equally; the idea of a 'true' reading is rejected and each possible interpretation is given equal weight; all indeterminacy is declared; and all previous theories and mistakes in restoration are considered part of the site's narrative. The effect is to allow each visitor to create their own narratives and to experience Hadrian's Villa beyond the conventional realms of time and space.

Jean Chiying Wang 2006

p 133
Shelf Life: The Preservation and Decomposition of a Political Border
Hypercontext model
The site of the National Produce Exchange and Market is the only point on the former border of the Panama Canal Zone that has been successfully reassimilated into Panama City since the 1999 handover. Wang proposes a revision of the market as an engine for preservation and decomposition that is able to straddle the former border and the extreme socio-economic divide it has left behind. Her proposal is scripted by the materialisation of time embedded in the relative shelf life of produce: the tomato decomposes rapidly, accelerating time, whereas citrus fruit slows it. Thus to house decomposing tomatoes in the same time–space structure as citrus fruit requires a folding of citrus time–space upon itself.

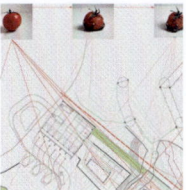

p 134
Shelf Life: The Preservation and Decomposition of a Political Border
Taking the literal to task, the waste produced by the market is composted to 'grow' bridges between the two (post-zonian and ex-zonian) communities that lie either side – spatially or temporally – of the zone. Scripted by the relative shelf life of fresh and preserved organic waste, slow and fast 'compost glaciers' transform the border landscape between the Panama Canal Zone and Panama City, over time transforming both the border and the access to and through the very market that generates them.

Images

p 16
Edouard Riou, illustration for Jules Verne's 1864 *Journey to the Centre of the Earth*; engraving by Pannemaker, Gauchard, Maurand, 1867

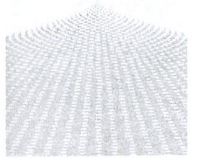

p 26
Agnes Denes, *Pascal's Triangle, Drawing No 3*, 1973–75 (detail), ink on graph paper, 15 x 15 x 10 inches (Copyright Agnes Denes, Courtesy Leslie Tonkonow Artworks + Projects, NY) Stations of the Pyramids

'In Pascal's Triangle (1973–74) a mathematical solution for the relative probability of accidental repetition of chance occurrences results in a dynamic, spiralling number system. Each line of this pyramid of binomial coefficients is constructed by writing the sum of each pair of adjacent numbers of the line above and putting "1" at each end. The relative probability is given by one particular term divided by the sum of all terms in that line.

Starting with the equilateral triangle, the expansion accelerates so rapidly that if the structure were continued to a height of 22.9ft, the base would be one mile long. If the base were extended from here to the sun (93 million miles), the tip of the structure would still be only 133 miles high.

Although Pascal's Triangle is known and discussed by mathematicians, it has never before been realised in visual form, exposing previously unknown properties that can lead to new discoveries. For example, the drawing reveals that the theory is a three-dimensional, spiralling number system that fits around a shell (shell mathematics), pointing to basic patterns unifying rational thought and nature.' (Agnes Denes)

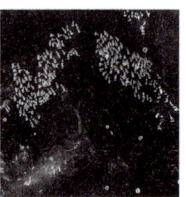

p 35
Plate b26816 of *Large Magellanic Cloud from Arequipa, Peru*, taken on 18 December 1900 with an eight-inch Bache Doublet, Voigtlander, reworked by Clark. Exposure 60 minutes centred on 5h09m47s RA and -67d22m51s declination. Henrietta Leavitt logbooks, research on Cepheid stars (Courtesy of the Harvard–Smithsonian Center for Astrophysics)

p 43
Mer de Glace, 1910
Auguste Couttet
(Copyright: Collection Yves Ballu)

p 50
Théodore Olivier, *geometric string figure of intersecting cones*, c 1856 (© Collection of Historical Scientific Instruments, Harvard University)

p 54
Athanasius Kircher, *Arca Noë: Inside of the Ark*, engraving, 1675, 35.5 x 23.2 cm (GC6.K6323.675a (A), Houghton Library, Harvard University)

p 57
Juan van der Hamen, *Still Life with Flowers, Artichokes, Cherries and Glassware*, oil on canvas, 1627, 81.5 x 110.5 cm (Prado Museum, Madrid)

p 62
JMW Turner, *The Devil's Bridge*, *St Gotthard*, oil on canvas, c 1803–04, 76.8 x 62.8 cm (Private collection, UK. Source: www.zeno.org)

p 69

The Diploma Table
Photography by Sue Barr

p 70

*MIT Science Reporter: Computer
Sketchpad*, John Fitch, Dir. Russell
Morash, WGBH-TV, Boston, 1963

p 72

Claude Lorrain, *Seaport with the
Embarkation of the Queen of Sheba*,
oil on canvas, 1648, 149.1 x 196.7 cm
(National Gallery, London)

p 73

JMW Turner, *Dido Building Carthage,
or The Rise of the Carthaginian
Empire*, oil on canvas, 1815, 155.5 x
230 cm (National Gallery, London)

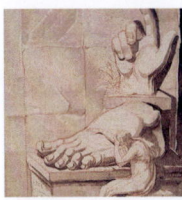

p 78

Johann Heinrich Fuseli, *The Artist
Moved by the Grandeur of Antique
Fragments*, red chalk on sepia wash,
1778–80, 41.5 cm x 35.5 cm

p 82

Anne Carson, *If Not, Winter:
Fragments of Sappho* (London:
Virago Press, 2003), 14.

p 85

Fragment of mural, from
Herculaneum (Courtesy of
Herculaneum Conservation Project)

p 94

Giovanni Battista Piranesi &
Francesco Piranesi, *Pianta delle
Fabriche esistenti nella Villa Adriana*,
1871, etching on paper, 6 double
plates, together 80 x 320 cm

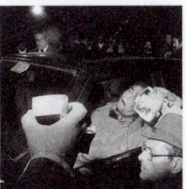

p 102

Letizia Battaglia, *Bagheria, 1979,
March 9. The secretary of the
Christian Democratic Party in
Palermo, Michele Reina, forty-six
years old, was assassinated in front
of his wife by two killers*, silver gelatin
print on baryta paper, 50 x 60 cm
(Maes & Matthys Gallery, Antwerp)

p 116

Joel Sternfeld, *Lovers parking
beneath a pyramidal tomb of the
second century AD*, Via Appia Antica,
Rome, *November 1990*, digital
C-print, negative: 1990; print: 2006,
56.52 x 71.12 cm (Courtesy of the
artist and Luhring Augustine, New
York)

p 117

Giovanni Battista Piranesi, *Vedute
di Roma*, Plate 58 – *Veduta
del'Anfiteatro Flavio, detto il
Colosseo*, 1751, 44.4 x 70.1 cm

p 130

James Ricketson and Jesse Ricketson, *Philippe Petit Tightrope Walk on Sydney Harbour Bridge*, 1973. (Courtesy of the artist)

p 138

Baz Ratner, *A Palestinian boy climbs through an opening in Israel's controversial barrier in Shuafat in the West Bank, near Jerusalem, 17 February 2009* (Reuters/Baz Ratner)

p 140

Geo R Lawrence Co, Union Stock Yards, Chicago, Illinois, photographic print, gelatin silver, 1907, 20.5 x 49.5 in (Library of Congress Prints and Photographs Division, Washington, DC)

p 148

Eadweard Muybridge, *Animal Locomotion*, 1887, plate 527, vol IV, Females (nude), A, B, C; 1, spanking child 104 (Courtesy of the Trustees of the Boston Public Library/Rare Books)

p 150

Construction of the Ferris Wheel at the World's Fair, St Louis, 19 April 1904, photograph by Official Photographic Company, 1904 (Missouri History Museum, St Louis)

p 153

Nineteenth-century Mer de Glace stereoscopic slide

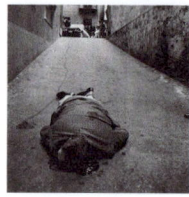

p158

Letizia Battaglia, *Palermo, 1976 – They killed him while he was going into the garage to get his car*, silver gelatin print on baryta paper, 60 x 50 cm (Maes & Matthys Gallery, Antwerp)

p 161

Samuel van Hoogstraten, *A Peepshow with Views of the Interior of a Dutch House*, oil and egg tempera on wood, c 1655–60, 58 x 88 x 60.5 cm (National Gallery, London)

p 170

Sylvester Stallone, *Rambo: First Blood Part II*, George P Cosmatos, Tri-Star Pictures, 1985; still at 1 hour and 10 minutes.

Acknowledgements

The speculative productions of Diploma Unit 15 would not have been possible without the help of many individuals, both from inside and outside the AA, who enthused about, intellectually fed or administratively supported our working discourse. Our thanks to: Anne Save de Beaureceuil, Mary Beard, Peter Carl, Mark Cousins, Marilyn Dyer, David Edgerton, Homa Farjadi, Belinda Flaherty, David Greene, Christine Hawley, Jonathan Hill, Catherine Ingraham, Christopher Lee, George L Legendre, Antonia Loyd, Jim Mallett, Jonathan Meyer, Mohsen Mostafavi, Ciro Najle, Hugh O'Shaunessy, Theodore Spyropoulos, Brett Steele, Charles Tashima, Mike Weinstock, Humberto Velez and Alan Zeigler.

For the annual workshops that drove the in-house refining of the large drawing, thanks to: Karl Kjelstrup-Johnson, Gergely Kovács, Sang Hoon Oh, Matthew Potter, Jean Wang and Yeena Yoon.

Thanks also to the many institutions that generously received us and exchanged research with us: The Ministry for Education and Employment in Gibraltar; Panama Canal Authority, Ministry of Housing, The City of Knowledge, Marine Traffic Control Centre, and the University of Panama Department of Architecture in Panama; HANU, The World Bank, UN-Habitat, Urban Rural Solutions Saigon, and Hanoi University of Civil Engineering in Vietnam; Herculaneum Conservation Project, Univertsità degli Studi Roma Tre and the British School in Rome in Italy; The Paul Mellon Centre for British Art and The British Museum in the UK.

In the AA Print Studio, thanks to Thomas Weaver and Pamela Johnston for their editorial insight, wit and attentive care; to Claire McManus and Zak Kyes for the beautiful design of this book; and to Sue Barr for her photograph of the AA table.

Special thanks to Gergely Kovács who in his capacity as editorial assistant undertook the enormous task of compiling and preparing all the material for this publication. His help has, as usual, been invaluable.

Lastly my personal thanks to Brett Steele who first invited this book into being and who has been an unequivocal supporter of the work it contains.

As any teacher will know, a studio is the sum of its students; their daring, their trust, their sweat and tears. To all the past students of Dip 15 and most especially the 18 whose projects are presented here, this book is for you.

Contributors

Noam Andrews is an architect and former unit master at the AA. He is currently pursuing doctoral research on the role and signification of geometrical models in the material culture of early modern Europe at the Department of the History of Science, Harvard University. He is also the director of Wunderkammer Studio.

Mary Beard is one of Britain's best-known Classicists – a distinguished Professor of Classics at the University of Cambridge and Fellow of Newnham College. She has written numerous books on the Ancient World, including the 2008 Wolfson Prize-winner, *Pompeii: The Life of a Roman Town*, *The Roman Triumph*, *Classical Art from Greece to Rome*, as well as popular books on the Parthenon and Colosseum. Her interests range from the social and cultural life of the Ancient World to the Victorian understanding of Antiquity. She is also Classics editor of the *Times Literary Supplement* and writes an engaging blog, *A Don's Life*. Her academic achievements were acknowledged, in 2010, by the British Academy which elected her as a Fellow.

David Edgerton will (from mid-2013) be Hans Rausing Professor of the History of Science and Technology and Professor of Modern British History at King's College London. He is the author of a sequence of books on twentieth-century Britain: *Science, Technology and the British Industrial 'Decline', 1870–1970* (1996), *Warfare State: Britain, 1920–1970* (2005), and *Britain's War Machine: Weapons, Resources and Experts in the Second World War* (2011), and his first book, republished as *England and the Aeroplane: Militarism, Modernity and Machines* (2013). He is also the author of *The Shock of the Old: Technology and Global History Since 1900* (2006).

Francesca Hughes has taught architecture since 1993. After running design units at the Bartlett School of Architecture for several years, she taught at the AA between 2003 and 2011 during which time she was unit master of Dip 15. She has lectured internationally and the work of Hughes Meyer Studio, an art architecture practice, has been widely published and exhibited. Following on from *The Architect: Reconstructing her Practice* (MIT Press: 1996), her new book, *The Architecture of Error*, is forthcoming from MIT Press.

AA Agendas is an ongoing series of books launched in 2006 and produced by the Architectural Association School of Architecture. The series is designed to capture work generated through any number of the school's design units, courses and other AA events and initiatives. Through the range of projects illustrated, the series reveals the breadth of the AA's teaching practices and the vitality of the resulting student and staff work.

Agendas 1: A Manifesto for a Cinematic Architecture
Agendas 2: Bodyline
Agendas 3: Before Object, After Image
Agendas 4: Morpho-Ecologies
Agendas 5: Typological Formations
Agendas 6: Environmental Tectonics
Agendas 7: Articulated Grounds
Agendas 8: Nine Problems in the Form of a Pavilion
Agendas 9: Making Pavilions
Agendas 10: London +10
Agendas 11: Mediating Architecture